To Lo [illegible]

[illegible]

7 June 2011

PENGUIN BOOKS

Published by the Penguin Group

Penguin Books India Pvt. Ltd, 11 Community Centre, Panchsheel Park, New Delhi 110 017, India

Penguin Group (USA) Inc., 375 Hudson Street, New York, New York 10014, USA

Penguin Group (Canada), 90 Eglinton Avenue East, Suite 700, Toronto, Ontario, M4P 2Y3, Canada
(a division of Pearson Penguin Canada Inc.)

Penguin Books Ltd, 80 Strand, London WC2R 0RL, England

Penguin Ireland, 25 St Stephen's Green, Dublin 2, Ireland (a division of Penguin Books Ltd)

Penguin Group (Australia), 250 Camberwell Road, Camberwell, Victoria 3124, Australia
(a division of Pearson Australia Group Pty Ltd)

Penguin Group (NZ), Penguin Group (NZ), 67 Apollo Drive, Rosedale, North Shore 0632, New Zealand
(a division of Pearson New Zealand Ltd)

Penguin Group (South Africa) (Pty) Ltd, 24 Sturdee Avenue, Rosebank, Johannesburg 2196, South Africa

Penguin Books Ltd, Registered Offices: 80 Strand, London WC2R 0RL, England

First published by Penguin Books India 2009

Book design by Ka Designs
Illustrations by Ka Designs

10 9 8 7 6 5 4 3 2

ISBN 978 01430 68 419

Printed at Manipal Press Limited, Manipal

PHOTO CREDIT AND COPYRIGHT

The publisher would like to thank the following for permission to reproduce their photographs in the book:

[Key: Top=T; Bottom=B; Left=L; Right=R; Centre=C]

DK Images: 12TL1, 12TL2, 12TR1, 12B, 13, 14, 16, 17, 23TL, 23TR, 24, 26, 27, 31, 32TR, 32CR, 37, 39, 40, 44, 46, 47, 48R, 49BR, 50, 51, 53, 54, 56, 57, 59, 61, 63, 65, 66, 69, 70, 71, 72TR, 77, 78, 79TR, 81, 83B, 85, 86, 87, 88, 89, 91, 92, 93, 94, 95, 96, 97, 98, 99, 100T, 101, 108, 118, 124, 126, 134, 144, 145, 166, 174, 179, 194, 196, 197, 199TL, 199TR, 199CL, 199C, 206TL, 207, 209, 210, 211, 224, 232, 245, 249, 252, 254, 255, 256, 257, 262, 263, 265, 270, 272, 277, 278, 280, 282, 283, 284, 285, 288, 289, 292, 293, 295, 299

Penguin Group (Australia): 9, 10TR (second row), 15, 19, 23B, 25, 64BL2, 103, 107, 114, 119, 121, 127BL, 128, 132, 136, 137, 140, 148, 150, 153, 157, 159, 161, 163, 165, 167, 168, 171, 177, 178, 182, 186, 189, 192, 200, 202, 204, 205, 212, 213, 214, 215, 216, 221, 226, 230, 233, 235, 237, 238, 239, 240, 258, 260, 261, 290,

Pernod Ricard India: 10, 12TR2, 32TL, 32BL, 32BR, 35, 36, 38, 41, 42, 43, 45, 48L, 52, 64BL1, 64BR1, 64BR2, 65T1, 65T3, 65T3, 73, 74, 75, 76, 79 BR, 80, 82, 83T, 84, 86, 104CL, 104BL, 104BR, 127TL,127TR, 127CR, 127BR, 129, 138, 151, 152, 156, 158, 164, 169, 170, 172, 173, 175, 199B, 219, 241, 242, 244, 246, 248, 251, 253, 269, 273, 274,

Shutterstock Images: 4, 49TR, 104TL, 104TR, 104CR, 105, 106, 109, 110, 111, 112, 113, 116, 117, 120, 122, 131, 133, 141, 142, 146, 147, 154, 155, 162, 176, 180, 181, 185, 188, 190, 201, 206TR, 222, 229, 266, 267, 268, 275, 297

Vishesh Shourie: 100B

To my grandson, Lucas,
who will have his first legal drink
in a New York bar on 28 April 2026.
Cheers!

CONTENTS

INTRODUCTION

I drink it when I am happy and when I am sad,
Sometimes I drink it when I'm alone,
When I have company, I consider it obligatory.
I trifle with it if I am not hungry and drink it when I am,
Otherwise I never touch it—unless I'm thirsty.

—Madame Bollinger, 1961

I love a good drink. At home, if I am alone, I make myself something uncomplicated. On most evenings, it is whisky on the rocks, sometimes a Gin-and-Tonic. When I have company, I tempt my guests with a Mai Tai, a Mojito or jugfuls of Margarita. These cocktails and the many, many others that can so easily be made at home are a delight to mix, serve and drink. When I am in a bar that I trust, I order something that calls for an exotic liqueur or spirit that I do not have in stock.

A nomadic life, such as the one I have led, might have its disadvantages but it gave me the opportunity to mingle with people from different cultures and backgrounds and to taste and experience an unimaginable variety of food and drink. I had my first shot of tequila in Acapulco. I learnt how to mix a great Bloody Mary from Walter the barman in the delegates' lounge at the UN headquarters in New York. The best beer I have tasted was in the town of Ceske Budejovice in the Czech Republic. This book, perhaps the first and most comprehensive publication on cocktails and spirits to be published in India, is thus the result of years of research on the subject of drinks—research that, I have to admit, was mostly carried out in a state of bliss, in the most pleasant circumstances and in the most unlikely places.

You will find in the following pages all you need to know about maintaining a bar at home and the techniques of preparing the perfect drink; about a variety of alcoholic beverages, their history and production; and an extensive section on cocktail recipes, over 600 of them, for you and your friends to delight in. Some of these might seem complicated but most are devilishly simple and fun to prepare. The recipes are not my original inventions; many of them, such as the Dry Martini or Singapore Sling, have been around for a long time. I have included the ones I like to drink and those that can be easily prepared in Indian homes. I have also modified a few ingredients and measurements. For instance, I have made allowances for the fact that our lemons (the most important fruit when it comes to mixing cocktails), or what we call lime, are smaller and less juicy than the ones available abroad but tend to be sourer.

While this book remains largely a celebration of spirits and liqueurs and the wonderful cocktails you can make out of them, I have, because I feel it is important, also touched upon the dangers of excessive drinking and the need to enjoy alcohol responsibly and sensibly.

Although I can say in all honesty that I mix cocktails better than most bartenders I know in India—they tend to be too generous with the sweeteners, not so generous when it comes to adding spirits and liqueurs—I was trained to practice law, not mix drinks. I was put on this path by Vir Sanghvi, editorial director of *Hindustan Times*. He suggested my name to Poonam Saxena, the editor of Brunch, the paper's Sunday supplement, who called one afternoon and asked if I would write a column on drinks. I said I would think about it, but called her back five minutes later with an enthusiastic 'Yes!' My column, 'High Spirits', ran for over three years before I ran out of ideas, and it considerably expanded my knowledge and palate. In Poonam I found a very encouraging and supportive editor, and her colleague Veenu Singh made my pieces glow with innovative designs.

When Penguin India commissioned me to put this book together, Diya Kar Hazra bullied me into completing the manuscript. Had it not been for her, it would still have been sitting on my desk in bits and scraps. Poulomi Chatterjee, my copy editor with a talent for expunging flights of fancy, has been both patient and understanding. Sherna Wadia performed the tedious task of meticulously checking the recipes and measurements. Thank you. Also, Anisha Heble and her team at Ka Designs for designing the perfect look for the book.

I enjoy a good whisky and I like fine wines but some of my most memorable evenings have been spent drinking feni on Delhi's rooftops or what we call barsaatis. (At that point in our lives that was all my friends and I could afford.) So, let me leave you with a thought. When you are entertaining, you should always remember that it is your generosity of spirit, the mix of the people you invite and the mood and atmosphere that you create that will ensure the success or failure of an evening – not the price on the bottle of the drinks you serve. And if a guest complains, do not invite the person again.

BAR BASICS

JACOB'S CREEK
CHARDONNAY
Orlando Wines
Named after Jacob's Creek, site of Johann Gramp's
first vineyard in the Barossa Valley
Established 1847

KAHLÚA

Ballantine's
FULLY MATURED
QUALITY GUARANTEED
EST^D 1827
VERY OLD
SCOTCH WHISKY

CHIVAS REGAL
18
SCOTCH
WHISKY
GOLD SIGNATURE
PRODUCE OF SCOTLAND

RON PURO CUBANO
FUNDADA
EN 1878
Havana
Club
Ron Tradicional
HECHO EN CUBA
Ron Tradicional
HECHO EN CUBA

Seagram's
The King of the Forest
ROYAL
STAG
DELUXE
WHISKY

Tia Maria
LIQUEUR

ABSOLUT
Country of Sweden
VODKA
This superb vodka
was distilled from grain grown
in the rich fields of southern Sweden
It has been produced at the famous

THE
GLENLIVET
FRENCH OAK RESERVE
SINGLE MALT SCOTCH
WHISKY
GUARANTEED 15 YEARS OF AGE

MARTELL
V.S.O.P
MEDAILLON
OLD FINE COGNAC

Seagram's
100 PIPERS
DE LUXE
SCOTCH WHISKY

STOCKING THE BAR

spirits, liqueurs and wine

If you entertain at home and serve alcohol, here are four words for you: whisky, vodka, gin and rum. With these four bottles in your cupboard, or on your kitchen shelf, you are in business. You can please just about anyone as long as you also have some ice, bottles of soda water, tonic water and Coca-Cola, and of course lemons.

In India guests normally ask for whisky with soda, Gin-and-Tonic, vodka with something and, maybe, rum and Coca-Cola. Very few say, 'I will have wine.' Instead, they ask, 'Do you have any wine?' If you reply that you don't, the guest will happily settle for something else. In fact, most Indian hosts in middle-class homes are not expected to serve wine. What about a glass to go with the meal? I would not bother, unless it is a special event when a bottle or two of decent wine will lend elegance to the evening. Don't believe everything the promoters of wine and some of our food experts say. Wine is not a necessary accompaniment to Indian food. Our masalas tend to overpower wine. However, if you are serving something like pork chops or pasta, the meal will be incomplete without wine.

So, as I said: whisky, rum, vodka and gin. These constitute the basic bar. Of course, you will be required to stock much more than that if you live on Prithviraj Road or Carmichael Road and drive around in a Mercedes. The well-heeled should always have some bottles of good single malt. Glenlivet is available in our liquor stores and is popular worldwide. People will expect you to serve Chivas Regal or Black Label, two of the best-known premium brands, but cheaper blended Scotch labels like Ballantine's, 100 Pipers and Famous Grouse are equally fine.

Ideally you should also stock some tequila. You know how to make Margaritas, don't you? And cognac—Martell or Rémy Martin, for instance, or any other popular brand—and any liqueurs you can lay your hands on. Personally, I have a soft corner for Bénédictine, Tia Maria, Cointreau and Kahlúa.

HOW MANY BOTTLES?

Ideally, you should stock three bottles of whisky for every bottle of gin, rum and vodka. Indians love whisky, especially the men, and more so if Scotch is on offer. Unless the crowd is very macho, two bottles of whisky should be sufficient for a party of twenty men and women. But it is always advisable to keep an extra bottle handy. An unopened bottle will last a long, long time. And keep in mind that you cannot measure out more than twenty drinks from a standard 750 ml bottle unless you are a stingy host.

If you have decided to serve wine and if you are moneyed, don't buy those awful French table wines that bootleggers flog. The French label won't impress anyone once they've taken a sip. And remember there will be more guests asking for red wine than white, even in the summer months. Keep some beer handy, too. Indians are not beer drinkers the way the Australians and Germans are, but guests do ask for it, more so if it is a lunch spread. The local beer is good these days if you stick to the better labels.

Most important, whatever you serve has to be the same for all your guests. Never serve Scotch to favoured guests and Indian whisky to the rest at the same party!

sugar syrup

Sugar does not dissolve readily in alcohol. Professional bartenders have enough on their hands when the bar is crowded and, to speed things up, they use simple sugar syrup when they mix cocktails. You can also make it easily at home. Just add two cups of sugar to one cup of cold water in a pot and heat it for five minutes or so until all the sugar is dissolved and the syrup is clear. When it cools down, pour it in a bottle and keep it in the refrigerator. It can be stored for fairly long, and will save you time when you are in the mood for cocktails and prove especially useful when you are entertaining a large number of guests. Another simple solution is to use superfine sugar instead of regular sugar for making cocktails. Or pound the sugar in a mortar till it turns powdery. It will dissolve faster.

juices

Juices are essential ingredients in a wide range of cocktails, the most common being lemon and orange juices. Freshly squeezed juices are infinitely preferable to anything poured out of a carton, bottle or can. Freshly squeezed orange juice makes a world of difference to a Mimosa, for example. And squeezing lemons is easy and hardly time consuming. I suppose, one of the few exceptions in this regard is tomato juice. A good brand poured from a carton is quite acceptable for a Bloody Mary. I do not know anyone who makes tomato juice at home, though it might be worth a try.

Sometimes, of course, using packaged juice is unavoidable. Many fruits, like mango and lychee, are seasonal and some fruits, such as cranberry, do not grow in India. In such cases it is quite acceptable to pour it out of a carton or bottle.

sauces, syrups, condiments and cream

No Bloody Mary will be complete without a dash of two sauces: Tabasco and Worcestershire. The ones made in our country leave much to be desired, so it is better to buy the imported brands. They are not that expensive.

When it comes to a professional bar, the list of things that are required can be endless. Syrups such as grenadine, which is made from pomegranates and lends a sparkling red glow to many cocktails, or orgeat, an almond-flavoured syrup, always come handy. Some of the sweeter cocktails and hot drinks, Irish Coffee for instance, call for light cream.

A good bartender will also have in his cupboard cinnamon sticks, horseradish, ground nutmeg as well as ground pepper, powdered sugar and coarse salt, which work wonderfully as elegant garnishes to very many mixed drinks.

mixers

Most Indians like their whisky with club soda. Unless it is a big party, you should get the club soda available in small bottles since the fizz will disappear once the bottle is opened. Club soda without the fizz is just plain water. For those who like their whisky with water, mineral water is preferable to tap water even if it is boiled.

Tonic water goes well with gin. Some people also prefer it with light rum. Ginger ale is a popular mixer for some drinks as are lemon-lime sodas, such as Seven Up.

TO MAKE ORNAMENTAL ICE CUBES

An attractive, if somewhat elaborate, option is to freeze fruits and other garnishes like raisins or mint leaves in ice cubes. To do this, half fill each compartment of an ice tray with regular water or water flavoured with fruit juice, sugar syrup or bitters. Then dip the fruits and/or other garnishes in water before placing them in the ice tray and setting it to freeze. Once they have frozen, top up the compartments and place in the freezer again to complete the process.

Nothing dampens the mood of a party more than the host running out of ice. When whisky runs out one can switch to rum, but there is no substitute for ice. It is indispensable in our climate, and good ice is imperative for making appetizing drinks, especially cocktails. When it comes to ice, always stock up on more than you think you might need.

The ice should be clear, not cloudy. If your water produces cloudy ice try using bottled mineral water. In any case do not use water straight from the tap. There is a myth that freezing water kills the impurities in it, but that is not the case. The water should be boiled or filtered properly before pouring it in the ice tray. Small cubes are better than large ones. They chill drinks faster and fit more comfortably in glasses.

It is always safer to make ice at home for small parties. For big gatherings buying ice from an outside source is unavoidable, but you must ensure that you buy it from someone reliable. You will find your foreign guests asking for drinks without ice. They do not trust our ice and I don't blame them.

Do not buy a large block of ice and break it into pieces at home. These blocks are almost always made from tap water. They are intended to cool things and not meant for consumption. For that very reason at parties it is wise to refuse ice that is not in the form of cubes.

Many cocktails call for crushed ice. Unlike in the West, you cannot buy crushed ice in our markets. You can crush ice manually by wrapping the cubes in a clean piece of cloth and crushing them with a hard, blunt instrument in the kitchen. Or you can crush the cubes in a blender provided you have one that is sturdy.

Punches sometimes call for a large block of ice to be placed in the punch bowl. You can make this by placing the water in a handi and keeping it in the freezer compartment of your fridge. To remove it from the handi just turn it upside down and run tap water, preferably warm, over the bottom of the handi. The block will dislodge from the handi soon enough.

BAR EQUIPMENT

Unless you are running a professional bar or are seriously into cocktails, you don't really need much by way of equipment. You will find most of the tools you need in your kitchen, but you might want to invest in some essential pieces.

cocktail shaker

If you like to serve more than just whisky–soda or Gin-and-Tonic, you will need a cocktail shaker, the most important and flamboyant of the bar equipment. A regular cocktail shaker is made of either stainless steel, hard plastic or tough glass. It has three parts: the cup, which is the largest part, the top with a built-in strainer and the cap. First, pour the ice cubes and the liquids into the cup. Then screw on the cap. Now shake it vigorously. Remove the cap and strain the chilled liquid into the glass. The excess ice will remain in the cup.

The Boston shaker is less elegant. It consists of a stainless steel cup (a bit like the one used for lassi in dhabas) and a similarly shaped one made of glass. Ice and the liquids are placed in the steel section and the glass is then placed tightly over it, mouth to mouth, forming a seal. The ingredients are shaken and served. The strainer for the ice comes separately. Whichever cocktail shaker you use, don't fill it completely. The drink inside must have room to move and mix.

measure

In America the jigger is the most commonly used device for measuring drinks. It is a small glass with markings on the side that measures up to one and a half ounces of liquid. In India we have something similar to the jigger in the double-sided metal peg. One side measures a single peg (30 ml) while the other measures a double peg (60 ml).

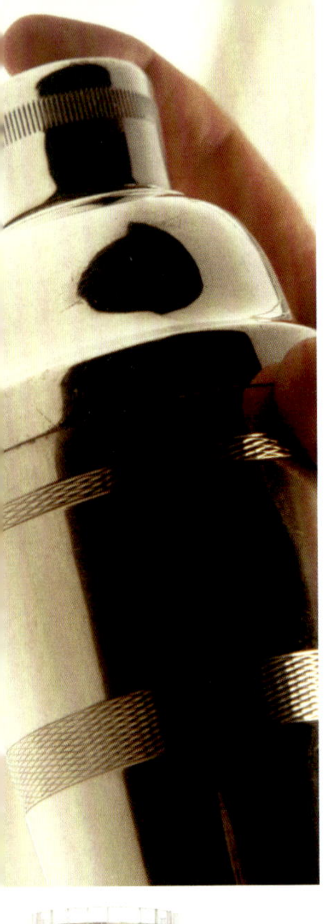

corkscrew

Corkscrews come in a range of shapes and sizes. The old-fashioned corkscrew with a wooden handle requires you to place the bottle between your legs, insert the screw into the cork and pull it out carefully without spilling the wine all over the floor. I find it cumbersome and, more often than not, I make a mess of the procedure.

The sommelier's corkscrew looks like a Swiss army knife and holds a corkscrew, a bottle opener as well as a small knife for removing the sealing material from around the cork. It fits easily into your pocket but, again, it's not easy to use.

The best of all is the wing type which has two arms that rise when the screw is inserted into the cork. You then press down on the wings and the cork pops out. It is reliable in the hands of the inexperienced, though a bit expensive.

bar spoon

A bar spoon is a small teaspoon with a very long handle. It has a number of uses. It can be used for stirring cocktails and can reach the bottom of any glass. It is also useful when you want to float liqueur or cream on top of a cocktail by pouring it over the back of the spoon.

ice bucket

An ice bucket with a fitted lid is essential in any home, whether you drink or not. It saves you running back and forth from the refrigerator.

ice tongs

Ice tongs prevent you from using your hands to pick up ice. I am uncomfortable when hosts or waiters use their fingers to do this.

blender

Every middle-class home has a blender these days. You will need it for making frozen drinks such as Margaritas. A blender is also a good substitute for a cocktail shaker. Be careful while grinding ice. It is a heavy-duty job and you should put cracked or crushed ice in the blender instead of ice cubes. Otherwise you are likely to damage it.

strainer

A strainer proves very handy to strain cocktails that do not call for ice cubes in the glass. Some shakers come with strainers built into them. These are usually the best. Or you can buy a Hawthorn strainer, a flat-topped device that has a continuous metal coil on the underside. It fits comfortably across the mouth of a shaker and mixing glass when the drink is poured out. You don't really need a special strainer if you make cocktails only occasionally. Just wash the tea strainer in your kitchen thoroughly and use it. It will also come in handy for removing seeds when you squeeze lemons.

knife

Keep a superior quality, sharp knife handy for cutting fruit into wedges and slices and for removing skin from lemons for that twist in the Martini.

GLASSES

Get yourself some nice glasses. They are not very expensive these days if you stay clear of crystal and cut pieces.

Some years ago, when I was on a lecture tour, I found myself in the bar of the Empress Hotel on Vancouver Island sipping my drink out of a ceramic mug. I don't recall which drink I had ordered but the mug was shaped like an elephant and it had a straw sticking out of its back. Normally I would not drink anything with a straw but here I had no choice since the drinking end had a narrow opening. I got to keep the ugly mug as a souvenir and for years I used it to store the pens and pencils on my desk.

Good glasses are essential for the enjoyment of cocktails as well as something as simple as whisky on the rocks. They enhance drinks. They lend panache and flair to parties. I hope I don't sound like a snob when I say I hate drinking anything out of a paper cup. Plastic containers are only marginally better. Americans are notorious for using paper plates and cups at their parties. Indians have no excuse since most of us have paid help who can clean up afterwards. Hand-blown crystal is always lovely to own but machine-made glasses are fine for day to day entertaining. The glass need not be crystal but it should be a cut or two above what you use in the kitchen for water.

Thanks to easing of imports, good-looking glassware is available these days in any decent crockery shop. They come in a mind-boggling range. Apparently, there are as many as 572 kinds of glassware for drinks. In practice, however, only a few basic types are necessary for your bar.

Glasses of various shapes and sizes are described below. I have not mentioned special-purpose glasses for serving the more esoteric beverages such as Irish Coffee and parfaits.

highball or collins glass

The tallest of the tumblers, this glass is used more than any other. The Collins glass is used to serve juices, fizzy, aerated drinks and any long drink that requires a sparkling mixer, whisky–soda, Gin-and-Tonic, etc. The

height and narrowness of the glass serve to hold back the bubbles longer and there is always room for ice cubes. It's best to invest in ones that are heavy-bottomed. While buying, tap one of them with your fingernail or a spoon and if it produces a sound of high register you are on the right track.

shot glass

This glass is for drinking neat shots of alcohol in one gulp, such as frozen vodka or tequila. You have probably seen them displayed in saloon bars in hundreds of cowboy movies. It holds no more than 60 ml (4 tbsp) and can also be used for measuring drinks.

martini or cocktail glass

The Martini or cocktail glass has a wide conical or V-shaped bowl on a long stem and is essential for anyone who enjoys mixing cocktails. The glass is used to serve chilled concoctions that do not have ice floating in them. The stem prevents your hand from warming the cold drink.

old-fashioned glass

This is your 'on the rocks' glass. Old-fashioned glasses are usually no more than four inches tall and hold 250 ml. These glasses are used to serve whisky and also drinks that are served with ice. At a pinch, they can be used for just about any drink. My old-fashioned glasses are an inch thick at the base. A bit macho perhaps, but I like the feel of a heavy, robust glass in my hand, sparkling with ice.

liqueur glass

Also known as the 'pony' because it is small and holds no more than 90 ml or six tablespoons. It is used for after-dinner drinks which are served straight, such as Bénédictine and Cointreau.

brandy balloon or snifter

You cannot fully enjoy a good cognac, armagnac or other brandy without this glass. Also known as the 'snifter', its wide middle and narrower opening traps the fragrance of the drink and allows you to inhale the wonderful aroma of a good brandy. For the purest pleasure you are meant to cup your hand around the glass to gently warm the drink and release its aroma. Never pour more than a few tablespoons at a time into the glass. It is advisable not to buy snifters the size of flower bowls. They look pretentious and impair the enjoyment of the drink.

goblet

Similar in shape to the brandy balloon, this one also has a stem but its rim is much larger than that of a snifter. It is good for serving frothy drinks that contain cream or crushed fruit, such as Piña Coladas. The wide rim will also allow you to use fancy garnishes like pineapple and orange wedges.

champagne flute

The flute, shaped like a tulip, has now become the more acceptable glass for serving sparkling wines. Since less surface area is exposed to air, it conserves the bubbles better. This glass too must always be held by the stem. It can also be used to serve champagne cocktails like the Kir Royale.

champagne saucer

It is no longer fashionable to use the saucer for champagne. Use them by all means if you are ancient like me and still have them around. But they are more useful for cocktails that have crushed ice or fruit slices floating in them, as also for Frozen Margaritas.

red wine glass

It holds about 500 ml but should never be filled more than a third full. This will allow the wine 'to breathe' and release its bouquet. I also use them for my Gin-and-Tonics and Bloody Marys.

white wine glass

This one is smaller than the red wine glass, with a capacity of 150–200 ml. Unless you are a connoisseur of wine, it is perfectly acceptable to serve white wine in red wine glasses. If you plan to buy only one type of wine glass, you will be better off buying the larger red wine glass.

beer glass

There are two kinds of beer glasses. The big, thick pint-sized mugs with handles, which were once popular in London pubs and the beer halls of Munich, and the tall, narrow glasses without handles which hold the same quantity and are more commonly used now. The latter also come in a smaller size that holds a half pint of suds. The Pilsener glass, which is shaped like an elongated, lightly curved V and holds about 300 ml, is more elegant.

TIPS ON GLASSWARE

- If you buy sturdy glasses and handle them carefully they will last for years.
- Glasses must be colourless. Let the drink shine through unimpeded. A clear, uncomplicated glass is the best showcase for a drink.
- Glasses should be cleaned thoroughly, preferably polished.
- Serving drinks in pre-chilled glasses has a distinct advantage. Keep the glasses in the fridge, not in the freezer, for an hour or so before you begin serving your guests. This will give the glass a nice frosted look. Or you can simply fill a glass with cracked ice and stir it around. You can create an aura of romance by serving a cocktail in a goblet instead of an ordinary glass. Something as simple as Gin-and-Tonic will look more inviting in a wine glass. And, in fact, wine glasses are frequently used to serve all kinds of cocktails. For straight liquors and liqueurs you will need some small 60–90 ml glasses. As for beer, you could just use the highball. Always remember that the most important thing about glasses is what you put in them.

GARNISHES

A garnish is something that decorates a drink and often contributes to its flavour. The **pineapple wedge** in a Piña Colada, for instance, is there just as a decoration while the **grated nutmeg** floating on a Brandy Alexander serves two purposes: it decorates the drink and adds to its taste. Both are garnishes, something added at the final stage in preparing a cocktail. A Martini is not complete without a **lemon twist** or an **olive**. **Lemon and orange slices** and **wedges** are also used in many cocktails. A gin-and-tonic is not the same without a slice of lemon. **Cucumber peels** and **mint leaves** are used for Pimm's. You will find flowers in rum cocktails ordered in tropical resorts. **Celery sticks** are put in Bloody Marys. **Coffee beans** are dropped in Sambucas.

One of the most popular garnishes is **maraschino cherry**. You can make it at home from fresh cherries but most of us prefer to buy it in small jars. They are bright red and are essential in the preparation of Manhattans, Shirley Temples and a wide range of other cocktails. They also enhance the look of simple cocktails like the Tom Collins.

Many cocktail recipes call for the use of lemon or lime juice, and **lemon or lime wedges.** In the recipes included in this book I have not differentiated between a 'lemon' and a 'lime' since all one can find in our markets are those round things, the shape and size of golf balls, which you buy for the kitchen. They are widely known as 'cagdi nimboo'. They look like limes, but unlike the green limes found in the rest of the world they are yellow in colour, like lemons. So, are they limes or lemons? Well, I'm not quite sure.

TO MAKE A TWIST

Use a knife to cut a small strip of the rind of a lemon or an orange, starting at the top of the fruit and continuing as long as you can towards the bottom. If done properly you will get a strip that is a quarter inch to a half inch wide. Cut carefully so as not to slice the pulp of the fruit and keep as little of the white part as possible on the rind. Hold it between both hands over the cocktail and twist it to release the fragrant oils. Rub the twist on the rim of the glass and gently drop it in the glass so that it floats.

TO MAKE A WEDGE

Slice the fruit through the middle with the skin intact; not too thin, not too thick. Now cut it into four equal sections and remove the seeds. You will have four wedges. Wedge one on the rim of the glass after the cocktail has been poured. You may prefer to squeeze the citrus wedges into the drink and then drop it in the glass. It's your choice.

As long as they are juicy and sour you can use them whenever 'lemons' are required in any of the recipes.

Then there are the **twists**, long strips of lemon or orange skin more precisely known as **rind** or **peel**. Twists are twisted over a cocktail releasing their oils into the drink. The lemons that grow in the cooler regions of the world produce much more oil than the lemons we get in India, and you will have to make that extra effort to squeeze out a little oil. As for oranges, it's always better to use the imported ones found in our markets.

Wedges are another popular cocktail garnish. Fruits that are commonly used as wedges are lemon, orange and, for an exotic tropical drink, pineapple. Ensure that you use good, fresh, ripe fruit that will enhance the taste of the cocktail with its flavour and aroma.

HOW TO ...

measure

I have stuck to metric measurements for the recipes in this book. However, if you prefer the widely used 'ounce', approximately 30 ml make an ounce. If you don't have these measures handy, all you have to do is remember that two tablespoons make about 30 ml.

When it comes to measurements, drink recipes are much simpler than food recipes. Accurate measurements are not all that important in mixing drinks. A lot depends on personal tastes. I, for one, add lots of lemon juice to my Bloody Mary because I prefer it on the sour side. Others may not. The measurements used in this book are there as guidelines and to give you some degree of confidence when you try out a new cocktail. Otherwise, you might go and add equal parts of vodka and tomato juice and make a right mess of a Bloody Mary!

When you are preparing cocktails the following guide will be helpful:

Teaspoon: It is the spoon you use for stirring tea. Its capacity is about 5 ml or a third of a tablespoon. Six teaspoons will make 30 ml or an ounce.

Tablespoon: Three teaspoons make 15 ml or one tablespoon. Two tablespoons make 30 ml or an ounce.

Peg: It is equivalent to 30 ml or an ounce. Two tablespoons or six teaspoons make a peg. A large peg is twice that.

Dash: A dash is about one-eighth of a teaspoon. You never measure a dash. It is just a little bit of something that is added through guesswork, or should I say instinct. This measurement is used for the more potent ingredients, such as Angostura bitters or Worcestershire sauce, too much of which will overpower the mix.

shake, stir and blend

Mixed drinks that have juices and sugar are usually shaken. Shaking with ice is the most common way of mixing the various ingredients of a cocktail. Not only does it chill the drink but it also dilutes it slightly. Diluting a mixed drink helps release the flavours. Shaking, instead of stirring, also produces a nice froth. Never fill the shaker more than half with ice. Use ice cubes instead of crushed ice unless the recipe states otherwise. Shake the contents vigorously until the outside is frosted and cold to the touch.

Drinks are usually stirred when the ingredients mix easily and you don't want the cocktail to get cloudy. The basic principle is the same as shaking: you want the ingredients to mix and chill quickly. You can stir the contents in a shaker or mixing glass with a bar spoon and pour it into the serving glass, or even stir inside the serving glass.

Ingredients of a cocktail may also be blended. Using a blender chills the mix more than the other methods since a blender crushes the ice, but at the same time the cocktail will become more dilute. Many people prefer it this way. Blenders are indispensable for

making frozen drinks at home. The process can be tricky but it will only take a few failed attempts for you to get the hang of it.

rim

Some drinks require the rim of the glass to be coated with salt or sugar, Margaritas for instance. The method is quite simple. Cut a piece of lemon and run it along the rim of the glass to moisten it with lemon juice. Now place the glass upside down on a small, flat plate containing salt or sugar so that the rim gets coated. If you are using salt, it is preferable to use coarse salt. Otherwise the salt you use in your kitchen will suffice. Professionals recommend that only the outside of the rim should be coated. Otherwise granules of salt or sugar may fall into the drink and affect its balance. Rimming only the outside is a more cumbersome exercise and, frankly, one need not be too fussy about it.

muddle

Some recipes, such as that of the popular cocktail Mojito, require muddling. The process involves mashing or pressing the ingredients together. This is done at the bottom of the glass itself, often with bitters, sugar, fruits, herbs, etc. To do this, you can borrow the pestle you use to pound dry spices such as black pepper and jeera. Then crush the ingredients firmly, making sure you don't break the glass. When pressing a herb do it gently, making sure you just bruise it and don't turn it into paste.

float

Brightly coloured syrups or cream may be floated on some drinks like Irish Coffee and Tequila Sunrise. This gives the drink an attractive, layered look and divides it into distinct levels of taste in the mouth. To layer a drink place the back of a spoon over the rim of the glass and pour the syrup or cream very slowly over the drink. This will allow the liquid to gently spread over the top of the drink and the desired effect will be achieved.

MODERATION

I have enormous respect for people who abstain from alcohol for religious or other reasons—I am myself a product of one such family—but it has been medically established that drinking in moderation can be good for you.

Alcohol reduces stress and doctors have gone so far as to recommend one to three glasses of wine a day. Among alcoholic beverages, red wine is the best for you. It contains potassium, iron and antioxidants which protect the heart by breaking down 'bad' cholesterol that can clog the arteries. In fact, most alcoholic beverages help in this to some extent.

On the downside, alcohol is virtually worthless when it comes to nutrition. And when drunk in excess it can be very harmful, even fatal. Excessive drinking can put a strain on the normal functioning of your liver and sometimes damage it beyond repair. Too much alcohol also depletes the body of valuable nutrients such as vitamins A, B and C. It is important to remember that alcohol is an intoxicant and a powerful one, less dangerous than tobacco maybe but an intoxicant nevertheless.

It may be useful to understand how alcohol works on your body. After you drink it, the liquor spends some time in the stomach before travelling to the intestine. Some of it gets absorbed into the bloodstream by passing through the walls of the intestine. The blood carries alcohol through the body and some of it gets transferred to the lungs, which is why your breath continues to smell of alcohol for quite a while after you have been drinking and the breath analyser used by the police can detect the amount of alcohol in your blood.

For an average person, weighing around seventy kilos, the body can handle about one drink per hour without any noticeable signs of drunkenness. As a general rule a woman's capacity is said to be two glasses for every three for a man.

So, how much is moderate consumption? Alcohol tolerance varies from person to person but, generally speaking, one to three

TO AVOID GETTING DRUNK

- Before you start drinking alcohol, drink a glass of milk or a tablespoon of olive oil. Olive oil tastes better than other edible oils. This will line the stomach and slow down the effects of alcohol.
- Munch something with your drink. High protein foods like kebabs and nuts will slow down the absorption of alcohol in the bloodstream. If you're at a party, bully your host into serving dinner early.
- Sip your drink, don't guzzle. Be careful while drinking fruit-based drinks like a Bloody Mary or a Screwdriver. They go down all too easily and can be deceptively potent.
- Drink a glass of water for every peg of alcohol. If you forget, then drink lots of water before going to bed to avoid discomfort the next morning.

drinks a day is considered moderate for most people, when the 'drink' is measured as a can or small bottle of beer or 30 ml of any liquor. A glass of wine should be no more than 125 ml, no matter how large the glass is.

Emotional problems and stress can sometimes lead to alcohol abuse. An alcoholic is someone who is so preoccupied with drinks that it interferes with his work and family life. Alcoholism is a disease, not a weakness, and it should be treated as such with professional help. An important thing to remember: under no circumstances should you drink and drive. Keep in mind that by indulging in such irresponsible behaviour you are not only endangering your own life but also the lives of others.

HANGOVERS: THE MORNING AFTER

Unless you are a teetotaller or always drink in moderation, hangovers are inevitable. Following a night of excessive drinking, your head will ache, noises will make you wince and bright lights will hurt your eyes.

You may even suffer complete loss of memory of the events of the previous night.

Hangovers are mainly caused by the body producing too much insulin, which results in low blood sugar levels. The brain swells up and starts rubbing against the skull, resulting in an excruciating headache. Chemicals that are formed in the production of alcohol, called congeners, also contribute to the hangover. Congeners are poison and your body recognizes them as such. As a rule, the darker drinks, whisky and brandy, for instance, have more congeners than white drinks like gin and vodka. Cheap drinks made with cheap ingredients are more likely to give you a hangover than more expensive ones.

It is always good to know what and how much your body can tolerate. Genes play a major part in this. Some people seldom, if ever, have hangovers, no matter how much they drink, and there are others who are hopeless after a bottle of beer.

Human beings have been in search of a hangover cure for a long time. The ancient Romans were partial to owl eggs. Mint tea seems to work for Moroccans. Jews go for chicken soup. There is a school of thought that believes that inhaling pure oxygen is a sure cure for a hangover. Kingsley Amis, the novelist, once suggested vigorous sex as the perfect remedy. Since alcohol also dehydrates your system and causes general discomfort, most doctors agree that drinking lots of water or anything that helps rehydrate the body will have a beneficial effect. Aspirin and other painkillers are not a good idea. You have already given your liver a hard time with all that drinking. Popping pills will just give it more work to do and might even cause damage.

Officials in the KGB, the secret service of the former Soviet Union, had allegedly invented a pill to keep its spies sober so that they could drink their opponents under the table and steal their secrets. It is still made in Russia and marketed in the United States as RU-21. It is apparently popular among Hollywood stars. It helps them party all night and still deliver their lines on the film set the next day without any distraction or discomfort. But no medical tests have been conducted to prove its effectiveness.

Scientists are reluctant to come up with a cure for hangovers since the subject raises ethical questions. A foolproof cure might encourage people to drink excessively, knowing they can take a pill and avoid suffering the next day. The idea that an airline pilot or a bus driver can take something for a hangover and go to work is a frightening one.

THE
GOOD
STUFF

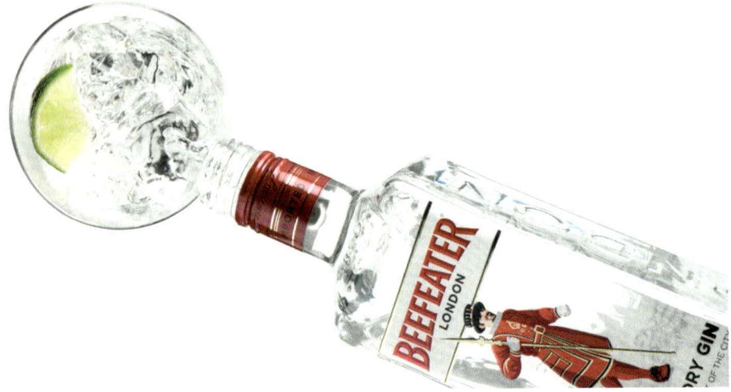
BEEFEATER
LONDON

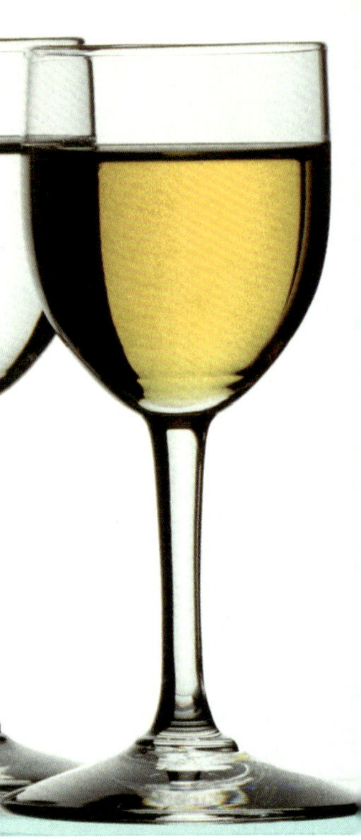

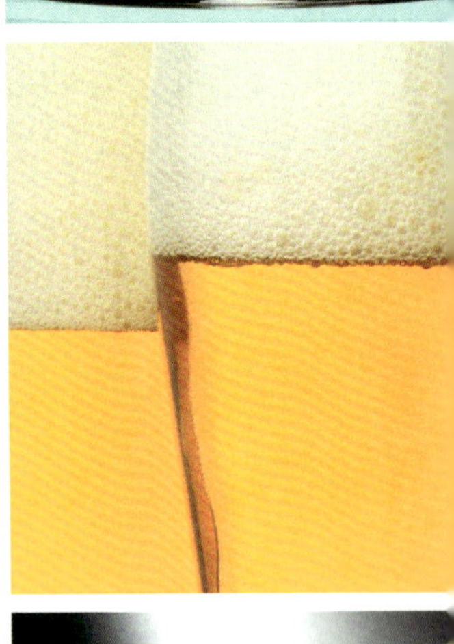

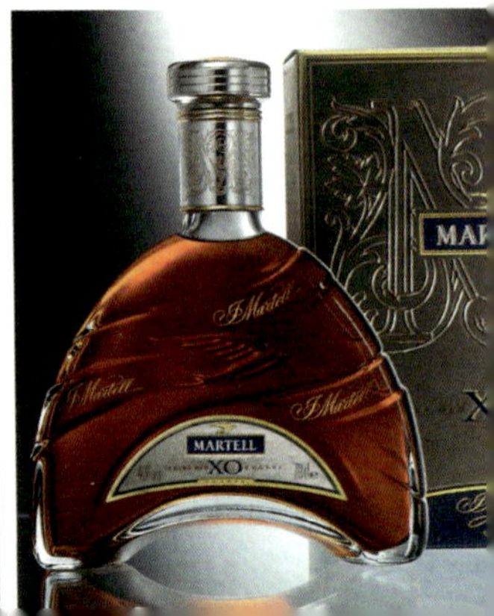

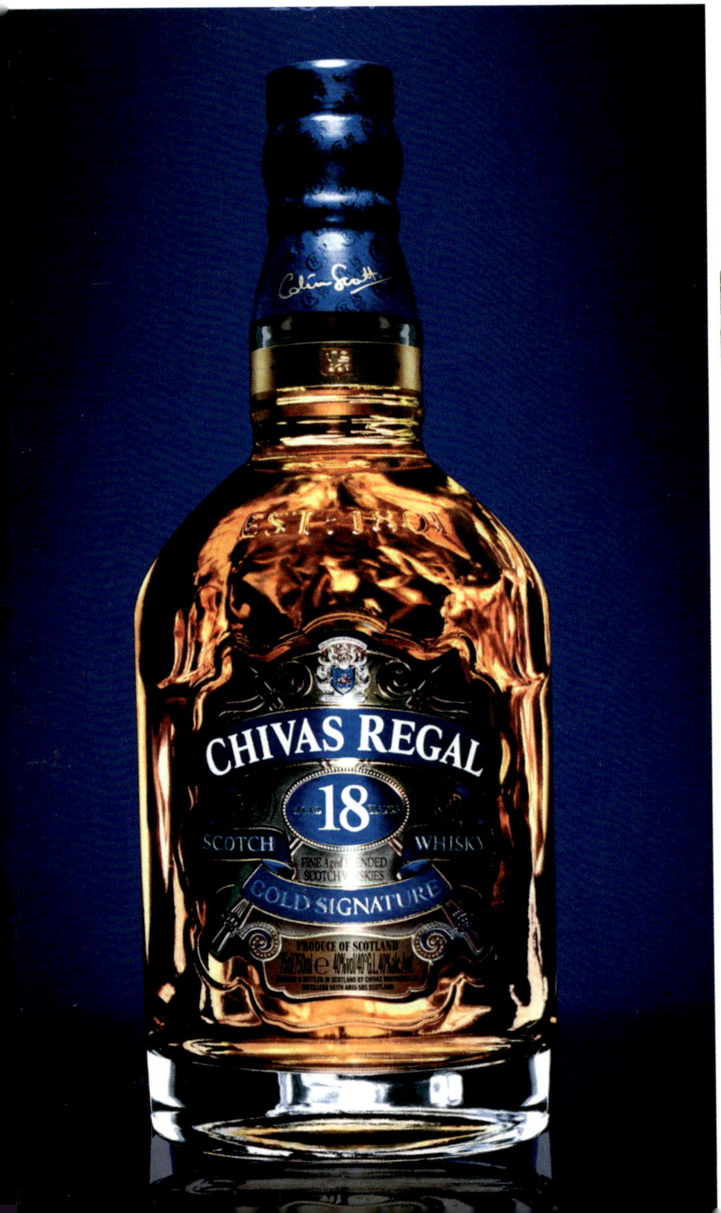
CHIVAS REGAL
18
SCOTCH
WHISKY
GOLD SIGNATURE
PRODUCE OF SCOTLAND

MARTELL
XO

SPIRITS

We know that wine is produced by fermenting grapes and beer is brewed from grains and hops. Spirits, on the other hand, are products of distillation. There is a good reason why distilled liquors are known as spirits: A good brandy will capture the spirit of the grape from which it is made; a good Scotch will do the same for the grain from which it is prepared. Plainly put, a spirit is the result of humble ingredients such as grain, fruit or vegetable being transformed by an intricate process into something splendid and pleasurable.

You cannot drink spirits the way you can drink wine or beer. A bottled spirit is usually 40 per cent alcohol, sometimes more, while wine and beer have a maximum alcohol content of 15 per cent. It is wiser therefore to slowly sip a spirit even when it has been diluted with a soft mix such as a juice or a carbonated drink. Otherwise it can get you into trouble.

The early Egyptians, Greeks, Chinese and Indians knew how to make wine and brew something equivalent to modern-day beer thousands of years ago. They also knew a thing or two about distillation. Aristotle, the Greek philosopher, wrote that 'sea water can be made drinkable by distillation'. In fact, ancient civilizations learnt how to make perfumes, medicines and flavourings through distillation. What they probably did not know was how to distill alcohol. When it comes to things alcoholic, historians are very loose with facts and make all kinds of claims on behalf of their countries.

It is fair to say that serious distillation of alcohol did not begin until the tenth century. If spirits were produced before that, it was not on a significant scale. Credit for inventing the distillation process is most often given to the Arabs, and that may be true. But it was the Italians who, roughly around the twelfth century, turned

TO PRESERVE SPIRITS AND LIQUEURS

- Store in a cool, dark space, away from direct sunlight. Brown spirits like whisky and rum stored in transparent bottles lose their colour over time with exposure to sunlight. Bottles with spirits or liqueurs need to be stored upright.
- Once opened, spirits will last quite long at room temperature, but it will be wise to refrigerate liqueur bottles, specially the milk- and egg-based liqueurs. The trick of course is to consume a liqueur within six months of opening the bottle. Spirits can be kept in the freezer as long as they contain 40 per cent or more alcohol. A liquor with a lower percentage of alcohol will freeze.
- Decant. If you have half a bottle of something precious it is best to decant it into a smaller bottle up to the top so that it does not come into contact with air. You could also place a bunch of glass marbles in a bottle so that the liquid reaches the top.

PROOF AND ABV

'Proof' indicates the strength of a liquor, ranging from 1 to 200; 200 proof alcohol is pure alcohol. 'Proof' is twice the percentage of alcohol in a drink. For example, Scotch whisky usually has 40 per cent alcohol and is therefore 80 proof. The average wine is 20 to 30 proof and an average beer about 8 proof. Increasingly, fewer and fewer labels on liquor bottles indicate proof. This is because 'ABV' is simpler to figure out.

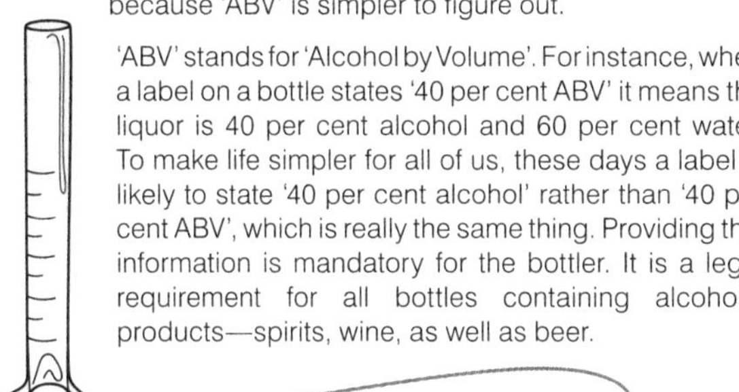

'ABV' stands for 'Alcohol by Volume'. For instance, when a label on a bottle states '40 per cent ABV' it means the liquor is 40 per cent alcohol and 60 per cent water. To make life simpler for all of us, these days a label is likely to state '40 per cent alcohol' rather than '40 per cent ABV', which is really the same thing. Providing this information is mandatory for the bottler. It is a legal requirement for all bottles containing alcoholic products—spirits, wine, as well as beer.

the process into an industry by mass-producing brandy from wine.

The actual method of distillation has not changed much over the centuries. The first step is to ferment the principal ingredient with yeast and water to draw out the sugar and then separate the resulting alcohol from the rest of the mush. Distillation itself is a relatively simple procedure based on the fact that water and alcohol have different boiling points. Water boils at 100 degrees Celsius while alcohol boils at a lower temperature of 78.3 degrees Celsius. To separate the water from the alcohol, all you have to do is to heat something that contains alcohol in a still to a temperature of more than 78.3 degrees Celsius but less than a hundred. As the alcohol boils, it rises in the form of vapour to the top of the still where it collects and condenses into liquid form. Traditionally, onion-shaped copper pots have been used to boil alcohol and the vapours are captured in pipes emerging from them. Modern distilleries have designed their equipment keeping functionality and economy of space and budgets in mind. Most of them construct long steel columns that perform the same functions and are as efficient as the traditional copper pots.

What follows is the tricky part: making the alcohol drinkable. Also, since some of the water vaporizes early and some of the alcohol vaporizes late, the result of the first distillation is not exactly firewater. It is only about 25 per cent alcohol, not much stronger than wine. If redistilled, it will, of course, end up as something more potent. This stuff, however, will not taste great unless you are accustomed to buying liquor in plastic bottles from bootleggers. Badly distilled spirits contain methanol, which can be poisonous, as well as foul-smelling by-products of the ingredient that has been fermented to produce the spirit. It takes a great deal of expertise to turn this liquid into something you would want to drink.

Except for the Saudis, the Iranians and the Gujaratis, just about everyone else makes spirits of some kind from something that has sugar in it: potato, beetroot, sugar cane, even banana skin, and rotting fruits and vegetables. Some of this stuff is not good hooch, but it is hooch nevertheless.

Fruits are the easiest to work with because they have high sugar content, their own supply of liquid and ferment very easily. Grape is the most popular fruit in southern Europe. Further north, where grapes do not grow too well, spirits are distilled from a variety of grains: whisky and vodka, for instance. In the tropics sugar cane is used to make rum.

A sealed bottle of hard liquor can be preserved almost indefinitely but a five-year-old Scotch won't become a superior ten-year-old Scotch just because you have resisted opening the bottle for five long years. Spirits age in barrels, never in bottles. A feature of many good spirits, such as whisky and brandy, is that after distillation they are matured in oak barrels for several years, which contributes enormously to both the colour and flavour of the spirit.

whisky

SCOTCH

'Scotch whisky is a mystery, a magic of locality. The foreigner may import not only Scottish barley, but Scottish water, Scottish distilling apparatus, and set a Scot to work on them, but the glory evaporates; it will not travel.'

—Ivor Brown in *Summer in Scotland*

India's passion for Scotch whisky remains unmatched anywhere in the world. The Chinese are big on cognac, the French stick to wine and Americans are partial to white spirits, and even an Englishman or English woman is more likely to order a pint of bitter or wine instead of a peg of whisky. But give an Indian a glass of Scotch and he is in high heaven. It is the fuel that propels our parties.

If you ask me, when it comes to Scotch whisky the magic is in the water used to make it. How else do you explain that no one outside Scotland has been able to replicate Scotch? Some whiskies from Ireland, Canada and the United States are quite good. So is the Suntory brand from Japan. But all of them pale in comparison to Scotch.

HOW SCOTCH IS MADE

Malt whisky in Scotland is made exclusively from barley. Earliest records of production go back to 1494 and the process has remained unchanged for hundreds of years. The oldest of the existing distilleries date from the 1700s. When whisky production began, the notion of brands was unknown and whisky was sold by the barrel to merchants who dispensed it in whatever container was available. Johnnie Walker was one such merchant and George Ballantine another. The Chivas brothers were partners in another shop. John Dewar started his business in 1806 and was the first to sell branded whisky in bottles.

Let me try to explain how Scotch is made without getting into too much detail. Before distillation, barley is softened in water, germinated (made to sprout the way we sprout green moong) and then dried by heating in a kiln or a furnace over peat (vegetable matter used for fuel). The smoky flavour you find in malt whiskies comes from the peat. The aim is to ferment the barley, and the malt that is produced is heated with water and mixed with yeast. After two days the liquid is strained and the brew that is obtained has about 5–8 per cent alcohol. It is a little like beer.

As I have mentioned earlier, the water used in the process plays a crucial role. The quality of the water in the Scottish Highlands is influenced by the rock from which it rises and also by the land over which it flows before it reaches the distillery. It may pass over heather, peat and land rich in minerals. The site for setting up a new distillery is primarily determined by the source and quality of water.

This brew, known as wash, is then distilled in a large onion-shaped copper pot and heated to a temperature at which the alcohol vaporizes and passes into a cooling plant where it condenses into liquid form. This is the first distillation and it separates out the alcohol. The product is now about 28 per cent alcohol by volume. The second distillation takes place in a smaller still and the resulting colourless spirit contains about 70 per cent alcohol. It is diluted with water and then aged for several years in oak casks. The quality of the cask determines the colour and aroma of a whisky. The minimum period for ageing, required by law, is three years. It is estimated that up to 60 per cent of a whisky's flavour comes from the cask it has been aged in. The colour too comes mainly from the cask.

Often, casks which have previously been used to mature sherry are used. This will give the whisky a darker colour than one which has been matured in refilled whisky casks. A tiny amount of colouring, from caramelized sugar, will also be added to bring consistency to a particular brand. J&B is known for its light colour while Johnnie Walker Red Label, in the same price range, is darker. Here is a bit of trivia: the part of whisky that evaporates from the casks is called the 'Angel's Share'.

Now we come to **grain whisky**. This is distilled mainly from corn and wheat. The process is less complicated. Instead of pots, a continuous still is used which makes industrial production possible. The grain is boiled and mixed with yeast to enable fermentation. In a relatively short time pure, neutral-tasting alcohol is produced, which is mixed with malt whisky to produce blended Scotch. Grain whisky has been dismissed sometimes as nothing more than Scottish vodka, a mere addition to the malts to make Scotch more affordable.

SINGLE MALT

About thirty years ago one rarely came across a bottle of single malt whisky in India. The few who had discovered its pleasures had their stock hidden in cupboards and seldom offered it to guests. Glenlivet and Glenfiddich were the first brands to gain a wide following and now there are dozens of brands to choose from. All of them are good if they come from Scotland. I am told that Australia, New Zealand, Japan and even the distillery in Murree in Pakistan produces single malts. But since I have not encountered them, all I can tell you is that you cannot go wrong with Scottish single malts.

Traditionally, there were four distilling regions in Scotland: Lowland, Highland, Islay and Campbeltown. Now, more than half of Scotland's malt distilleries are located in Speyside, a modern sub-division of Highland. It is the home of Glenlivet and Glenfiddich, two of the world's best-selling single malts. Laphroaig, one of my favourite single malts, comes from the island of Islay. I love the flavour of salt and seaweed it has acquired from the ocean washing against the distillery's walls.

THE
GLENLIVET
FRENCH OAK RESERVE
SINGLE MALT SCOTCH
WHISKY
15
ESTD 1824
OAK RESERVE
ESTD GEORGE & J.G. SMITH LTD 1824

THE
GLENLIVET
18
SINGLE MALT SCOTCH
WHISKY
ESTD 1824
ESTD GEORGE & J.G. SMITH LTD 1824
DISTILLERS of SCOTCH WHISKY
SCOTLAND

18

HOW SINGLE MALTS ARE MADE

Single malts are made only from barley, as all malt whiskies are. A single malt whisky is whisky that has been produced in one distillery and is not a mixture of malt whiskies from several distilleries. Single malt Scotches are produced in more than a hundred distilleries. Each distillery uses malted barley as the base, but variations in the atmospheric conditions, the water used during the distillation process, the shape of the still and features of the ageing barrels are factors that determine the characteristics of the final product. The produce of two distilleries located next to each other can taste quite different.

Whiskies which are labelled 'Pure Malt' are made from malted barley, like the single malt whiskies. They are not blended with whisky made from any other grain, but are mixtures of malt whiskies produced in several distilleries. I prefer single malt whiskies to the pure malts because the former are of superior quality marked by a particular distillery's subtle individual touches.

Most single malts are aged for at least eight years, some for considerably longer. As with all other whiskies, or spirits for that matter, the ageing takes place in oak barrels, not in bottles.

SERVING AND DRINKING

Single malts are a slow pleasure, to be drunk in moderation. Whatever you do, never, ever drown a single malt whisky in soda. The gods that look after whisky drinkers will smite you for the sacrilege. You are allowed a drop or two of water, or a solitary ice cube, if you must.

BLENDED SCOTCH

While connoisseurs prefer single malts, blended Scotch whiskies are far more popular because the addition of light-bodied grain whiskies reduces the intensity.

Indeed, 95 per cent of the Scotch drunk around the world is blended. Chivas Regal and Black Label are among the more expensive brands available in India. Other popular brands of blended Scotches in the middle price range include Ballantine's, Famous Grouse, Red Label, 100 Pipers and Passport.

HOW BLENDED SCOTCH IS MADE

Blending is done by combining a number of single malt Scotches with neutral grain whiskies. A normal blend consists of thirty to forty different whiskies with the portion of malt whiskies varying from 5 per cent to 70 per cent in each. An expensive brand such as Chivas Regal has more of malt whiskies in it. A brand like VAT 69 has more of grain whiskies, which are less complicated to produce.

SERVING AND DRINKING

A Scotsperson would not dream of drinking his or her whisky any other way but straight, without the interference of any added ingredients. This is understandable because in their climate the whisky bottles on their shelves are readily cold. Those of us living in warmer climates and ever so often in urgent need of a cool, refreshing drink prefer blended whisky with a dash or two of club soda and ice cubes. A smaller number prefer it with water. There is absolutely nothing wrong with this as long as you do not overdilute the whisky. As for me, I prefer blended Scotch with lots of ice cubes. No water, no soda. The ice cubes melt quite rapidly and leave me nursing a chilled drink, which is just the way it should be.

BOURBON

Bourbon is America's only native spirit. It is a type of whisky, except that the Americans spell it differently: whiskey.

Bourbon is quintessentially American, like baseball, apple pie and, of course, corn, which made bourbon possible. Early settlers from Scotland and Ireland began distilling whisky as a side business to farming. Corn grew in abundance in their new homeland and the farmers put the surplus to good use. In the late eighteenth century there were over 5000 stills operating in Pennsylvania alone, but it was Kentucky that was to become the hub of America's whisky industry. In fact, the name 'bourbon' is derived from Bourbon County in eastern Kentucky, which in turn was named after the Bourbon royals of France.

Among the better known bourbon brands are Wild Turkey, Jim Beam, Knob Creek and Maker's Mark. Tennessee whisky is a first cousin of bourbon. It is different in that, before barrelling, the whisky is filtered through charcoal made from sugar maple wood. This gives it a distinct smoky flavour. By far the best known brand is Jack Daniels

INDIAN WHISKY

India is the world's largest consumer of whisky. We drink about 600 million litres of the spirit in a year, 40 per cent more than the United States, the second largest consumer of whisky. No other spirit or brew comes close to such popularity.

Almost 90 per cent of the whiskies produced in India are in reality close relatives of rum and not 'whisky' as the rest of the world defines the product. Whisky is, by definition, made from grain—mainly barley, but other grains like wheat and rye are also used. Almost all Indian whiskies are made from molasses, a by-product of the process of extracting crystal sugar from sugar cane juice. Molasses can be used to make ethanol, as Brazil does, or for making what the liquor industry calls 'extra neutral alcohol', which is tasteless and colourless.

The low-end Indian whisky available for around a hundred rupees is alcohol to which caramel has been added to give it an acceptable colour, and essence and tinctures to approximate the taste of genuine whisky. One step up the ladder is alcohol to which, in addition to all of the above, a small amount of locally produced malt whisky is added. In India malt whisky is produced from barley that is grown mostly along the Haryana–Rajasthan border. So, why don't our distilleries switch from molasses to grain? It is a question of cost. Molasses is a waste product and is cheap and readily available. Grain is expensive. And who wants to go through the process of ageing the spirit in oak barrels for four years or more?

Fortunately, we do have a few distilleries that make whisky from grain. Seagram's Blenders Pride and Royal Stag, for instance, have no molasses alcohol content, they are a blend of Scotch malts and Indian grain spirits. India also makes single malts exclusively from local barley: Solan's No. 1 is marketed only within the country while Amrut, a brand from Bangalore, has found a niche in the Indian restaurants of Scotland.

which has the second highest whisky sales worldwide. Only Johnnie Walker Red Label Scotch sells more.

HOW BOURBON IS MADE

American whiskies are grain spirits that are produced by mixing different proportions of corn, rye, barley, wheat and other grains. In America the law requires that a particular whisky must contain at least 51 per cent of the primary grain along with lesser amounts of other varieties. For instance, American rye whisky should contain 51 per cent rye and lesser amounts of corn and barley. Since bourbon is made from corn it must contain at least 51 per cent corn. Both have to be aged for a minimum of two years in new charred barrels. In practice, almost all American whiskies are aged for at least four years and many of the brands are made with quite a bit more than 51 per cent of the required grain.

SERVING AND DRINKING

Indians will probably find the taste of bourbon harsh compared to that of Scotch. Bourbon can be drunk the same way as other whiskies but I have seen American bartenders serving it on ice, with a lemon twist. Give it a try. After all, you are not likely to drink bourbon every evening.

OTHER WHISKIES

There are a number of other countries that produce whiskies, among them Canada, Ireland, Japan, United States and, to a limited extent, France and Germany. Of these, Irish whiskey is the best known. Though the Scots may deny it, they probably learnt the process of distilling alcohol from the Irish. At one time, the quality of Irish whiskey was considered superior to the product of Scotland. That is why they started spelling it 'whiskey', with an 'e', to distinguish it from the stuff produced by their northeastern neighbour.

To be called Irish whiskey, the liquor must be distilled in Ireland from Irish grain and it must be stored in wooden casks for at least three years. In practice, the storage period is much longer. While Scotland has nearly a hundred distilleries, Ireland has only three, in Middleton, Bushmills and Cooley. They produce blended whiskies as well as single malts. Scotch is mostly distilled twice, while Irish whiskey is always distilled three times. This gives it a smoother flavour.

Jameson is the best known of the Irish brands. Over 30 million bottles are sold annually worldwide, with Ireland and United States consuming most of it.

If you ever decide to make Irish Coffee, a delicious, hot, winter cocktail, I suggest you use Irish whiskey. Otherwise it would be anything but Irish Coffee!

PROHIBITION

It is hard to believe that for over a decade, beginning 17 January 1920, America implemented Prohibition against what they termed 'the demon drink'. The law was put into effect to prevent the manufacture, sale and transportation of alcohol for consumption. As with all absolute laws, people found various means to circumvent this one as well. In fact, the term 'bootlegging' originated at this time, from the practice of smuggling bottles of liquor in one's boots. Finally, in 1933, when the failure of Prohibition was apparent, President Franklin Roosevelt announced the repeal of the law with the words, 'What America needs now is a drink'.

India is one of the few non-Islamic countries in which Prohibition is still in effect, even if it is only in certain states. Gujarat, for instance, has been a Prohibition state right from the time of our Independence. But take it from me, a thoroughbred Gujarati, more Scotch is drunk in Ahmedabad than in most state capitals of India. Prohibition seems to rear its head in Tamil Nadu too from time to time, depending on which political party is in power. Haryana tried Prohibition in the 1990s before the malls came up. The results were disastrous. The government lost out on crucial revenue while residents of Haryana bought their booze in Delhi and smuggled it across the border in the boots of their cars. The law encouraged bribery and corruption as well.

AND IF YOU HAVE THE MONEY ...

On 4 December 2002, when an anonymous bidder paid £25,877 (close to Rs 80,000 a peg) for a bottle of Dalmore at an auction house in Glasgow, the sixty-two-year-old Highland single malt became the most expensive bottle of whisky in the world. I would love to take a sip but, most probably, I would not be able to tell the difference between it and whisky that is sold for $100 a bottle. This was not the first time the price of premium Scotch had gone through the roof. Earlier, a sixty-year-old bottle of Macallan went for the astonishing price of £20,150. It was distilled on Speyside in 1926 and bottled in 1986 in a limited edition of twelve.

Rare bottles of cognac too can fetch fancy prices but they don't quite reach the dizzy heights that single malts do. In 2000, to celebrate the beginning of the new millennium, Hennessy blended eleven of its cognacs dating from 1900 to 1990 and sold them for $5000 a bottle. If you are a high roller, you can order a single shot of Louise XIII cognac in some of the finer bars abroad for anywhere between $100 and $200. If you have money to burn, you can buy a bottle of the 1865 cognac for Rs 15,000.

gin

The word 'gin' comes from the Dutch word for juniper berries: *genever*. As with many other spirits, gin was originally intended as medicine and was invented in 1650, in Holland, by Dr Franciscus Sylvius, a medical professor. While seeking a treatment for kidney disorders, the good doctor mixed the oil of juniper berries with alcohol and called the concoction 'genever'.

From Holland, the drink travelled to England and became popular when King William, a Dutchman, ascended the English throne and banned the import of French goods. The English, deprived of brandy, which till then was their staple, turned to 'gin' (the name by now shortened from 'genever'). The popularity of gin can be attributed to the fact that it was penny-cheap, since, like country liquor in India, it could be distilled from anything that ferments. Today the Dutch continue to make their own style of gin called Genever gin. These are of two types: *oude* (old), which is distilled twice and aged in wooden barrels, and *jonge* (young), a lighter version. Both are usually drunk neat and ice-cold. These gins are heavier, sweeter and distinctly different from London-style gin.

The gin that London distilleries eventually developed was very different from its Dutch ancestor. It was smoother and quickly became a respectable drink among the upper classes. The London dry gin that we drink today was invented in 1831. The phrase 'London dry gin' is generic and is used to describe a style of gin. Beefeater is the only brand that is still distilled in London.

The primary flavour of gin comes from juniper berries but other herbs and spices also go into its making. The makers of Bombay Sapphire claim that they flavour it with ten different botanical ingredients, including almonds, coriander and lemon peel. There

are dozens of other possible ingredients such as cardamom, nutmeg and ginger, though juniper berries is the constant, which gives the best brands (the imported ones, I have to admit) their unique aroma. Old Raj gin uses saffron flavouring while Hendrick's gin uses cucumbers. Both are from Scotland.

Over the last few decades gin has somewhat lost ground to vodka. But it is still a very popular ingredient for cocktails. The fact that it is colourless, like vodka, helps. It has the added advantage of having the scent of spices and herbs that blend well with a wide range of liqueurs.

HOW GIN IS MADE

The method of making gin varies. The alcohol is distilled from grain, usually 75 per cent corn and 25 per cent barley. Some distillers combine the spices and herbs with the alcohol and distill the mixture while others suspend the botanicals above the still, which holds the spirit, and let the vapours pass over the flavouring agents.

Indian gin is not really gin. It is neutral alcohol produced from molasses, a by-product of sugar production, to which extracts of herbs and spices are added to attain the flavour of gin. The method is far less costly.

SERVING AND DRINKING

Gin is mostly drunk with tonic water.

The production of tonic water is, I often feel, almost completely sustained by gin drinkers. It is said that the Gin-and-Tonic combination was invented to make more palatable the quinine in the tonic water that British troops stationed in India had to take as an antidote to malaria. Quinine has a very bitter, unpleasant taste and so the soldiers would mix it with gin and lemon juice to make it more palatable. Over the years they got a taste for the drink, more so when soda was added to the mixture. The tonic water that you get in the shops today has no medicinal value since it has very little quinine.

Gin is, of course, indispensable in the mixing of a Dry Martini, a classic and popular cocktail.

Vodka may be colourless, tasteless and odourless, but it can leave you breathless in more ways than one. Being the most neutral of all liquors, it has the unique ability to take on the characteristics of whatever mixer it is added to. If you add tomato juice to it, as you would in a Bloody Mary, it will enhance the taste of the tomato juice; mix it with orange juice, as in a Screwdriver, and it will taste like orange juice, with added zing, no doubt.

For a liquor that was practically unknown fifty years ago outside Eastern Europe and Scandinavia, vodka is remarkably popular around the world and is the reigning king of spirits when it comes to sales. In recent years vodka sales have even overtaken the combined fortunes of blended and malt whiskies!

Popular vodka brands include Stolichnaya, which comes from the interiors of Siberia, Wyborowa from Poland and Absolut from Sweden. Among the various brands bottled in India, Smirnoff is the most popular. Interestingly, although the bottle's red label is emblazoned with czarist crowns and regalia the licenced product has no Russian connection. It is an American brand named after the Smirnoff brothers, Vladimir and Nicolai, who made vodka exclusively for the Russian court.

MAKE YOUR OWN FLAVOURED VODKA

Drop some green chillies into the vodka bottle and leave it in the fridge. After a week it will turn into a delicious, fiery drink. You can even add lemon peels, black pepper and coriander (dhania) seeds to a bottle of Absolut for a zesty, spicy mix with overtones of citrusy freshness.

HOW VODKA IS MADE

Some countries like to define vodka as nothing more than diluted ethyl alcohol which is what it is: about 40 per cent alcohol and 60 per cent water. This means it could be made from just about any fruit or vegetable. If you must know, all vodka produced in India began life in sugar cane fields since Indian vodka is made from molasses.

This upsets countries like Russia and Poland which insist on the use of grain and potatoes, according to tradition. East Europe is vodka's spiritual home. The Poles claim they discovered the drink. The Russians, who have a deep affinity for vodka, will tell you it was invented in 1503 by monks in the Kremlin. And in one memorable advertisement the makers of Finlandia claimed that 'real Russian vodka comes from Finland'!

In the days of the czar the Russians produced vodka from potatoes. These days it is distilled mainly from grain, fermented wheat, corn or rye. There is a body of opinion that insists that vodkas can be divided into two, only two, categories, pure and impure; good vodka has no taste, bad vodka tastes like rubbing alcohol. The essential difference in taste from one brand of vodka to another is determined by the type of grains used, the techniques used during distillation and filtration and the water used to control the alcoholic strength.

Flavoured vodka has now become popular in the cocktail circuit. You will find vodkas flavoured with lemon, lime, even mango and vanilla. Absolut's Kurant, flavoured with blackcurrant, leads the pack. Since the flavours play no part in the process of distillation and are added afterwards, these vodkas can be said to fall under the category of liqueurs.

SERVING AND DRINKING

Vodka is best consumed straight out of the freezer. Top quality vodka, frozen and drunk neat from ice-cold glasses is a much better drink than vodka and tonic. If you put a bottle of any spirit in the freezer its alcohol content will prevent it from freezing but it has to be at least 40 per cent alcohol. You can also make any liquor ice cold by placing the bottle in an ice bucket filled with cubes. It serves the purpose of chilling the drink and looks particularly enticing on a buffet table.

Vodka is essential in making many cocktails. In fact, vodka-based cocktails are more popular than cocktails made with other spirits, especially in the United States.

Unlike gin, vodka and whisky, rum is unmistakably a tropical spirit, produced as it is from sugar cane, a plant that grows only in the tropics. It is one of the oldest spirits in the world. In the relative roughness and heaviness of its flavour and aroma, rum never lets you forget where it comes from.

Beneath rum's benign image lurk dark, though often alluring tales. Rum has always been associated with the fiercest of pirates and shadiest of adventurers. Almost every Caribbean island of any consequence still makes its own rum and only part of the total volume produced is meant for export. Jamaica, Barbados and Martinique specialize in dark rums. Puerto Rico and the Virgin Islands make lighter rums which mix better in cocktails.

When I embarked on a misguided career as a lawyer in Bombay in the late 1960s the only booze I could afford was rum. The naval base in Colaba provided sailors with rations of rum at eight rupees a bottle. I would buy a bottle from my bootlegger, who also happened to be my chemist, for twenty-five rupees. Hercules, the most popular brand of indigenous rum at the time, was not bad to taste for that kind of money, though I haven't seen a bottle of it in years. Of late, Old Monk, another dark rum, has taken on the mantle of the most popular brand. It is facing competition from an American interloper, Bacardi, which began life in Cuba in 1862, and the recent entry of Havana Club.

High-quality brands, like the twenty-one-year-old Appleton Estate and Mount Gay Extra Old, should be treated like fine cognac and drunk neat, not wasted on Piña Coladas and punches. The Mount Gay distillery in Barbados traces its origin to 1703, making it the world's oldest rum brand. The island, with a population of 265,000, is said to consume more than 200,000 cases of rum every year!

HOW RUM IS MADE

Most countries that grow sugar cane make rum. Once the juice is extracted by crushing the cane, it is boiled. Part of it becomes the crystallized sugar you buy in shops; the rest is a thick, sweetish by-product known as molasses. This is fermented with yeast and then distilled to separate out the alcohol from the solid wastes. The result is a clear, colourless liquid which is about 80 per cent alcohol. White or light rum is produced by diluting this product to 40 per cent alcohol. The gold and dark rums have a richer, heavier flavour. They get their colour from ageing in oak casks but some producers cheat by adding caramel to white rum.

SERVING AND DRINKING

Rum is a very versatile liquor. You can drink it cold or you can drink it hot. You can mix it with just about anything, Coca-Cola, tonic water, any fruit juice, even ginger ale. (I prefer the more robust local brands to Canada Dry.) I like my rum with soda and a dash of lime cordial. You can also add it to a pudding or a cake or pour it over ice cream. You can even set it alight over gulab jamuns to make an exotic, desi dessert.

tequila

Tequila is Mexico's most famous export, if you do not count the illegal immigrants who cross the border into the United States. Within Mexico, too, it is only produced in two designated provinces, one of them around the town of Tequila and the other around Guadalajara.

Tequila is most commonly found in two colours: gold and white. The golden liquor tends to be smoother and is usually drunk by itself or with ice. It is more expensive. The colourless tequila is far more widely consumed as the base for Margaritas. Good quality tequila is now available and can be bought quite readily in India.

CACHAÇA

Brazilians produce something called cachaça (pronounced kah-shah-sah) which is probably a closer relative to brandy than rum since it is distilled directly from fermented sugar cane juice and not molasses. First, the juice is allowed to ferment naturally for three weeks in pots or barrels. After that it is boiled down to a third of its original volume and then distilled in a still.

Cachaça is best known as the main ingredient in a very popular cocktail, the Caipirinha, a blend of the spirit with lime and sugar. The sweetness of cachaça and the intensity of the lime make the drink especially enticing in the hot summer months.

Roughly translated, the name cachaça means 'farmer's drink'. It is the national drink of Brazil, and I love it.

HOW TEQUILA IS MADE

Tequila is made from the juice extracted from the *Agave tequilana* plant, which is then fermented and distilled twice. Tequila is aged in wooden casks, like brandy and whisky. While the spirit improves with age, four years is the limit. After that it may even begin to deteriorate.

Cheap brands of tequila are often mixed with distillates extracted from sugar cane. If the bottle says '100 per cent agave' it is the best you can buy.

SERVING AND DRINKING

I had my first tequila shot in 1968 in Acapulco, a resort town on the western shores of Mexico. The waiter brought us a bottle of raw tequila, wedges of lime, by no means freshly cut, and a pile of salt on a plate that might have been washed once. Then began the ritual of the 'Mexican itch'. Using sign language, the waiter taught us to grasp the wedge of lime between the thumb and forefinger of our left hand and place a pinch of salt on the back of the same hand. We lifted the shots of tequila, deftly licked the salt off the back of our sweaty hands, gulped down the tequila and sucked the lime. It was an indescribably messy procedure but the effect on the gullet was amazing and we promptly dispatched the waiter to serve more of the same. The rest of the afternoon remains a blur.

Tequila is the main ingredient of a Margarita.

brandy

The word 'brandy' comes from the Dutch word *brandewijn* (burnt wine), that is wine that has been boiled (burnt) in order to distill it. Brandy can be made from the juice or pulp of any fruit. Grape brandies, such as cognac for instance, are made from fermented grape juice or crushed grapes. While these brandies are mostly drunk straight, they also make great ingredients for some delectable cocktails.

There are a number of stories about the invention of brandy, though you have to be really gullible to believe some of them. The one that comes closest to the mark concerns a wily sixteenth-century Dutchman who was in the business of transporting wine from France to Holland. It occurred to him that by removing the water from the wine through distillation he could concentrate the product and ship more of it on each trip. The idea was to add water to the concentrated wine when the product reached its destination. His friends in Holland, however, tried the concentrated stuff and liked it the way it was.

It doesn't take a genius to make brandy. Just about every country that produces wine has its version. The more prominent ones are made in Australia, Germany, Italy, Greece, Spain, Israel, South Africa, Chile, United States, mainly in California, and some of the countries of the former Soviet Union. Surprisingly, Mexico also makes brandy and, believe it or not, it outsells the country's tequila in the domestic market. Whether these brandies are any good is an entirely different matter. Most of them are meant for home consumption, not for export. Producers in some of the countries use short cuts—adding caramel and wood chips, for instance—in a futile effort to hurry the ageing process. Such shenanigans result in cheap liquor and you will be able to notice the difference right away.

HOW BRANDY IS MADE

Like rum and tequila, brandy is an agricultural spirit. While whisky, vodka and gin are made from grain that can be harvested and stored, brandy is dependent on the seasons for the ripening of the fruit. Brandies are, therefore, more location specific.

Like all spirit distillation, brandy distillation is based on the fact that alcohol and water boil at different temperatures. When fermented juice is heated, the alcohol is first released and then trapped and eventually condenses into a clear liquid. The colour of a brandy comes from the wooden barrels, usually made of oak, in which the spirit is aged. Of course, the skills of the distiller and the cellar master who oversees the ageing process play a huge role in the quality of the final product.

COGNAC

There can be no argument. Cognac is the best brandy in the world. It is produced only in the area surrounding the town of Cognac in northwest France, where they have strict controls by government decree. Brandy distilled anywhere else in the world can be given any name but 'cognac'. Hence all cognac is brandy but all brandy is not cognac.

Distillers have come up with a system to help consumers differentiate various cognacs. Starting at the bottom, the first category is VS (Very Special) cognac, sometimes also known as Three Star. It is a blend of brandies that have been aged a minimum of two years, although many may have been aged longer. VSOP (Very Special Old Pale), which is superior to the VS category and more expensive, refers to blends that are aged not less than four years. XO (Extra Old) denotes a blend of considerable age. XOs are frightfully expensive and sometimes come packaged in crystal bottles.

Frankly, you can't really go wrong with a VSOP bottle from any of the leading companies. But feel free to buy XO cognacs if you have suitcases full of black money under your bed. The interesting thing about these initials is that they are in English rather than in French, which makes it apparent that they are intended for the export market. Stars on cognac labels no longer offer any meaningful information on quality. You can buy French brandy bottles with five stars on the label and they might turn out to be completely unpalatable.

As for the brands, the famous four are Courvoisier, Hennessy, Martell and Rémy Martin, though some of the lesser known brands, Bisquit, Camus and Hine, for instance, are also outstanding cognacs.

HOW COGNAC IS MADE

To understand what makes cognac such a great spirit you have to understand the French concept of 'terroir' or how the characteristics of a wine, or brandy, directly result from the effect of soil, climate, altitude and the vine's exposure to the sun. The Cognac region has many distinct terroirs producing diverse spirits from which the distilleries draw to make their distinctive cognac.

A lot of the spirit's success comes from the presence of chalk in the soil. Bands of chalk run through the area and the best cognac vines are grown in Grande and Petite Champagne regions which have the highest concentration of chalk. Only cognacs made from grapes of these two regions can be called Fine Champagne. Incidentally, the word 'Champagne' on a cognac bottle label has nothing to do with the bubbly wine other than that both are produced in the same part of France.

Now we come to the grapes. By law, cognac must be made from white grapes, specifically Ugni Blanche, Folle Blanche and Colombard grapes. The Ugni Blanche has been chosen for its late maturing while the Folle Blanche and the Colombard were selected because they produce thin white wines, unattractive on their own but ideal for distillation into brandy.

Cognac is always distilled twice in small copper stills. The colourless liquid, which by law cannot be more than 72 per cent alcohol at this stage, is pumped into oak casks for ageing for a legal minimum of two and a half years. Cognac cannot be aged more than seventy years since it loses its character if kept too long in casks. The ageing process gives the spirit its aroma, colour and smoothness.

Vintage labelling is rare in cognacs since blending usually includes brandies of different ages. The bottle you buy is a complex mix of many different cognacs from the region. Each cognac house has its own master blender who guards his blending secrets and controls the personality and consistency of a particular brand.

ARMAGNAC

Armagnac is that other great brandy which some connoisseurs consider being in the same league as cognac, if not better. The problem with armagnac is that it is difficult to find a bottle outside Europe.

Armagnac is distilled in southwest France, in Gascony, home of d'Artagnan, immortalized by Alexander Dumas in *The Three Musketeers*. Although it is made from the same grapes as those

used for making cognac—Folle Blanche, Ugni Blanche and Colombard—the peculiarities of the earth of southwest France and the oak barrels used in the ageing process result in a differently flavoured brandy.

One expert has described armagnac as 'full-bodied and nutty, with floral overtones of violets and a hint of fruit, such as plums, prunes, peaches or grapes'. I suppose he knows what he is talking about. But violets? All my taste buds have detected so far is a brandy that is somewhat pungent and as pleasant as the best cognac.

SERVING AND DRINKING BRANDY, COGNAC AND ARMANGAC

Cognac is the main ingredient in some cocktails but good brandies, cognac and armagnac included, are best drunk neat at the end of the evening to burn off the day's frustrations or reflect on a day well spent. Pour a small quantity in a snifter, a glass that was designed specifically to savour the taste and aroma of fine brandy. Swirl the spirit gently to release the wonderful aroma. Brandies should be drunk in moderation. In fact, you should not really drink cognac or armagnac; sip it, relish every moment, take in the glow.

OTHER GRAPE BRANDIES

Spanish: Spanish brandies cannot be compared with what the French produce but they are more reasonably priced. Brandy de Jerez is produced exclusively in southwest Spain, almost as a by-product in this heavily sherry-producing region. The spirit is matured in barrels that were previously used for maturing sherry. Maturation can take anything from one to twelve years. Young brandies are periodically transferred from their barrels and mixed with older brandies. If the bottle's label has the word '*Solera*' it means the brandy has been aged for a year. '*Solera reserva*' indicates an ageing period of at least two years, while '*Solera gran reserva*' brandies are normally over seven years old.

Unlike cognac, fruit flavours and caramel are added to Spanish brandies and they are not always distilled twice. They therefore tend to be sweeter. The Spanish are less strict than the French when it comes to quality control. Grapes for Brandy de Jerez are grown elsewhere in Spain. Apparently the local grapes are too valuable for making brandy and are reserved exclusively for sherry. Most of the distilling is also done at a different location and the raw spirit is then transported to Jerez for ageing in used sherry casks.

Greek: The Greeks produce a sweet brandy under the Metaxa label. It is fairly decent and has an aroma that comes from aniseed, or what we call saunf. I am more partial to their wine, Retsina, which goes very well with spicy food.

Pomace: Pomace brandy is a product of the fermentation of the pressed remains of the wine-making process, such as grape pulp, skin and stems—just about everything that would otherwise have been thrown away. Pomace brandy is rough, firewater stuff. It is seldom aged and is mainly meant for local consumption. The Italian brand Grappa is an example.

BRANDIES FROM OTHER FRUITS

In colder climates, where grapes do not grow, other fruits have been used to make superb distilled drinks. Such drinks are called eau de vie, French for 'water of life', a term now used to describe all spirits distilled from fermented fruit other than grapes. Their main distinction is that they are colourless since they are not aged in wood like their better-known cousins. These brandies are best served chilled or over ice.

An eau de vie should not be confused with a liqueur. Fruit brandies get their flavour from the articular fruit whose juice has been fermented and distilled and are hardly ever sweet. Liqueurs, on the other hand, are almost always sweet and the flavours are added to them after distillation.

Apple: The earliest reference to an apple spirit is from 1553 but it has probably been around much longer than that. Calvados from the Normandy region of France is the best known of the apple brandies and is known for its potency.

To make calvados, apple juice is first fermented into cider and then distilled twice, mostly in copper stills, in much the same way as grapes are distilled to make cognac. After distillation, the spirit goes into various-sized barrels of French oak where they are matured or, if you prefer, aged for two to six years, sometimes more. The younger the calvados the more likely it will smell and taste of apples. The older ones take the tones of the wood of the oak barrels. The apples used in making calvados tend to be small and tart. They are different from your table apples.

The best brands of calvados are produced in the Pays d'Auge area of Normandy which is prized for its soils and the lay of the land. While a VSOP will be aged for at least four years, three-star calvados spends a minimum of two years in barrels. Those aged for six years or more may be labelled Hors d'Age or Age Inconnu (age unknown).

In the United States, the apple brandy is known as **applejack** and its production dates back to the time when the Europeans landed there and found that apples took well to the New England soil. Applejack is more abrasive than calvados, in much the same way that bourbon is rougher than Scotch. Americans like their drinks that way. Laird's is one of the better known applejack brands. It is quite impressive but the devotees of calvados are unlikely to be fooled by it in a blind tasting.

Pear: Perhaps the most spectacular of the fruit brandies is Switzerland's pear brandy. It comes with a large pear in the bottle. When the pear is still on the tree as a bud, it is slipped through the neck of a bottle and allowed to grow there till it reaches its natural size. Then the bottle with the pear in it is detached from the tree and pear brandy is poured into the bottle.

Cherry: The Black Forest region of Germany is known for its cherry brandy, **kirsch**, which is also the German word for cherry. Genuine kirsch comes from black cherries but these days red cherries are also used. The French region of Alsace, across the border, produces something similar called **kir**.

Plum: One of the two local plum brandies of Romania is **palinca**, the other is **tuica**. Both are readily available locally, and inexpensive. They are basically poor man's drinks but you will find them served in all circles. Like most white brandies they can be drunk as an aperitif or as an accompaniment to the meal.

Tuica is made by fermenting and boiling plum juice and distilling it once in a copper pot. Generally palinca is produced from tuica which has been distilled twice to make it more potent. It can be concentrated, up to 90 per cent alcohol, and packs a wallop. Both palinca and tuica taste slightly peppery and fleetingly of plum.

Unlike in other countries, where distilling alcohol in backyards or sheds is an illegal activity, in Romania the production of palinca is not just legal, it is a thriving cottage industry. The drink is what we call 'moonshine'—distilled under cover of darkness. Farmers in Romania are very proud of the palinca they make at home. They send plastic Coca-Cola bottles full of the stuff to relatives and friends in cities to get them through the harsh winters. I have tried the moonshine variety when I was in Romania (the lady behind the counter at a local store grabbed hold of a grubby plastic bottle, which previously held mineral water, filled it up from a ten gallon cylinder and charged me the equivalent of less than two hundred rupees for it) and found it to be tastier and certainly stronger than the liqour bottled in large distilleries. Romania exports some twenty million bottles of its plum brandy every year.

Next door, the Hungarians too claim to make good fruit brandies. But they spell the name differently: palinka. Unlike the Romanians, the Hungarians will use any fruit for their brandy. The label on the bottle will tell you whether it is apricot, cherry or plum.

One of the better-known plum brandies is **slivovitz**, made in Serbia and Bosnia–Herzegovina, which were part of former Yugoslavia. Slivovitz is made from black plums. The fruit is crushed along with the pits and fermented slowly for around three months. It is then double distilled.

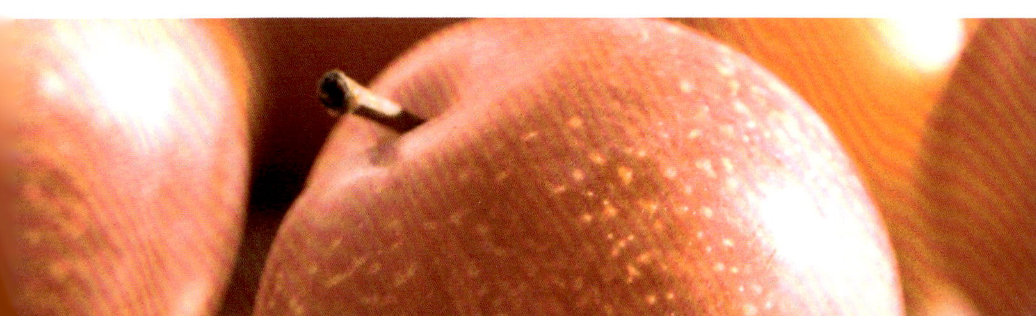

aperitifs and bitters

An aperitif is the less glamorous cousin of a cocktail. While you can get quite drunk on cocktails, an aperitif's intentions are more honourable. The word 'aperitif' comes from the Latin *aperire* (to open). An aperitif is meant to trigger your appetite, prepare your palate for the enjoyment of food yet to come. It is a prologue to a fine meal.

Aperitifs have one common characteristic; all of them are bitter, though in different degrees. Some of them are so bitter that, in my opinion, you would have to be mad, or an Italian, to drink them without adding fruit juice or club soda. A few aperitifs started out centuries ago as medicinal beverages prepared with wine to which herbs, roots and spices were added. But do not be put off by this information. They are really quite delicious.

Among the better known aperitifs are the **vermouths**, **Campari** and **Cynar**. Whisky, gin, vodka and other spirits do not fit the mould of an aperitif. Their high alcohol content tends to dull the taste buds rather than stimulate them. Aperitifs are lighter and contain between 16 to 24 per cent alcohol. In fact, most of them are just fortified wine, like sherry and port, which have been spiced up. Sherry probably qualifies as an aperitif, though port, which is taken after a meal, is a digestive, not an aperitif.

VERMOUTH

A good Martini is at least 90 per cent gin or vodka, but a few drops of dry vermouth are indispensable in its preparation. And you can't make a Manhattan without sweet vermouth. But the two vermouths can be drunk on their own as aperitifs.

Vermouth is a complex aromatized wine with a slightly higher alcoholic content than regular wines, 16 to 18 per cent. The best-selling brands, Martini & Rossi and Cinzano, come from Italy, though the French brands, Noilly Prat and Dubonnet, are considered classier. There is no connoisseurship in drinking vermouths. When you open a Martini & Rossi bottle it will be exactly the same as any other bottle from the company. The product is consistent and made from an unchanging recipe by the manufacturer.

There are two main centres of production, one in the Italian Alps and the other across the border in eastern France where the herbs that go

ceremonial bowl of liquor on special occasions.) The empty glasses will be set on the table, not to be lifted again until the host raises his. The same ritual is followed everywhere in Scandinavia, where aquavit is drunk with food, not as a cocktail or an aperitif.

CAMPARI

Few drinks taste more bitter than Campari. It may be something of a national drink in Italy but it is an acquired taste just about everywhere else. They say you have to drink it three times before you start to like the taste. I have drunk it more often than that and I still do not care much for it. It reminds me of a medicine my mother used to give me when I was a child. But there are people who swear by it, so it is certainly worth one try.

I should point out that Campari is a spirit and should not be confused with other bitters I mention here, which are used for flavouring. You can drink Campari on the rocks like whisky or vodka. You cannot do that with Angostura without getting violently sick.

Campari, a blend of aromatic herbs, was originally developed in 1860 by Gaspare Campari in his café in Milan. Campari is what the French call an 'aperitif' and the Italians 'aperitivo'. Its distinctive red colour is derived from the dried bodies of a species of Mexican bugs that feed on cactus (or so I am told)!

Campari is 24 per cent alcohol and is most often drunk with soda, with a twist of orange or lemon peel. Some people mix it with freshly squeezed orange juice. It is a bit like adding lots of sugar or gur to your karela subzi to mask the bitterness. It is also mixed with vermouth in a few cocktails such as the Americano or the Negroni (in the latter, along with gin).

CYNAR

Cynar is an aperitif that has been around since 1949. Produced by the same Italian company that makes Campari, it gets its bitterness from artichoke leaves. It is syrupy, dark brown in colour and tastes very bitter indeed. Makers of Cynar claim that it is good for health, especially for the liver, since, besides artichoke leaves, herbs are also used in its production.

Italians simply chill the drink before drinking it. I suspect that they drink it very slowly. While they would find it sacrilegious, you can always serve Cynar with tonic or soda water. And add a slice of lemon or orange if you do.

ANGOSTURA BITTERS

Angostura bitters is one of the most widely distributed bar items in the world. It is the most famous brand of bitters, but unlike Campari or Cynar it is by no means an aperitif. It is an addition to a drink, a modifier, never to be consumed on its own.

Angostura (not to be confused with rums that have the same name) contains numerous plant extracts, spices and herbs, such as cinnamon, cloves, nutmeg and dried orange peel. Over forty ingredients go into making Angostura, though the exact measurements remain a company secret. The mixture was originally developed in 1824 by a German military doctor in the port of Angostura in Venezuela, a city now known as Ciudad Boliver, as a medicine to fight malaria. These days the bottles come from a factory in Trinidad where, apparently, people still use it with hot water to fix upset stomachs. Angostura is sweet and bitter at the same time, has a pleasant aroma and gives any clear drink a soothing, light pink hue.

Angostura comes highly concentrated and is very potent. Go easy with it. A few drops in your drink is all you need. A 100 ml bottle will last you a long time since it has almost limitless shelf life even after the bottle has been opened. It is also available in larger bottles but these are best left to professional bartenders and people who use it to season food.

Just a few drops of Angostura lends zest to mixed drinks (add it to your Gin-and-Tonic and you will notice the difference in the taste) and improves just about any fruit punch. It is an essential ingredient in cocktails such as the Singapore Sling and the Manhattan and I know bartenders who mix

OTHER BITTERS

Peychaud's: An American product, it was concocted by a New Orleans doctor as a remedy for just about any ailment known to man. No one took the claim seriously but it became a local favourite as a mix in some of the local cocktails. Peychaud's is lighter bodied, more floral and sweet than Angostura bitters, and is used only a few drops at a time like the latter. But it is nowhere close to being as popular.

Fernet Branca: A brown liquid that is guaranteed to cure stomach upsets, this one comes from Italy and was first introduced in Milan in 1845 by a lady named Maria Scala. It is reputed to contain around forty herbs and spices, many of them from the Alpine foothills. Believe it or not, over a million cases are sold every year, most of it in Italy. Italians drink it on the rocks or straight. Some prefer it as an aperitif while others take it as a digestive.

Amer Picon: Of French origin, it has been around since 1837, when it was invented as a remedy for malaria by an army officer serving in Algeria. Quinine is one of its main ingredients, but the most prominent flavour is that of bitter orange. Its admirers drink this reddish brown liqueur with soda and ice cubes.

Gammel Dansk: Originating in Denmark, this is perhaps the most bitter of the bitters. The Danes drink it straight up at room temperature on festive occasions such as birthdays and weddings. It is supposed to contain twenty-nine herbs and spices, including cinnamon, nutmeg, anise and aniseed.

Underberg, Unicum, Melnais Balzams: From Germany, Hungary and Latvia respectively. The first is popular as a hangover cure while Unicum and Melnais Balzams both claim to have medicinal properties.

it in their Bloody Marys and Mojitos as well. When teetotallers at a party get bored of drinking endless rounds of Coca-Cola, serve them soda with a dash of Angostura and a slice of lemon. It makes for a pleasant change.

LIQUEURS

It is a pity that liqueurs are not very popular among Indians. We do not, as a norm, linger after a dinner party because Indian hosts tend to serve

food late. We gulp down our gulab jamuns as fast as we can and head straight home.

Liqueurs are delightful after-dinner drinks preferred by those who are not too fond of stronger alternatives such as cognac. At one time liqueurs were considered digestives with health-giving properties but the producers have given up such pretences long ago. Today we drink a liqueur for the sheer pleasure of sipping a drink whose sweetness contrasts nicely with our spicy main course. Most people drink liqueurs neat, sometimes chilled, but try pouring any liqueur on scoops of vanilla ice cream and you might get addicted.

HOW LIQUEURS ARE MADE

Liqueurs differ from spirits like whisky, gin or rum in the process by which they are made. The name comes from the Latin *liquefacere*, literally, 'to dissolve', indicating that some ingredient has been dissolved in alcohol to produce a liqueur. Let us take kirsch and cherry brandy as examples. Both are produced from the same fruit, cherry. Yet, while kirsch is distilled from the juice of cherries, making it a spirit, cherry brandy begins life as a tasteless, neutral spirit to which the cherry flavour is added afterwards. That makes cherry brandy a liqueur because the added ingredient (and not the spirit itself) takes centre stage. Again, cognac and port are also after-dinner drinks but they are not considered to be liqueurs.

In short, a liqueur has to have a base spirit to which flavours are added after distillation is complete. Almost all liqueurs are sweet since they get their sweetness from the fruit itself or are laced with sugar or honey. As you would expect, hundreds of combinations of all kinds of exotic herbs, spices, roots, seeds, flowers and fruit extracts result in a truly astounding range of liqueurs.

The Dutch make a liqueur by the name of advocaat which has egg yolks and looks like custard. Malibu liqueur from the West Indies gets its flavour from coconuts. Our thakurs may not have heard of the word liqueur but they have been making a liqueur from saffron (kesar) for centuries. It is known as aisha. In some liquour shops in India you will find a paan liqueur which is made

by soaking paan leaves and paan masala flavours in alcohol. It is not very popular, however, which does not surprise me in the least.

SERVING AND DRINKING

Europeans prefer to drink liqueurs neat after dinner while Americans tend to use them more in cocktails. Liqueurs form the base of some of the most popular cocktails and are usually sandwiched between a spirit and a non-alcoholic mixer like a juice or soda.

orange liqueurs

I cannot think of another fruit that is as appetizing as the orange. Its colour, taste and fragrance have no real comparison. I am referring here to oranges that grow abroad—in California, Australia and the Mediterranean—not the ones we find locally and call santra or keenu. The fruits that grow abroad are so orange in colour, both inside and outside, that they would make any BJP supporter blush with envy.

Before I move on to orange-flavoured liqueurs, let me tell you a thing or two about the fruit itself. If I remember my Greek mythology correctly, oranges were known as golden apples. The sacred fruit was the centerpiece in stories involving Atlas and Hercules. On the other side of the world, Confucius tells us that oranges grew in China in 500 BC, which is why a particular type of orange is still known as the mandarin. Oranges did not grow in Europe until the Arabs brought them to Spain in the fifteenth century. In France the orange tree was so rare that they called it the tree of kings. With that kind of lineage, the fruit was destined to lend its flavour to some of the best liqueurs in the world.

Grand Marnier is a very classy orange liqueur that originated in France. It does not come cheap since its alcohol base is top quality cognac. The flavour is extracted from bitter oranges grown in Haiti in the Caribbean. The rinds are soaked in brandy, redistilled, sweetened and aged in casks. It is amber in colour.

Grand Marnier should be served with as much reverence as you would give to your best cognac. Serve it neat in the balloon-shaped glass known as the snifter. The fumes that will hit your nostrils will convince you that the bottle is worth its price.

The liqueur is also an ingredient in a number of cocktails and is an indispensable ingredient in many pastry and cake recipes.

Cointreau does not have the complexity of Grand Marnier but it is the best known of all liqueurs. Over two million bottles of Cointreau are sold every year the world over. Launched in 1849 by the Cointreau brothers, it was initially marketed as 'Triple Sec White Cointreau', but when other companies started selling their liqueurs as triple sec the brothers decided to call their product Cointreau.

Cointreau gets its primary flavour from rinds of a variety of oranges, some bitter, others sweet. Grape brandy is first double distilled and the rinds soaked in them and sweetened. The aroma comes from the addition of herbs. The liqueur can be used as a substitute for triple sec in any cocktail, a Margarita or Mai Tai, for example.

Curaçao is a poor cousin of Grand Marnier and Cointreau and comparatively inexpensive. It is made by many companies in different countries and is not a proprietary product. Curaçao gets its name from an island off the coast of Venezuela, a Dutch colony that produces some of the best bitter oranges.

Curaçao is made more or less in the same way as the other two orange liqueurs, but with a neutral spirit or nondescript grape brandy. It comes in a range of colours, bright blue, dark green, red and yellow. The colours have novelty value and there is no significant difference in their flavour or alcohol content. Triple sec is curaçao that is colourless.

Curaçao is essentially a mixer. I do not know anyone who drinks curaçao or triple sec neat, although curaçao, tonic and ice make a very appealing long drink for hot summer days. It also works well over ice with an equal measure of sweet or dry vermouth.

whisky liqueurs

Drambuie is the most famous of the liqueurs produced in Scotland or, for that matter, anywhere in Britain. It is a concoction of aged malt and straight grain whiskies to which are added flavours from heather honey and herbs.

According to a story of dubious origin, the recipe for making Drambuie was given to one Captain John Mackinnon in 1746 by Bonnie Prince Charlie, the pretender to the English throne. The Mackinnon family continues to be the guardian of the formula and in 1892 the Mackinnons gave the liqueur its name, derived from the Gaelic *an dram buidheach* or 'the drink that satisfies'. It is 40 per cent alcohol and has been commercially available since 1906. Drambuie was earlier bottled in Skye and is now bottled near Edinburgh.

You can serve Drambuie neat or over ice. It is also used in mixing cocktails such as the Rusty Nail or the lighter Mackinnon, though it is used less than some of the other liqueurs.

Glayva is a lesser known brand of whisky liqueur. It is made outside Edinburgh and is of more recent origin, 1947. It is quite similar to Drambuie, being also flavoured with heather honey and herbs.

Famous Grouse liqueur seems to be an even more recent invention. It is pleasant to taste, with a tinge of orange, ginger and spices.

Southern Comfort is a peach-flavoured bourbon liqueur. As the name implies, it is from the American south where peaches grow in abundance. It is not quite as classy as the produce of Scotland. It is sipped on the rocks and sometimes mixed with either orange or peach juice.

It should come as no surprise that two of the best known

liqueurs are products of Catholic monasteries. Unlike puritanical Hindus and the Muslim community, Christians, especially Catholics, have never had much problem with alcohol. Wine plays a part in their religious service and I have met Irish priests who can drink anyone under the table.

Bénédictine: '*Deo optimo maximo* (To God, most good, most great)', proclaimed Dom Bernardo Vincelli when he first tasted the liqueur he had concocted in the year 1510. It still bears the name of the religious order to which he belonged: Bénédictine, one of the oldest liqueurs in the world. The monastery in the Normandy region of France continued making Bénédictine until the French Revolution in 1789 when it was closed down by the mob and production of the liqueur banned. For eighty years after that the liqueur remained extinct, until a descendant of the monastery's lawyers discovered the recipe in a bundle of yellowing legal papers. Soon a new distillery was up and running and the production of Bénédictine was on again.

The exact formula for making Bénédictine is known only to three people at any given time. It is believed to contain over twenty ingredients including thyme, clove, cinnamon, saffron and orange peels. These are left to marinate in cognac and the mixture is then redistilled to concentrate the flavour.

Bénédictine is a lovely yellow in colour with a very pleasant aroma and possesses the alcohol strength of whisky. Some people find it too sweet on its own and prefer to mix it in cocktails or dilute it with ice cubes. It is also perfectly acceptable to mix Bénédictine with an equal measure of cognac. In fact, in the United States, B&B, in which cognac and Bénédictine have been pre-mixed, has been known to outsell Bénédictine.

Chartreuse: Another set of monks, the Carthusians, came up with Chartreuse, probably the most famous of herb liqueurs, in a monastery near Grenoble in France. The original recipe not only specified the ingredients but also stipulated in what phase of the moon they should be harvested. This liqueur dates back to the beginning of the seventeenth century.

BUCKFAST TONIC

There are several other alcoholic beverages that are of ecclesiastical origin. Not to be outdone by their French counterparts, the Bénédictine monks in southwest England make something called Buckfast Tonic. It is black in colour, very sweet to taste and is rumoured to be made by adding tea, cocoa leaves and other odd stuff to wine. For reasons no one can fathom it is hugely popular in the slums of Scotland, although the wine correspondent of the *Times*, London, investigated it recently and pronounced that it tasted vile and hoped he would not have to drink it ever again.

The Carthusian monks take a vow of silence, which is probably the reason for the recipe remaining a secret over the years. All we know is that besides sugar and alcohol, it contains flavours of 130 different plants and involves a precise system of blending and distillation. It is aged in casks for up to five years. Proceeds from the sales of Chartreuse go towards charity. Green Chartreuse has a pungent smell and is strong stuff with an alcohol content of 55 per cent. The yellow version is milder.

Chartreuse is usually drunk neat, after dinner. Some people find the flavour overpowering and prefer to mix it with soda to make a refreshing summer drink. The French like to fortify their hot chocolate and coffee with Chartreuse.

crème liqueurs

Liqueurs that have 'crème' in their names are more syrupy and heavier than other liqueurs and contain about twice as much sugar. The word 'crème' implies that the flavour comes from a single source. **Crème de menthe** is a mint liqueur, **crème d'ananas** is pineapple based, and you do not have to be a rocket scientist to know what **crème de banana** has in it. These liqueurs, of course, have nothing to do with cream liqueurs.

The largest producer of crèmes is a French company, Marie Brizard, which has a range of over thirty different flavours. Raspberry (**crème de framboise**), strawberry (**crème de fraise**) and blackcurrant (**crème de cassis**) are among the more popular ones. All of them have rich, enticing colours. Other big producers of crèmes are Bols and De Kuyper companies of the Netherlands.

Crèmes are great for making all kinds of puddings. Or you can just pour a few spoonfuls over scoops of vanilla ice cream (since it is the most neutral of ice creams and will bring out the flavour of the liqueur) and serve it in wine glasses with teaspoons. You can do this with just about any liqueur but avoid colourless ones since they do not create the same effect on the table. When crèmes are used in mixing cocktails, there is no need to add sugar since they amply supply the sweetening element.

brandy liqueurs

There are three liqueurs that have the word 'brandy' attached to them: **cherry**, **apricot** and **peach**. But they are not brandies at all. True brandies obtain their flavours through the distillation process and ageing in barrels. In these brandies, on the other hand, the flavours are added after distillation. Strictly speaking, they belong to the crème category of liqueurs.

You need not lose sleep on that account, however, since these brandies, from reputable manufacturers, are quite delicious. Their flavouring is often not only from the fruit but also through the crushing of the kernels and pips inside them to give a slightly bitter taste.

The best of the cherry brandies is Cherry Heering from Peter Heering, a distillery in Denmark that has been producing it for over a hundred years. The company grows its own cherries. Cherry brandy is added to a wide range of cocktails, the Singapore Sling being the most famous. Marie Brizard and Bols manufacture all three fruit brandies with peach being the least popular and apricot somewhere in the middle. They have around 25 per cent alcohol.

cream liqueurs

'Creams' are liqueurs that have dairy products in them. They are thick and very sweet. I suppose you can describe them as milk shakes for grown-ups. But they are deceptively potent.

The most famous of the cream liqueurs is Baileys Irish Cream, which originated in Dublin in 1974. It is 17 per cent alcohol and is a blend of Irish whiskey, cream and cocoa. I sometimes like to serve it on the rocks to my guests before dinner, instead of a wine or a spirit. These days you will also find cream liqueurs that are flavoured with coffee or chocolate. Some confectionary companies, like Cadbury's, have also branched into liqueur production to get a share of the lucrative market. The downside is that these liqueurs contain artificial additives which prevent the cream from separating from the alcohol.

Cream liqueurs are best kept in the fridge once the bottle is opened, and even then not for too long.

anise liqueurs

ABSINTHE

'After the first glass you see things as you wish they were. After the second, you see things as they are not. Finally you see things as they really are, and that is the most horrible thing in the world.'

—Oscar Wilde, on the effects of absinthe

During the late nineteenth century, a very potent spirit, which bordered on being a poison, became very popular. Absinthe was the heroin of its day and was the drink of choice of artists like Manet, Lautrec and Degas. Van Gogh is said to have sliced off his ear and presented it to a prostitute after a glass or two. Absinthe pushed an entire generation over the edge. It was finally banned in Switzerland in 1905 when one of its citizens woke up from an alcoholic stupor and found his wife and children at his feet, slain by his own hand.

Absinthe was first concocted by Dr Pierre Ordinaire around the time of the French Revolution. The good doctor discovered that a narcotic herb by the name of wormwood could cure just about anything. He experimented with it and came up with absinthe that included fifteen other herbs including aniseed (saunf) and coriander (dhania). He found that the remedial effects of the mixture were heightened if it included an enormous quantity of alcohol: 68 per cent. That became the traditional strength of absinthe.

By the 1890s it became the drink of the European café society. Picasso painted absinthe bottles and absinthe drinkers. He drank it himself. But others railed against it and absinthe was finally banned in France in 1915 after the country suffered heavy losses in the First World War, partly due to the extensive use of absinthe by soldiers.

Absinthe has an emerald colour which has earned it its nickname, 'green goddess'. It has been considered an aphrodisiac but, as Ernest Hemingway correctly pointed out in *For Whom the Bell Tolls*, its erotic effects are purely in the mind. It remains prohibited in many countries, including France and the United States, though I had no problem buying a bottle in Prague. The Czechs spell the name a little differently: absinth.

There are several ways of sampling absinthe. You can strain it through sugar into a glass and sip it slowly. The more adventurous take advantage of its high alcohol content and put a shot of it in a glass, set it alight with a match, and drink it through specially designed straws.

ANISETTE AND PASTIS

The French government relented somewhat at the end of the First World War and decreed that absinthe could still be made so long as wormwood, by then known to be harmful to the liver and brain, was not one of the ingredients. Its chief manufacturer, Henri Pernod, then turned to making a similar product, anisette, without wormwood and at a lower proof. It is also known as anise. Today's Pernod is a sanitized, direct descendant of absinthe.

Another drink, the pastis, which originated in the south of France, was similar to absinthe and also contained wormwood. When that got banned, the company that marketed it, Paul Ricard, also removed the wormwood from it. In 1971 Pernod and Ricard merged and, between them, they now control almost 80 per cent of the world's twelve-million-case French anisette and pastis market.

There is some confusion as to the precise difference between anisette and pastis. Both are successors of the outlawed absinthe, contain aniseed, have the unmistakable flavour of anise and turn cloudy when water is added to them. And both have 39 per cent alcohol, a far cry from the strength of absinthe. The major difference is that pastis has liquorice in it while anisette does not. The other difference is the colour. Pastis does not have the green tinge of anisette.

Anisette and pastis should ideally be served in a small, thick-bottomed glass with an equal amount of water. The water should be very cold, so as to obviate the need for ice. If you have a sweet tooth you may add sugar. Frankly, to enjoy either of them, it helps if you are French.

ARAK

Anise-based liqueurs are common throughout the Mediterranean region, where they are generically known as **arak**. There have been claims that arak was widely drunk in ancient India, as far back as 800 BC. The name 'arak' comes from the Arabic word for juice, *araq*.

The Greeks have their own version, called **ouzo**. Ouzo evolved from a drink the ancient Greeks used to make from herbs and honey. Like most anise drinks, adding water makes the mix cloudy. Some consider it a brandy, but generally it is placed in the liqueur category because of its sweetness. The Turks make something similar and call it **raki**.

Some araks can be very smooth but most of them are quite raw and can contain up to 50 per cent alcohol.

other liqueurs

Liqueurs are, basically, easy to make, and hence the variety that is available. All you have to do is dilute pure alcohol to around 40 per cent and add flavouring. If required, you can also use sweeteners, such as honey or sugar. You can even make liqueurs at home using vodka as the base, since it is quite tasteless. But you will need a precise recipe and, frankly, it is not worth the effort because you will probably just ruin a good bottle of vodka. It is easier to just buy them. Given below are some of the more popular liqueurs I have not yet mentioned.

There are two coffee-based liqueurs that are well known. Kahlúa is from Mexico but is also made in Europe under licence. It comes in a distinctive high-necked bottle with a yellow label. It is dark brown in colour and uses white rum as the base spirit.

Tia Maria from Jamaica has more or less the same colour but is less sweet and a little lighter. As one would expect, it is made with Jamaica's famous dark rum, once favoured by pirates. Both Kahlúa and Tia Maria are used in making cocktails and can also be drunk neat after dinner or with crushed ice.

Malibu also comes from Jamaica, in an attractive opaque white bottle. The liqueur is made with white rum and flavoured with coconut. It is colourless and contains only 24 per cent alcohol. It is seldom drunk by itself. Bartenders in beach resorts use it for cocktails that require tropical fruits like pineapple.

There is a misconception that Italy's amaretto is made from almond extracts. That is not the case; it is made from pits of apricots which grow in the orchards around Milan. Admittedly, the pits do taste a bit like almonds. Amaretto's flavour is slightly bitter and very pleasantly so. It is deep amber in colour. Disaronno amaretto is the largest selling brand and you will find bottles in just about every airport in Europe. I use it in making the Mai Tai cocktail. It can also be enjoyed on its own and tastes best when chilled or poured over crushed ice.

Sambuca, also Italian, is a clear liqueur that has a distinct flavour of aniseed. It is flavoured with many other spices and herbs as well. If you order it in a bar or a restaurant after dinner you will find two or three roasted coffee beans floating in your drink. The waiter or bartender will then set it alight. You are supposed to blow out the flame and then drink the Sambuca, munching the beans as you go along. I'm not quite sure where this ritual originated, though. If you are drinking it at home make sure the glass has a narrow mouth, like a sherry glass. Better still, use a snifter. That way the drink will light up easily.

Midori has been around since 1978. It started out as a Japanese product but is now produced in Mexico. It is made from melons and has a bright green colour which comes from a dye. Midori is the Japanese word for green. I do not consider it a great liqueur though it does look attractive.

Galliano comes in a tall, narrow bottle that you will have difficulty storing in your liquor cabinet. The liqueur originated in Tuscany in 1896 and is named after an Italian war hero. Like many branded liqueurs, the makers of Galliano keep its contents a closely guarded secret but it is reputed to contain more that thirty herbs, roots and berries from the slopes of the Alps. Its chief claim to fame is that it is essential in mixing the cocktail Harvey Wallbanger, the other two ingredients being vodka and orange juice. I also use it with gin, fresh lime juice, club soda and sugar syrup to make a superb Tom Collins.

Chambord, a brand liqueur produced in the Loire Valley in France, has its admirers though I find it too sweet for my taste. It is made by steeping raspberries and blackberries in cognac and other spirits and flavouring the product with cinnamon, cloves, vanilla, honey, ginger and extracts from orange and lemon peel. It is only 16½ per cent alcohol and can be drunk straight or used in cocktails that call for a raspberry liqueur.

WINE, CHAMPAGNE AND FORTIFIED WINES

The only effective way to learn about wine is to drink it. Serious wine drinking involves the knowledge of a staggering amount of detail and years of drinking experience, but you need not know too much about wine to enjoy it. Drinking a glass of good wine is one of the great pleasures of life. The more you drink, the more you will be able to appreciate the difference between a good wine and something that is closer to vinegar than wine. Eventually you will settle on the wines you like and learn to match them to different foods. Wine appreciation is very subjective. Rather than depending on a wine writer or expert, you are probably better off following your own judgement by experimenting with different wines.

Some of the more prominent wine producing countries are, in no particular order, France, Italy, Spain, Romania, Greece, Yugoslavia, Germany, Austria, Hungary, Cyprus, Greece, Portugal, Turkey, Israel, Canada, United States, Chile, Argentina, South Africa, Australia and New Zealand. Many serious wine drinkers are dumping French and other snooty wines for bottles from the New World. Australian wine now outsells French wine in Britain.

There was a time when the only imported wine available in India, mostly bootlegged, was French, alongside a smattering of German and Italian wines. Now our local liquor shops are crammed with bottles from California and Chile, Australia and New Zealand. In addition, our lives have been made easier since the newcomers label their wine by the name of the grape from which it is made, that is, Cabernet Sauvignon or Chardonnay, Merlot or Shiraz. This trend of labelling remains

unpopular with French winemakers because they label their wines by the geographical area in which the wine is produced, that is, Bordeaux, Burgundy, etc.

Wines can be divided into four categories: still wine (red, white and rosé), sparkling wine (champagne) and fortified wine (port and sherry).

red, white and rosé wine

Still wine contains around 12 per cent alcohol. There are three types of stills: red, white and rosé.

Wines are also classified according to the grape variety, the vintage year and the place of origin. You will find the information on the label; unless it is a very cheap bottle, in which case the product is best avoided. For most of us vintage is less important than the place of origin and type of grape from which a wine is produced. Grape is a very versatile fruit. It will grow in just about any soil as long as the climate is mild and there is a dry spell for the grapes to ripen. It may come as a surprise to you to know that the juice of red grapes is clear, not red in colour.

Both red and white wines can range from very dry to very sweet. You may well ask how a liquid can be dry. Just bear in mind that, when it comes to wine, dry is the opposite of sweet. A very dry wine will not be sweet in the least. If your knowledge of wine is limited and you are buying for a party it is advisable to keep on the dry side.

Wine, like bread, is served from the beginning to the end of the meal, and unlike bread it can be served before or after a meal. Some wines go with certain kinds of food. There was once a rule, strictly observed, that white wine should be served with 'white' meat dishes such as chicken and fish. Red wine went with the red meats, beef and lamb. There is something to be said for this kind of pairing but feel free to order wine of any colour with your meal. You do not need a connoisseur to tell you which wine you should drink and with which dishes. I prefer red over white and I order red all the time with tandoori chicken and kebabs.

	COLOUR	HOW WINES ARE MADE	SERVING	COMMON VARIETIES
WHITE	White wines start very pale and approach gold as they age.	Ripe grapes are harvested, destemmed and crushed to extract the juice. To make a white wine the skins and all other solid matter are separated from the juice and transferred into large steel vats or wooden casks where fermentation begins. White wines ferment at around 12–18°C and sometimes require a second round of fermentation. They may be aged in oak barrels or bottled right away.	4–6°C for light whites; 10–12°C for full-bodied whites. Serve 100 ml max. or one-third of a glass.	Chardonnay, Chenin Blanc, Colombard, Muscadet, Pinot Blanc, Reisling, Sauvignon Blanc
RED	Reds can be maroon, purple, ruby, garnet or even brownish red.	To make red wine, once the ripe grapes have been crushed to release the juice, the skin and pips are left in contact with the juice, even during fermentation and sometimes for a few days after that. Red wines ferment at higher temperatures than whites (25–30°C). They may then be made to sit in stainless steel or oak barrels for six months to three years before they are bottled.	14–16°C for simple, fruity reds; 18–20°C for complex, rich reds. Serve 100 ml max. or one-third of a glass.*	Cabernet Sauvignon, Merlot, Pinot Noir, Shiraz, Zinfandel
ROSÉ	Rosés range from light pink or mauve to a mild orange.	Ripe grapes are harvested, destemmed and crushed to extract the juice. The colour in rosé wine is obtained by letting the skin and pips stay in contact with the juice for only a short time, usually less than 24 hours. Some rosé wines are also made by siphoning off some of the juice of red wines during fermentation.	4–6°C. Serve 100 ml max. or one-third of a glass.	

* Wine books often recommend that red wine should be served at 'room temperature' but you should remember that these books have been primarily written for readers in countries with colder climates.

CORKS VS SCREW CAPS

Increasingly, the traditional method of sealing wine bottles with cork is being abandoned in favour of screw caps. The fault lies with inferior quality cork which can taint or 'cork' the wine. The culprit is a chemical compound, trichloroanisole or TCA, which comes from chlorine bleach that is used to sterilize the cork and brighten its colour, but reacts with the wine and spoils it. When this happens the wine smells like wet cardboard and tastes mouldy.

Screw caps are a little more expensive but the most attractive alternative. With screw caps the wine remains the way the producer intended it to be. Quality does not vary from bottle to bottle and an added advantage is that the bottle need not be stored on its side since there is no cork that needs to be kept moist.

Whether one likes it or not, the wine trade seems to be heading towards screw caps. Seventy per cent of wine bottles from New Zealand now have screw caps; Australia is not far behind. European producers, who tend to be traditionalists, have been less receptive to screw caps, with Spain going as far as banning their use in eleven of its wine producing regions. This is understandable since the country's cork industry is under siege. Switzerland is perhaps the only enthusiastic user of screw caps in Europe though there is growing interest in France and Germany as well. Some of the American wineries have tentatively started using screw caps; they are waiting to see the customers' response to the innovation. Overall, the verdict seems to be that caps are fine for bottles that are to be consumed over a short period.

Is it necessary to taste the wine before pouring from a screw-capped bottle since the wine wouldn't have been tainted by a cork? Absolutely. The bottle may have been badly stored and could go bad through excessive heat, for example. In some cases wine spoils even before it is bottled due to careless fermentation or unhygienic conditions.

RITUALS AT A WINE TASTING

Experts will find tastes and aroma in a bottle of wine that you and I, as hard as we may try, have not the faintest hope of detecting. If you follow the five 'S's—see, swirl, sniff, savour and spit—you will do just fine when you are invited to a wine tasting.

See: Check the colour, intensity and clarity of the wine by tilting the glass against a white background (the tablecloth at tasting sessions is always white) or looking down on it from above. A good wine should be clear and have an intense hue; a cloudy wine may be unfiltered wine or may simply have not aged gracefully.

Swirl: Swirl the wine gently around the glass without spilling it. The movement increases the wine's surface area and releases more of its bouquet, that is, its aroma.

Sniff: Now dig your nose into the glass and inhale deeply without being embarrassed. The nose is very reliable in determining the quality of a wine. If it has turned to vinegar, you will smell it right away. Over time, you will learn to smell the nuances of wood, berries and other fruits, flowers and vanilla.

Savour: Take a small sip and roll the wine over your tongue. Let in air through the lips and let it pass over the wine. The combination of smell and taste will give you the full flavour of the wine at this stage.

Swallow or Spit: The trick is to let very little of the wine go down your throat, just enough to get the taste and see how long it lingers. Spit out the rest. Tasters are usually provided with small steel buckets for this purpose.

INDIAN WINES

Indian wine production is one of the great success stories of recent times. Until the early 1990s Indians hardly touched wine, and with good reason. Wines from abroad were not available legally and Indian wines of those days were a wine drinker's nightmare. There were two prominent brands, Bosca and Golconda, both notoriously bad. They came from somewhere in south India and had a closer relationship to vinegar than wine.

Things have changed for the better since that time, and dramatically so. Some of the better Indian vineyards are producing quality wines that are reasonably priced, award-winning wines in international circles. The wineries are owned by people who know wine. When they don't, they bring in outside expertise to help them. Maharashtra produces over 90 per cent of the wine bottled in India and in 2007 the state saw a phenomenal growth of 40 per cent with a production of 13.2 million litres from 40,000 hectares. Nashik is an important grape-growing area but other districts of Maharashtra have also been tempted into making wine. Goa, Karnataka, areas around Bangalore and as far north as Himachal Pradesh have also begun to produce wine.

Sula was the first winery to come up in Nashik. It produces some of the best wines in the country using mainly Sauvignon Blanc, Cabernet Sauvignon, Shiraz, Chenin Blanc and Zinfandel varieties of grapes. The other big boy in the Indian wine business is Grover, with their winery located just outside Bangalore. The vineyard sprawls over 200 acres and specializes in Cabernet Sauvignon and Shiraz and its product is good enough to be sold in France.

STORING WINE

It is a myth that all expensive wines get better with age. Sensitive as they are, they need to be stored in proper conditions, that is, in dark, slightly humid areas, away from heat and fluctuating temperatures.

The optimum temperature for storage is 10–12°C but a slow change in the range of 5–18°C between summer and winter months is not a problem.

While screw-capped bottles can be kept standing up, wines with traditional corks should be stored on their sides so that the cork remains moist. If the cork dries out, air will enter the bottle, and once the wine absorbs oxygen it will begin to turn into vinegar. Once opened, most wines will stay drinkable for a few days, but the best place for them, even red ones, is the fridge.

If wine has been stored for a number of years some sediment will form on the side of the bottle, particularly in a red wine. This is quite natural and does not mean the wine has spoiled. In that case it is best to decant the bottle slowly.

On a visit to a vineyard in Portugal I was presented with a set of pumps that come with rubber stoppers with small holes in the middle. You can place the contraption over the mouth of an unfinished wine bottle and pump out the air. This creates a vacuum in the bottle and I am told it adds another week or so to the life of the wine. Fancy bars use a more effective and expensive system for preserving wine they sell by the glass. The device pumps nitrogen into the bottle, sealing it from the effects of oxygen.

Champagne can be described as a sparkling wine, a fizzy wine or an effervescent wine. With few exceptions, when it comes to champagne you get what you pay for. Expensive bottles are likely to be better than cheaper ones. Champagne spells luxury, as it well should. In the West no celebration is complete without uncorking a bottle of champagne.

In the United States any sparkling wine can be labelled 'champagne', but the countries of the European Union are not allowed to do this. Genuine champagne can come from only one region, the eponymous

Champagne, which lies east of Paris. Thus, while champagne is a sparkling wine, all sparkling wine is not champagne. The largest and most famous producer of champagne is a company by the name of Moët and Chandon in Epernay.

Like still wines, champagnes too come in sweet and dry varieties, and there might be some confusion when it comes to distinguishing between the two. A sparkling wine which has the word 'sec' (the French word for dry) on its label is actually semi-sweet. 'Brut' and not 'Extra dry' is the least sweet of the champagnes. In fact, champagnes marked 'brut' may actually taste sour to the uninitiated. A champagne labelled 'doux' will be distinctly sweet and I would not recommend it. Sparkling wine is made by adding a small amount of sugar and yeast solution in the bottle and then corking it tightly. The yeast and sugar cause further fermentation in the tightly sealed bottle which results in the generation of gases in the form of bubbles, which have nowhere to escape until the bottle is opened. Bottles containing sparkling wine are therefore heavy and very sturdy to prevent them from exploding from the immense pressure within. And that is why a wire is needed to hold the cork in place. Champagne loses its zest after about ten years and does not age in the bottle.

Removing the cork without making a mess of the operation is an art. First, twist off the wire that is around the cork. That is easily done. Now hold the cork in your left hand and grab the bottom of the bottle firmly with the other hand. Keep the bottle slightly inclined and make sure that the cork is not facing anyone. Make sure your grip on the cork is firm; a flying cork is like a missile. Turn the bottle slowly with your right hand, holding the cork until it pops. If you are unsure of yourself, I suggest you place a napkin over the cork to prevent it from flying off in case you lose your grip.

Champagne can be served at any time; well, maybe not at breakfast but definitely for brunch on Sundays. It should always be chilled. You should always fill it less than half-full. As for glassware, the wide-rimmed saucer-shaped glasses have gone out of fashion and have been replaced by tulip-shaped glasses or flutes. These glasses trap the bubbles of the champagne better and keep it bubbly for longer. Hold the glass by the stem to prevent your fingers from warming the champagne.

fortified wines

PORT

Port is usually associated with doddering English gentlemen and their London clubs. It is almost always drunk in company and there are some antiquated English rituals surrounding its consumption. You are supposed to pass the decanter from the right to the left. Or is it the other way round? But don't be put off by such nonsense. Port is a sublime after-dinner drink, as good as cognac.

Most wine producing countries produce something similar to port but the genuine stuff comes only from one area, the Douro valley in northern Portugal. If the port is not made from grapes of this region of Portugal it is an imitation. You will find bottles of port produced in California, Australia and South Africa, but they taste nothing like the genuine thing. In the countries of the European Union you cannot call the wine port unless it is Portuguese in origin.

Outside of Portugal, the British have the port wine business firmly in their grasp and own all the good labels. The first port house was set up in England in 1670 by the Warre family. Ironically, the French today drink three times more port than the British. The Brits consider it a dessert wine. The French like to drink it before a meal as an aperitif.

Like so many life-enhancing creations, port was invented by accident. Thanks to their many wars with France the British were forced to import Portuguese red wine as an alternative to French wine. They added a small amount of brandy to the wine as a preservative to ensure that it did not spoil during the sea journey. The addition of brandy halted further fermentation and retained the sugar not converted by the yeast. The resulting 'fortified' mixture was both sweet and strong, a thicker product than a still wine, and the British found they preferred the taste of the wine in this form. The process was refined over the years and now brandy is added in the proportion of 100 litres of brandy to 450 litres of red wine while it ferments and still contains at least half its grape sugars to produce the finest port.

Port contains about 20 per cent alcohol while wine has about

12 per cent. In spite of its high alcohol content, a good port can be very smooth to taste. There are glasses designed for the consumption of port but any good wine glass is perfectly acceptable. It should be filled no more than a third to halfway to enable you to enjoy the aroma. It is best enjoyed with cheeses and nuts or, if you prefer, alongside a good cigar.

Unlike wine, bottles of port can be recorked once you have opened them without fear of the drink spoiling, though it is at its best when the bottle is first opened. Connoisseurs never recork the bottle.

Traditionally, ports may be classified as 'ruby', 'tawny' and 'vintage'. **Ruby port** is a young port, very fruity, that has been aged up to three years in wooden barrels. Needless to say, it gets its name from its colour. It is the cheapest and the most widely available among port wines. **Tawny port** is one level above the ruby and also takes its name from its colour, which is anything between gold and reddish brown. Most tawnies are aged for five years and then bottled but there are also exquisite tawnies that have stayed in barrels for as long as forty years. The information is usually given on the label.

At the top of the heap we have **vintage port**, the granddaddy of ports. Vintage ports are bottled in years when the grape harvest has been of exceptional quality. These do not need to be blended or improved in any way. Vintage port is kept for just two years in barrels and then bottled. The drink then ages in bottles, usually bearing the year of the harvest, and reaches maturity in fifteen or twenty years. Vintage port is best stored in a wine cellar with the bottle placed horizontally so that the drink always touches the cork. During the ageing process a sediment forms in the bottle. You will have to decant the drink before serving it.

There are also **late bottled vintage ports (LBVs)** which

are made from grapes harvested in the same year and have been kept in wooden casks or barrels for four to six years before bottling. These are more affordable than vintage ports and wonderful for everyday drinking. LBVs do not age in the bottle. For the novice, the best indication of the quality of the port is the price. There is also something called **white port**, which is light and dry and has limited popularity.

SHERRY

Sherry, it may be said, is Spain's greatest glory. The country produces seventy-five million litres of it in a year. Its home is a small region in southern Spain, the rolling countryside around the town of Jerez, which is how the drink got its name—the English couldn't pronounce the name Jerez. There are several countries, Australia, South Africa and Cyprus included, which make their own version of this wine, but it is genuine sherry only if it is produced in and around Jerez.

Sherry comes in three broad categories: dry, medium and sweet. Fino is the most common of the dry sherries. Amontillado and Oloroso are sweeter and can be served as an after-dinner drink the way port is.

Sherry comes mainly from the Palomino and Pedro Ximenez variety of grapes, with a splash of Moscatel thrown in. Making sherry is a complicated process. First, it is made exclusively from white grapes. The Jerez region produces only mundane table wines, thin and flabby, but these wines are great for making sherry. The harvested bunches of grape are laid on straw mats to reduce their moisture and concentrate the flavours. Then they are fermented and left in the open, in contact with air, for an extended period. This allows the wine to oxidize and develop a coating of yeast on the surface. It is the yeast that gives the sherry its distinctive, nutty flavour.

The secret of a fine sherry is in its ageing and blending. The wine is passed through

interconnected barrels which are piled on top of each other. The young wine starts at the top and eventually ends up in the bottom-most barrel from where part of it is drawn off and bottled. The barrel is then topped up from the one above it, the second oldest barrel, which in turn is replenished from the third oldest above it and so on. It takes about five years for the wine to get from the top to the bottom barrel. This constant, slow stream produces a complex drink which does not vary in taste and quality from year to year. There is therefore no such thing as vintage sherry.

Sherries contain 15 to 20 per cent alcohol. The bottles should be stored in a cool, dark place but not for too long. The more sensitive ones lose their character as early as a year after they are bottled. Once opened, the bottle should not be kept longer than a month, more so in our climate. There are special glasses for drinking sherry which are shaped like wine glasses but are smaller and narrower.

Few wines can match a dry sherry as a before-dinner drink with canapés and hors d'oeuvres. Roasted almonds and cashews also go very well with sherry. It is popular as an aperitif but the Spanish have been drinking it with food for centuries. In the sherry producing areas of Spain lunch never starts before three in the afternoon and dinner is rarely served before midnight. If you are fortunate to receive an invitation, the host will provide you with tapas: copious amounts of olives, anchovies, fried peppers, squid and other wonderful titbits to go with glass after glass of chilled sherry. Sherry can be served chilled or at room temperature. Dry sherries are probably best served chilled. I like to drink it neat, but there are cocktail recipes that make good use of sherry, like the Bamboo which has got its name from a 1902 hit song, *Under the bamboo tree*.

MADEIRA

Besides port the Portuguese produce another good fortified wine on the Madeira Islands off the coast of Africa. Madeira originated in the sixteenth century when the islanders started adding brandy to their wines so they could survive the long journey through the tropical heat and the ship's movements on its way to the Americas.

What makes madeira special is the way the wine is made. Madeira is made from five varieties of grapes: Sercial, Verdelho, Bual, Malmsey and Tinta negra mole. The grapes are first crushed and fermented, but before fermentation is complete and while it still has some of the sweetness, brandy is added to fortify the wine. The wine is then heated up to 55°C for a few months to help concentrate it.

Madeira wines that have been in casks for three years are considered to be inferior. Then come those that are five to fifteen years old. At the top of the heap are the vintage Madeiras, which can be quite expensive.

Since it is a fortified wine, with brandy in it, madeira remains drinkable for a long time after the bottle is opened. It may not be as well known as port, but this sweet wine works wonderfully as an after-dinner drink accompanying dessert. It tastes great with cheese as well and can be served as an aperitif.

DRINKS IN ANCIENT INDIA

With the exception of tribal communities, drinking alcoholic beverages has never been part of normal social interaction among Indians the way it has been in most non-Islamic countries. Opening a bottle of champagne to celebrate any occasion, drinking a peg or two before dinner or sipping wine at the dining table are recent introductions to our culture.

Hindus are more ambivalent about alcohol than people from other religious communities. There are no hard and fast rules as such, but we know from the shastras, sculptures, inscriptions and wall paintings that our forefathers knew a thing or two about making and drinking alcohol. The cosmic sea was composed entirely of amrit, the nectar of immortality sought equally by the gods and demons.

Wine and alcohol also find frequent mention in the Smritis, which laid down the laws of Dharma, as well as in renowned ayurvedic texts such as the Charak Samhita. While the Smritis decreed that women should avoid drinking when their husbands were away because alcohol lent a certain charm to women and created an urge for sexual intercourse, the Charak Samhita refers to the medicinal properties of wine as well as to its harmful effects.

Other accounts prove that though our forefathers did not know how to distill—they learnt that later from the Arabs—they were quite inventive when it came to fermenting and brewing. Sugar cane juice, barley, rice, beans, flowers, herbs and all kinds of fruit were used to make intoxicants. There were as many as fifty different kinds of liquor in ancient India. Sura was made by mixing grain and jaggery, and was distributed as rations to soldiers on the battlefield; madira was a rice beer; madhvi was made from honey; sidhu was a predecessor of modern rum; and kadambari was produced from sour milk. There is also a mention of a drink called kohola, made from barley. It is believed that when that name was later combined with the Arabic prefix 'al' it became the origin of the word 'alcohol'. There is reference in the Rig Veda to a drink made from snake's milk that was left to mature under moonlight.

Though some brahmins drank, it was more common among the kshatriyas, vaishyas and the sudras. Drinking was a way of life in Aryan and Dravidian cultures. Women drank as much as men. The Aryans were particularly fond of a brew produced from a mix of rice, jaggery and mahua blossoms while the Dravidians were partial to toddy tapped from palm trees.

The consumption of alcohol became less acceptable in Indian society after the advent of Buddhism, which considered drinking among five cardinal sins. Hindu society too began condemning it around this time. The brahmins were by now forbidden to drink; Kautilya had declared it a penal offence as he considered it unworthy of their calling as teachers and the guardians of moral values. The lower castes, however, were allowed to drink as much as they pleased.

BEER

There are countries where people drink beer and little of anything else. In Australia, for instance, you will be looked upon with suspicion if you order whisky in a pub.

It has been established that both the Chinese and the Egyptians were making and drinking beer well over 5000 years ago. A 4000-year-old tablet, found in what was once Mesopotamia, shows that beer brewing was a highly respected profession of the time. Beer mugs dating back 3000 years have been unearthed in Israel as well. The Egyptians showed the Greeks how to make beer who, in turn, taught it to the early Romans. Then the word spread to all corners of the Mediterranean region. It also became the drink of choice of the ancient tribes of Britain.

Brewing beer started late in India. Before the invention of refrigeration our hot climate was a major stumbling block. Until the middle of the nineteenth century beer was imported from England, by sea, primarily as rations to quench the thirst of British troops stationed here. Since ordinary beer could not survive the climate changes on the long journey, a brewer by the name of George Hodgson developed a highly hopped beer which could withstand the long trip. He realized that a higher alcohol content would prevent spoilage. The extra dose of hops gave the beer the backbone it needed. This beer became known as India Pale Ale. It is robust and still popular around the world.

India's first breweries were set up around 1850 in the hill stations of Murree, now in Pakistan, and Solan in Himachal. Dyer and Company, which ran one of them, had connections with General Dyer, made infamous by the Jallianwala Bagh massacre. The other company, Meakins is known today as Mohan Meakins. It produces Golden Eagle, a brand name that has seen better times.

My favourite beer is the bitter that you get in pubs in England and is pulled straight from a barrel. It is frothy, reddish amber in colour and not at all heavy. It has an alcohol content of 3 to 5 per cent, though stronger versions also exist and are referred to as 'Best' or 'Special'. The British innkeepers of my student days used to serve it warm but these days you get it a bit chilled. The English bitter does not travel well. You need the pub atmosphere and inclement weather to appreciate it fully. The English also drink stout, a very dark beer.

The best beer I have drunk was in the Czech Republic. The Czechs, apparently, drink more beer per capita than any other nationality—German, Irish and Australian included. They were the pioneers in the development of the beer that is commonly referred to as Pilsener.

In India we get mainly lager beer. Apart from Kingfisher, India's best-selling brand at the moment, and Haywards, a number of foreign brands are also available in our shops: The South African brand, Castle, and the Australian Fosters, which is rapidly losing ground even in its home country. Singapore's famous Tiger beer has now reached our shores and we have Cobra beer which started life as the beer of choice in Indian restaurants in Britain. These beers also have 3 to 5 per cent alcohol. Then there is Corona, which comes from Mexico. It is unusual in that you are expected to drink it straight from the bottle after a wedge of lime has been squeezed into the bottle.

TYPES OF BEER

There are, more or less, three types of beers.

First, there is the ubiquitous **lager**. It is golden yellow in colour and is by far the most popular kind of beer in the world. Just about every country makes it; some make it very well, like the central Europeans, others produce dreadful stuff.

Then we have the **ale or bitter** which is more bitter than lager and usually has higher alcohol content. It is darker in colour, more brown than yellow. You get ale when you ask for a pint of bitter in an English pub.

Stout beers are not for everyone. They are dark and velvety, have a thicker texture than other beers and are almost medicinal to taste. Guinness is the Holy Grail of stout beers and outsells all other brands combined. The beer requires a slow pour. When you order Guinness, the

bartender will fill the glass three-quarters full and put it aside for a few minutes to allow the beer to settle. Once the brownish liquid turns almost black he will fill the rest of the glass. If you like a good 'head' on your beer Guinness is for you. In fact, in 1988 the company invented and patented what it calls a 'widget', a plastic device that sits at the bottom of the can and releases nitrogen when a can is opened, forcing a surge of bubbles. Quite clever, I think.

Most stouts, however, are quite weak in alcohol content. Guinness, for instance, contains only 4.2 per cent alcohol and its bitter taste can be quite overpowering. Like other stout beers, it should be drunk as cold as possible.

Brewers of stout beers have long claimed that their products are beneficial for health. In Britain, stouts have a reputation for giving strength to dedicated drinkers. Guinness has been running advertising campaigns for years with slogans like 'Guinness is Good for You', 'My Goodness, My Guinness' and 'Guinness is Strength'. 'Stout' itself is an archaic word for strong. Until quite recently English doctors would recommend stout beer as a pick-me-up for people recovering from illness and for nursing mothers. There is a good reason for this. Sweet or cream stouts have lactose, the sugar that is found in milk.

HOW BEER IS MADE

Beer is made from malt, hops, yeast and water. At its best it is a fine balance between malted grains and hops.

Hops is a flowering vine whose oils give the beer its bitter taste and aroma. There are varieties of hops, with different tastes, just as there are different kinds of grapes. The hops used in Indian breweries are imported in the form of pellets from hop-growing countries like Germany, Poland and Britain. Interestingly, a small amount of hops is also grown in Himachal. It used to be cultivated in Kashmir as well until the liquor-hating militants put an end to it.

Variations between different beers result from the type of yeast that is used to ferment the malt. The malt comes from germinated barley, which is allowed to sprout. Sometimes wheat, corn or rice is used instead of barley.

The brewing process consists of four steps. First, the malt is boiled with water. Then hops are added and the mixture boiled further. In the third step, the hops are removed and yeast is added to ferment the brew. Finally, after fermentation, the beer is aged. Of course, it is not as simple as it sounds. Many brewers employ their own particular techniques to add character and nuance to their brew.

SERVING AND DRINKING

Generally, hand-pumped or draught beer is better than what you pour out of a bottle. This is how it is served in pubs and good bars unless the customer insists on a bottle. The closer the pub or the bar is to the brewery the better the beer.

Bottled beer should be stored in a cool place, away from sunlight. If you open a bottle and there is no fizz, I suggest you discard the bottle since it is more than likely that the beer has spoiled.

While pouring beer, waiters have a habit of tipping the neck of the bottle gingerly against the side of the glass and pouring the beer slowly into the glass so as to get as little of the frothy head as possible. This is not how it should be done, since most of the carbon dioxide gets trapped in the glass. Beer should be served with a high head of foam. It should be poured straight to the bottom of the glass. This builds a rich creamy cap and the beer loses just enough of its carbonation to make it soft and mellow. You should take the first drink through the head rather than wait for the suds to subside.

WHY IS ONE BEER DARKER THAN ANOTHER?

During the brewing process the barley is roasted. At low heat the colour is light and with more heat, since you are closer to burning the barley, it turns dark. The beer that results from this barley will also be dark. Like dark roasted coffee dark beers attracts a special kind of crowd. It is for people who drink beer like wine, not like water.

CIDER

In certain parts of the northern hemisphere where grapes cannot be cultivated with success, other local fruits are used to produce fermented drinks. In Britain, for instance, apple is the fruit of choice. Cider, or fermented apple juice, has been appreciated for centuries in England. It is not drunk much anywhere else, though in India in recent years some apple growers, mainly in Himachal, have been producing it in small amounts.

Cider is a relative of wine, with almost as ancient a history. When the Romans landed in England as unwelcome guests 2000 years ago, they found the locals drinking cider in large quantities. The conquerors did not care much for it and stuck to drinking wine. Although Americans have learnt to make cider, especially in New England, the British are still masters when it comes to producing a nice bottle. English cider is fruity and sparkling and, when properly chilled, is a great thirst quencher. The production of cider is concentrated in Devon, Somerset and Herefordshire.

French cider, from Normandy, is quite different from the English product. It tends to be thinner in texture and has lower alcohol content.

HOW CIDER IS MADE

Making cider is not a difficult art. Any farmer can make it at home. Earlier, the fruit was first beaten to a pulp in a stone trough. These days the apples are placed between two cylinders that have sharp knives which, when rotated at high speed, perform the same operation much more quickly and efficiently.

Good cider is always made from ripe apples. Although any variety of apple can be used to make cider, the quality of the cider depends on the proper blending of different types of apples. Some need to have high acid content while others should be sweeter. Over a hundred types of apples grow in Britain alone as apple trees thrive in wintry conditions. Broadly speaking, cider apples are categorized as sweet, bitter-sweet, bitter and acid. Yeast is added for fermentation. The more expensive ciders are aged and vintage-dated like wines. But, unlike wine, there is no significant improvement to cider if you keep the bottle for a long period.

SERVING AND DRINKING

Cider does not have much of a kick and can be completely non-alcoholic, in which case it is simply referred to as 'cider'. It can be drunk by everyone, including children. When it has alcohol in it, it is called 'hard cider'. Cider should always be served chilled, preferably in tall glasses that you would normally use for beer.

THE LOCAL STUFF

feni

Feni is really country liquor that has risen from its lowly status. It is the only widely known spirit that is uniquely Indian. It is produced only in Goa.

Whatever claims the Goans may lay to its potency, feni is no stronger than whisky or vodka. It is distilled either from the cashew fruit or from toddy obtained from the coconut tree. Neither the cashew nut nor coconut milk plays any part in the production of feni. Cashew feni is made in northern Goa, where the crop is grown, while coconut feni is a product of the south. Cashew feni is by far more popular, having captured about 70 per cent of the market. It is also a little more expensive than coconut feni. Foreign tourists, especially Germans, seem to prefer coconut feni for its dubious aphrodisiacal properties.

While it is bottled commercially, feni continues to be distilled mostly in the villages. There are two major distilleries, Madame Rosa and Global Spirits, in Goa while about 6000 cottage distilleries spread across the state continue to produce feni. Goa is trying to change the image of feni and has started marketing it aggressively in the United States, for instance, under the brand name Kazkar. And you will find feni in cities like Mumbai and pockets of the Middle East where there is a Goan presence.

The rule of thumb is that more expensive bottles are better than the cheaper ones. In any case you should avoid the temptation of buying anything that is really cheap. Its production is likely to have been compromised. I would also avoid feni in plastic bottles unless you intend to drink it within a week or so. In the long run the plastic will react and have a negative effect on the alcohol.

So, how is feni made? First let's take cashew or kaju feni. The fruit (from which the cashew nut protrudes at the lower end) is crushed in a stone bowl to extract the juice, which is then fermented in a copper or clay pot for a few days. When it is heated, the vapours that rise from it are led through a pipe and trapped in liquid form in a small pot that is attached to it. As far as I know, no other country has thought of using the fruit's juice to make alcohol. They are probably put off by the smell. For Goans the aroma is an integral part of the pleasure of drinking feni.

The first product of this process is called urrack, which has low alcohol strength. It is quite popular locally during distillation season (April and May). You can drink urrack neat. This spirit is distilled twice over to turn it into feni which is stronger. The process is the same for coconut feni where toddy is used instead of cashew fruit juice. Unlike cashew feni, its coconut counterpart is distilled throughout the year.

Feni is among those drinks that have an essentially acquired taste. I prefer cashew over coconut feni. I drink it with club soda, lots of ice cubes and a dash of lime juice. But you can mix it with tonic water, lemonade or Coca-Cola. It can also be used in making cocktails where you follow the recipes and substitute gin, vodka or tequila with feni. That way you can make yourself a Feni Daiquiri or a Feni Fizz.

bhang

Technically, bhang is illegal but since it has a cultural resonance Indian authorities turn a blind eye to it. It is drunk in enormous quantities in the best of homes on Holi, a day when even teetotallers don't mind indulging themselves a bit. It is homemade and as safe as anything you can buy in a liquor shop.

Bhang is deceptive. It tastes like any drink made with cold milk that has some spices in it, but the effect it has on the brain is quite something else. The recipe I have calls for water, green marijuana leaves and its flowers (also known in its dry form as cannabis, hemp or ganja), milk, almond, cardamom, a touch of garam masala, powered ginger, rosewater and sugar. If I drink too much bhang I start giggling.

toddy

Toddy is another desi drink beyond government control. It is made from palm trees, coconut and date palms (khajuri). In West Africa it is known as palm 'wine' and it is the staple drink of millions. Nigerians call it *ogogoro*. Toddy is drunk in rural areas since it does not travel well and perishes very fast.

The sap for toddy is collected by the tapper who climbs the tree and makes cuts between the kernels. A plastic bottle or a matka is left hanging there to collect the draining sap. The white liquid that oozes out is sweet and not alcoholic. We call it neera. When I was much younger, neera was sold by the glass in the mornings in government-run kiosks in Bombay. Neera begins fermenting quite rapidly, within a day. Before you know it, it becomes mildly intoxicating but is still sweet. With time it becomes stronger and sour in taste. If you keep it too long it turns into vinegar. Some people prefer the vinegary flavour.

desi liquor

Most of the Indian middle class drinks what is known as 'foreign' liquor: whisky, gin, vodka and so on. But indigenous or desi liquor, prepared from recipes passed down through centuries, is the mainstay of India's village population and the urban poor.

Desi liquor is fermented and distilled from papayas, bananas, pineapples, jackfruit and just about any fruit that has high sugar content. In south India a very potent liquor made from green betel nuts (supari) is popular. Rajasthanis produce a saffron (kesar)-flavoured liqueur. There was a time when a distillery in Sikkim produced paan liqueur which tasted vile but was popular with homesick Indians abroad. In the north, orange-flavoured spirits are common. You can buy some of this stuff in shops but much of it is produced in the backyard and is illegal.

Mahua is among the better-known desi liquors. It is made from the mahua flower that grows all over central India. When the flowers drop from the trees, around April, they are gathered by the tribals and dried and sold in the markets. The dried flower is soaked in water for four days in order for it to ferment and distillation follows. I have not had the opportunity to taste mahua but I am told it has a flowery smell and can be quite heady. Animals are known to get drunk just by chewing on the flowers strewn on the forest floor.

HOOCH: THE DRINK THAT KILLS

In 1981, in a deadly tragedy in Bangalore, recorded in James Manor's fine book *Power, Poverty and Poison*, over 300 people died and hundreds of others were left paralysed or had their eyesight damaged after consuming hooch or illicit liquor. Over the years innumerable such incidents have claimed lives in almost every state across India.

Why would anyone want to drink something that can kill you? In India hooch is the drink of the poorest of the poor more out of necessity than anything else. It is cheaper than what you can get in shops since it is bootlegged and not subject to taxes. If you live in a slum you don't have to travel a great distance to get a bottle. Someone in the neighbourhood will be distilling it or selling it. Illegal bars with relaxed hours abound in various localities. Moreover, hooch gives a bigger high than the legal desi drinks.

The word 'hooch' entered the English language in the mid-nineteenth century from the Hoochinoo tribe of Alaska, known for making homemade liquor. Americans call it 'moonshine' because, in the days when Prohibition prevailed, the distillation process was usually carried out at night under moonlight to avoid attracting the attention of the authorities. Moonshine continues to be produced in the United States, mainly in the region of the Appalachian Mountains in the south. The American product is far safer than what you will find in our slums. Incidentally, there are countries, New Zealand for instance, where it is perfectly legal to brew or distill your own liquor at home.

Why is Indian hooch so poisonous? First, it is made in the most unsanitary conditions without government supervision. Second, all sorts of things are thrown into the mix that ends up as the final spirit: chicken shit, cow dung, dead cockroaches and lizards, battery acid, pieces of discarded rubber tyres and footwear, rotten fruit and vegetables, even urea fertilizer. Anything and everything is first boiled and then distilled. Often, methanol is added afterwards to give the liquor more kick. Methanol is capable of causing blindness and sometimes death. It is best to keep away from drinks with such dubious antecedents.

MIXING IT UP

ROYAL SALUTE
21
BLENDED
SCOTCH WHISKY

BLENDERS PRIDE

ABSOLUT
Country of Sweden
VODKA
This superb vodka
was distilled from grain grown
in the rich fields of southern Sweden.
It has been produced at the famous
old distilleries near Åhus
in accordance with more than
400 years of Swedish tradition.
Vodka has been sold under the name
Absolut since 1879.
40% ALC./VOL. (80 PROOF) 700 ML.
IMPORTED
PRODUCED AND BOTTLED IN AHUS, SWEDEN
BY THE ABSOLUT COMPANY
A DIVISION OF V&S VIN&SPRIT AB.

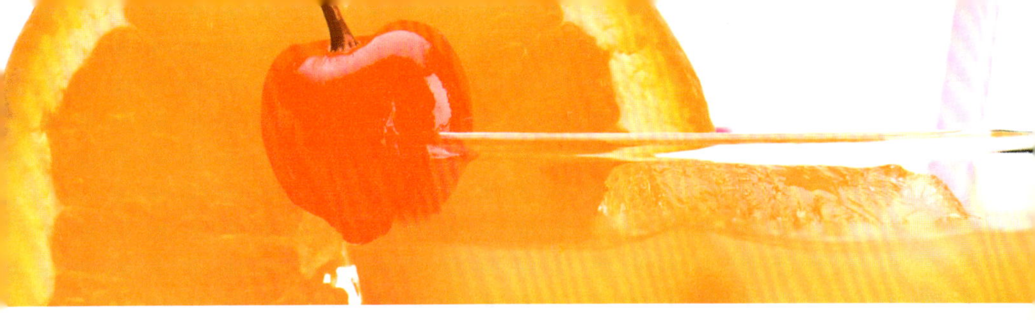

COCKTAILS

There was a young lady of Kent
Who said she knew what it meant
When men asked her to dine
Gave her cocktails and wine,
She knew what it meant—but she went!

It is true—and I know this from experience—cocktails bring people together. There is something in the heady mix of tastes and aromas, colours and garnishes that have stimulated social discourse for over two hundred years.

At its most basic, a cocktail is a mixed drink. Broadly, it is made up of three parts: a **base** (liquor, such as gin, vodka or rum, even wine or champagne); a **mixer**, which binds the drink together (soda, for instance); and **flavouring** (perhaps a fruit juice or a liqueur). There is usually a garnish which could be a cherry or a fruit wedge. Of course, it is not as simple as that. Mixing a cocktail is an art as well as a craft, and an evolving one at that. A good cocktail should satisfy the eyes, the nose as well as the palate. A cocktail should be a balanced drink where no single element is overpowering. The blend of acids and essences, if done properly, transforms the mixture into something smooth and bracing.

Mixing cocktails can be fun. Don't get intimidated. Keep a reliable recipe handy and track down the ingredients. Always remember that a cocktail recipe, or any other recipe for that matter, is a guide, not a rule. Feel free to alter proportions and ingredients according to your personal tastes. That is the first rule for cocktails: Mix them how you like them.

A WORD ON THE RECIPES BEFORE YOU PICK YOUR FAVOURITES:

- Some cocktails require more than one spirit. Such instances have been listed only once in the following pages. Singapore Sling, for instance, requires gin as well as cherry brandy, a liqueur. It is listed here under gin but not under liqueur. Similarly, the recipe for a Margarita calls for tequila and triple sec. It is listed only under tequila. If you are looking for a particular recipe, just search for it in the Index.
- Many of the drinks are served strained or without ice, but you may prefer to have them on the rocks. And why not? Just pour the mix into an old-fashioned glass filled with ice cubes.
- The measurements used are

1 cup = 250 ml (8 fl oz)
1 teaspoon (tsp) = 5 ml
1 tablespoon (tbsp) = 3 tsp or 15 ml (½ fl oz)
A pinch = 1/8 tsp (literally a pinch)
A dash = 1-2 drops

WHISKY

scotch and bourbon

Use blended whisky in making these cocktails. Single malts should not be wasted on cocktails and, in any case, some of the smokier ones would be too overpowering. American, Irish or Canadian whiskies are perfectly fine substitutes for Scotch. Bourbon and whisky recipes are, in most cases, interchangeable, so just take your pick.

aberdeen sour

60 ml Scotch whisky
30 ml Cointreau or triple sec
2 tbsp orange juice
2 tbsp lemon juice

Mix all ingredients with ice in a shaker or blender.

Pour into an old-fashioned glass.

45 ml Scotch whisky
30 ml dry vermouth
2 tbsp pineapple juice
Pineapple wedge

Shake all ingredients with ice cubes.

Strain into a chilled cocktail glass.

Garnish with pineapple wedge.

basin street

60 ml bourbon
30 ml Cointreau or triple sec
1 tsp lemon juice

Shake all ingredients with ice cubes.

Strain into a chilled cocktail glass.

beadlestone cocktail

45 ml Scotch whisky
45 ml dry vermouth

Stir Scotch and vermouth with ice cubes.

Strain into a chilled cocktail glass.

beals

45 ml Scotch whisky
15 ml dry vermouth
15 ml sweet vermouth

Stir all ingredients with ice cubes.
Strain into a chilled cocktail glass.

black hawk

45 ml Scotch whisky
30 ml gin
Maraschino cherry

Stir Scotch and gin with ice cubes.
Strain into a chilled cocktail glass.
Garnish with cherry.

blizzard booster

60 ml bourbon
1½ tsp cranberry juice
1 tsp lemon juice
1 tsp sugar
Lemon slice

Shake all ingredients, except lemon slice, with ice cubes.
Pour into an old-fashioned glass.
Garnish with lemon slice.

HIGHBALLS OR TALL DRINKS

An alcoholic drink in a tall glass, brimming with ice, can refresh you like nothing else can on a hot summer day. So let me tell you about highballs. A highball is, in essence, a small amount of something strong mixed with a larger amount of something weak in a tall glass with ice. The 'something strong' could be any hard liquor. The 'something weak' is usually club soda but it can be ginger ale, Coca-Cola or any other mixer. Highballs are devilishly simple to make, and therefore a very safe bet when you are entertaining. And you can make them according to your taste, without bothering too much with measurements. If you or your guests like your drinks strong, you can add more liquor and go easy on the non-alcoholic part. If you prefer them weak, do just the opposite.

Highballs are also known in some circles as built drinks; you pour a spirit in a glass and then build on it with other ingredients and serve the mix in the same glass. Highballs are, of course, always served in highball or Collins glasses. Tall and narrow, these glasses hold the bubbles of a soda or any other carbonated drink longer.

Our humble nimboo–soda becomes a highball if you add gin to it and give it the fancy name, Gin Fizz or Tom Collins. Other popular tall drinks are Cuba Libre (rum and Coca-Cola), the classic gin-and-tonic and of course the very potent Long Island Iced Tea.

blood-and-sand

15 ml Scotch whisky
15 ml cherry brandy
15 ml sweet vermouth
2 tbsp orange juice

Shake all ingredients with ice cubes.

Strain into a chilled cocktail glass.

bobby burns

15 ml Scotch whisky
15 ml Bénédictine
15 ml dry vermouth
15 ml sweet vermouth

Mix all ingredients with ice in a shaker or blender.

Strain into a chilled cocktail glass.

boilermaker

45 ml Scotch whisky
Mug or glass of beer

Drink the whisky in one gulp and immediately follow with a beer chaser.

Some prefer to pour the whisky into the beer and quaff them together.

bourbon and water

60 ml bourbon
120 ml water
Lemon peel

Pour bourbon and water into an old-fashioned glass.

Add ice cubes and a twist of lemon peel if desired and stir.

bourbon collins

45 ml bourbon
½ tsp lemon juice
1 tsp sugar
Club soda
Lemon peel

Mix bourbon and lemon juice with ice in a shaker or blender.

Pour into a highball glass half-filled with ice.

Add club soda and lemon peel.

bourbon gin fizz

1 tsp sugar
1 tsp lemon juice
45 ml bourbon
30 ml gin
Club soda
Lemon slice
Maraschino cherry

Mix sugar, lemon juice, bourbon and gin in a highball glass. Add ice cubes and mix. Add club soda.

Garnish with lemon slice and cherry.

Fizz drinks date back to the nineteenth century when they were taken to cure hangovers. All you need for a fizz is a spirit, lime juice, sugar and club soda. And ice, lots of it.

bourbon highball

60 ml bourbon
Ginger ale or club soda
Lemon peel

Fill a highball glass with bourbon, ginger ale or club soda, and ice cubes.

Add lemon peel. Stir gently.

bourbon side car

45 ml bourbon
25 ml Cointreau or triple sec
1 tsp lemon juice

Mix all ingredients with ice in a shaker or blender.

Strain into a chilled cocktail glass.

bourbon sour

60 ml bourbon
Juice of ½ a lemon
½ tsp sugar
Orange slice

Mix all ingredients, except orange slice, with ice in a shaker or blender.

Strain into a chilled cocktail glass.

Garnish with orange slice.

braemar cocktail

45 ml Scotch whisky
15 ml sweet vermouth
Dash of Bénédictine

Mix all ingredients with ice in a shaker or blender.

Strain into a chilled cocktail glass.

cablegram

60 ml Scotch whisky
1 tsp sugar
½ tsp lemon juice
Ginger ale

Mix all ingredients, except ginger ale, with ice in a shaker or blender.

Pour into a chilled highball glass.

Fill with ginger ale.

chapel hill

45 ml Scotch whisky
15 ml Cointreau or triple sec
½ tsp lemon juice
Orange slice

Mix all ingredients, except orange slice, with ice in a shaker or blender.

Pour into a chilled cocktail glass.

Garnish with orange slice.

churchill

45 ml Scotch whisky
15 ml sweet vermouth
15 ml Cointreau or triple sec
1 tsp lemon juice
Lemon slice

Shake all ingredients, except lemon slice, with ice cubes.

Strain into a chilled cocktail glass.

Garnish with lemon slice.

continental perfect

30 ml Scotch whisky
30 ml dry vermouth
30 ml sweet vermouth
Several dashes of Angostura bitters
Orange slice

Mix all ingredients, except orange slice, with ice in a shaker or blender.

Pour into an old-fashioned glass.

Garnish with orange slice.

croton

60 ml bourbon
10 ml dry sherry
Lemon peel

Stir whisky and sherry with ice cubes.

Strain into a chilled cocktail glass.

Twist lemon peel over the drink and drop into the glass.

daisy dueller

45 ml bourbon
1½ tsp lemon juice
1 tsp sugar
15 ml Cointreau or triple sec
Club soda
Maraschino cherry

Shake all ingredients, except soda and cherry, with ice cubes.

Strain into a highball glass.

Add ice cubes and fill with soda.

Garnish with cherry.

danny's downfall

30 ml Scotch whisky
30 ml gin
30 ml sweet vermouth

Pour all ingredients into a mixing glass and stir with ice cubes.

Strain into a chilled cocktail glass.

dinah cocktail

60 ml Scotch whisky
Juice of ¼ of a lemon
½ tsp sugar
Fresh mint leaf

Shake all ingredients, except mint leaf, with ice cubes.

Strain into a chilled cocktail glass.

Garnish with mint leaf.

dixie whisky cocktail

60 ml bourbon
10 ml Cointreau or triple sec
15 ml crème de menthe (white)
½ tsp sugar
Several dashes of Angostura bitters

Shake all ingredients with ice cubes.

Strain into a chilled cocktail glass

dizie dram

60 ml Scotch whisky
15 ml crème de menthe (white)
½ tsp lemon juice
½ tsp sugar
Several dashes of Cointreau or triple sec

Mix all ingredients with ice in a shaker or blender.

Pour into an old-fashioned glass.

dry mahoney

60 ml bourbon
30 ml dry vermouth
Lemon peel

Stir bourbon and vermouth with ice cubes.

Strain into a chilled cocktail glass.

Twist lemon peel over the drink and drop into the glass.

dundee dram

30 ml Scotch whisky
30 ml gin
15 ml Drambuie
1 tsp lemon juice
Lemon peel
Maraschino cherry

Mix all ingredients, except lemon peel and cherry, with ice in a shaker or blender.

Pour into an old-fashioned glass.

Twist lemon peel over the drink and drop into the glass.

Garnish with cherry.

eric the red

45 ml Scotch whisky
15 ml cherry brandy
15 ml dry vermouth

Mix all ingredients with ice in a shaker or blender.

Pour into a chilled old-fashioned glass.

flying scotsman

45 ml Scotch whisky
30 ml sweet vermouth
½ tsp sugar
Several dashes of Angostura bitters

Mix all ingredients with ice in a shaker or blender.

Pour into a chilled cocktail glass.

forester

45 ml bourbon
30 ml cherry brandy
1 tsp lemon juice
Maraschino cherry

Mix all ingredients, except cherry, with cubes in a shaker or blender.

Strain into a chilled cocktail glass.

Garnish with cherry.

french twist

45 ml bourbon
45 ml cognac
15 ml Grand Marnier
1 tsp lemon juice

Mix all ingredients with ice in a shaker or blender.

Strain into a chilled cocktail glass.

frisco sour

45 ml Scotch whisky
25 ml Bénédictine
1 tsp lemon juice
Dash of grenadine (optional)
Lemon slice

Mix all ingredients, except lemon slice,with ice in a shaker or blender.

Strain into a cocktail glass.

Garnish with lemon slice.

godfather

45 ml Scotch whisky
30 ml amaretto

Mix Scotch and amaretto with ice cubes in an old-fashioned glass.

gretna green

1 tbsp honey
45 ml Scotch whisky
15 ml Chartreuse (green)
2 tbsp lemon juice

Mix honey with a little water and stir till it dissolves.

Pour into a shaker or blender with remaining ingredients and ice.

Mix thoroughly.

Strain into a chilled cocktail glass.

highland cooler

1 tsp sugar
60 ml Scotch whisky
Club soda or ginger ale
Maraschino cherry

Put sugar and a little club soda in a highball glass and stir till sugar dissolves.

Add ice cubes and Scotch.

Fill with club soda or ginger ale and stir again.

Garnish with cherry.

(Sugar is optional if you are using ginger ale.)

highland fling

45 ml Scotch whisky
15 ml sweet vermouth
Several dashes of Angostura bitters
Maraschino cherry

Mix all ingredients, except cherry, with ice in a shaker or blender.

Pour into a chilled cocktail glass.

Garnish with cherry.

highland morning

60 ml Scotch whisky
30 ml Cointreau or triple sec
½ cup fresh grapefruit juice
Grapefruit peel

Shake all the ingredients, except grapefruit peel, well with ice cubes.

Pour into a highball glass.

Garnish with grapefruit peel.

hole-in-one

45 ml Scotch whisky
10 ml dry vermouth
¼ tsp lemon juice
Dash of Angostura bitters

Shake all ingredients with ice cubes.

Strain into a chilled cocktail glass.

A guy meets a beautiful blonde in a bar and after a great evening he volunteers to drop her home. She invites him in for coffee and one thing leads to another.

When he wakes up the next morning he sees a photograph of a man on the bedside table.

'Is that your husband?' he asks nervously.

'No,' she replies.

'Is he your boyfriend?'

'Don't be silly,' she purrs, 'that's me before the operation.'

horse's neck

Lemon peel	*Place the peel in a highball glass.*
60 ml Scotch whisky	*Pour whisky and add ice cubes.*
Ginger ale	*Add lemon juice.*
Juice of ¼ lemon	*Fill with ginger ale and stir gently.*

imperial fizz

60 ml Scotch whisky
15 ml light rum
Juice of ½ a lemon
1 tsp sugar
Club soda

Shake all ingredients, except club soda, with ice cubes.
Pour into a highball glass.
Add ice cubes if required.
Fill with club soda and stir gently.

invercauld castle cooler

45 ml Scotch whisky
30 ml Bénédictine
Ginger ale

Pour Scotch and Bénédictine into a highball glass.
Add ice cubes.
Fill with ginger ale and stir gently.

italian stallion

45 ml bourbon
15 ml Campari
15 ml sweet vermouth
Dash of Angostura bitters
Lemon peel

Stir all ingredients, except lemon peel, with ice cubes in a mixing glass.
Strain into a chilled cocktail glass.
Twist lemon peel over the drink and drop into the glass.

john collins

60 ml Scotch whisky
Juice of ½ a lemon
1 tsp sugar
Club soda
Maraschino cherry

Shake all ingredients, except club soda and cherry, with ice cubes.

Strain into a highball glass.

Add ice cubes.

Fill with club soda and stir gently.

Garnish with cherry.

kentucky colonel cocktail

45 ml bourbon
15 ml Bénédictine
Lemon peel

Stir bourbon and Bénédictine with ice cubes in a mixing glass.

Strain into a chilled cocktail glass.

Add lemon peel.

kentucky cooler

45 ml bourbon
30 ml brandy
1 tsp lemon juice
2 tsp sugar
Club soda
15 ml dark rum

Mix all ingredients, except club soda and rum, with ice in a shaker or blender.

Pour into a highball glass. Add ice cubes.

Fill with club soda.

Add a float of rum.

key biscayne

45 ml Scotch whisky
15 ml Cointreau or triple sec
15 ml sweet vermouth
Juice of ½ a lemon
Fresh mint leaves

Mix all ingredients, except mint leaves, with ice in a shaker or blender.

Strain into a chilled cocktail glass.

Tear the mint leaves to release their aroma and drop into the glass. Stir.

kiss on the lips

60 ml bourbon
60 ml apricot brandy

Pour bourbon and brandy over ice cubes in an old-fashioned glass. Stir.

loch lomond

45 ml Scotch whisky
1 tsp sugar
Several dashes of Angostura bitters
1 tsp lemon juice

Shake all the ingredients well with ice cubes.

Strain into a cocktail glass.

louisville cooler

15 ml bourbon
2 tbsp orange juice
1 tsp lemon juice
1 tsp sugar
½ orange slice

Shake all ingredients, except orange slice, with ice cubes.

Strain into an old-fashioned glass over more ice.

Garnish with orange slice.

mamie gilroy

60 ml Scotch whisky
Juice of ½ a lemon
Ginger ale

Combine all ingredients in a highball glass filled with ice cubes.

Stir gently.

manhattan

60 ml Scotch whisky
15 ml sweet vermouth
Dash of Angostura bitters
Maraschino cherry

Mix all ingredients, except cherry, with ice cubes in a mixing glass.

Strain into a chilled cocktail glass.

Add cherry.

(The amount of vermouth should be adjusted to individual taste.)

manhattan bourbon

60 ml bourbon
15 ml sweet vermouth
Dash of Angostura bitters
Maraschino cherry

Mix all ingredients, except cherry, with ice cubes in a mixing glass.

Strain into a chilled cocktail glass.

Add cherry.

(The amount of vermouth should be adjusted to individual taste.)

mint julep

1 tsp sugar
8 fresh mint leaves
1 tsp hot water
60 ml bourbon

Place the sugar in a strong bowl or mortar.

Tear the mint leaves into small pieces and add them to the sugar.

Bruise them with a pestle or use a muddler to release their flavour and colour.

Add the hot water and grind together.

Spoon the mix into an old-fashioned glass and half-fill with ice cubes.

Add bourbon. Stir till the outside of the glass has frosted.

Allow to stand for a couple of minutes till the ice melts slightly and dilutes the drink.

new yorker

45 ml Scotch whisky
½ tsp lemon juice
1 tsp sugar
½ tsp grenadine
Lemon peel

Shake all ingredients, except lemon peel, with ice cubes.

Strain into a chilled cocktail glass.

Twist lemon peel over the drink and drop into the glass.

painted pony

30 ml Scotch whisky
30 ml Grand Marnier
2 tsp orange juice
1 tsp lemon juice
1 tsp grenadine

Mix all ingredients with ice in a shaker or blender.

Strain into a chilled cocktail glass.

park lane

45 ml Scotch whisky
15 ml gin
1 tsp lemon juice
½ tsp sugar

Mix all ingredients with ice in a shaker or blender.

Strain into a chilled cocktail glass.

presbyterian

60 ml bourbon
Ginger ale
Club soda

Pour bourbon into a highball glass and add ice cubes.

Fill with equal parts of ginger ale and club soda.

purple heather

45 ml Scotch whisky
15 ml crème de cassis
Club soda

Mix Scotch and crème de cassis in a highball glass half-filled with ice cubes.

Fill with soda and stir gently.

red raider

30 ml bourbon
15 ml Cointreau or triple sec
1 tsp lemon juice
Dash of grenadine

Shake all ingredients with ice cubes.

Strain into a chilled cocktail glass.

red rover

45 ml bourbon
15 ml gin
1 tsp lemon juice
1 tsp sugar
Lemon slice

Mix all ingredients, except lemon slice, with ice in a shaker or blender.

Strain into a chilled cocktail glass.

Garnish with lemon slice.

rob roy

60 ml Scotch whisky
15 ml sweet vermouth
Dash of Angostura bitters
Maraschino cherry

Shake all ingredients, except cherry, with ice cubes.

Strain into a chilled cocktail glass.

Garnish with cherry.

royal rob roy

45 ml Scotch whisky
45 ml Drambuie
10 ml dry vermouth
10 ml sweet vermouth
Maraschino cherry

Mix all ingredients, except cherry, with ice in a shaker or blender.

Strain into a chilled cocktail glass.

Garnish with cherry.

rusty nail

45 ml Scotch whisky
30 ml Drambuie

Pour Scotch and Drambuie into an old-fashioned glass with several ice cubes. Stir.

s.s. manhattan

45 ml bourbon
15 ml Bénédictine
4 tbsp orange juice

Mix all ingredients with ice in a shaker or blender.

Pour into a chilled cocktail glass.

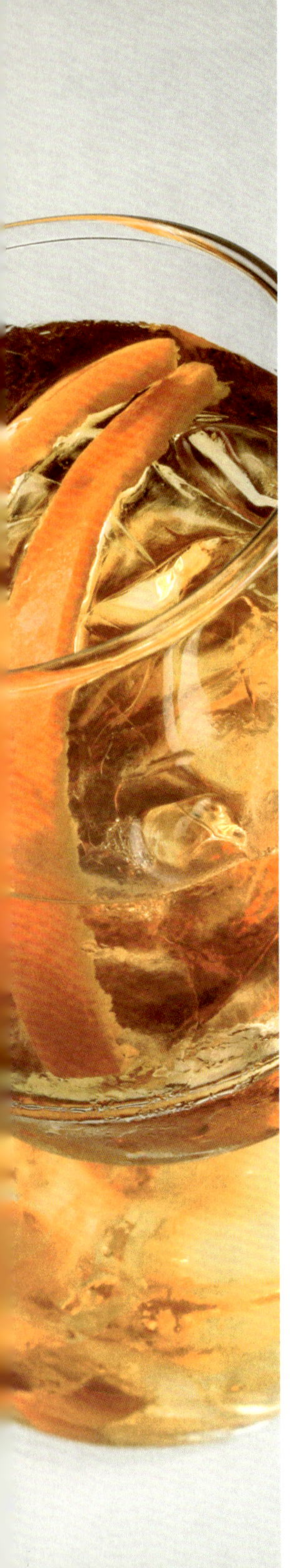

saratoga fizz

45 ml bourbon	Mix all ingredients, except club soda and cherry, with ice in a shaker or blender.
1 tsp lemon juice	
1 tsp sugar	Pour into a highball glass.
Club soda	Fill with chilled club soda.
Maraschino cherry	Garnish with cherry.

scotch highball

60 ml Scotch whisky	Pour Scotch into a highball glass half-filled with ice cubes.
Ginger ale or club soda	Top with ginger ale or club soda.
Lemon peel	Add lemon peel. Stir gently.

scotch old-fashioned

1 cube sugar	Muddle sugar cube and bitters with a spoonful of water.
Several dashes of Angostura bitters	Add Scotch and stir.
60 ml Scotch whisky	Add lemon peel and ice cubes. Stir.
Lemon peel	Garnish with cherry.
Maraschino cherry	

scotch rickey

60 ml Scotch whisky	Pour Scotch and lemon juice into a highball glass over ice cubes.
Juice of ½ a lemon	Fill with club soda.
Club soda	Add lemon peel. Stir.
Lemon peel	

scotch stinger

45 ml Scotch whisky
15 ml crème de menthe (white)

Shake Scotch and crème de menthe with ice cubes.

Strain into a chilled cocktail glass.

seaboard

30 ml Scotch whisky
30 ml gin
½ tsp lemon juice
1 tsp sugar
Fresh mint leaves

Shake all ingredients, except mint leaves, with ice cubes.

Strain over ice cubes into an old-fashioned glass.

Tear several mint leaves to release their aroma before dropping into the drink. Stir.

shoot

30 ml Scotch whisky
30 ml dry sherry
1 tsp orange juice
1 tsp lemon juice
½ tsp sugar

Shake all ingredients with ice cubes.

Strain into a chilled cocktail glass.

southern belle

45 ml bourbon
15 ml Cointreau or triple sec
4 tbsp orange juice
½ cup pineapple juice
Dash of grenadine

Combine all ingredients, except grenadine, in a highball glass half-filled with ice cubes.

Top with grenadine. Stir.

spirit of scotland

60 ml Scotch whisky
25 ml Drambuie
1 tsp lemon juice

Mix all ingredients with ice in a shaker or blender.

Strain into a chilled cocktail glass.

stirling sour

45 ml Scotch whisky
½ tsp lemon juice
1 tsp sugar
Several dashes of Cointreau or triple sec

Mix all ingredients with ice in a shaker or blender.

Pour into a chilled cocktail glass.

stone fence

60 ml Scotch whisky
Several dashes of Angostura bitters
Club soda or sparkling apple cider

Fill a highball glass with ice cubes.

Add Scotch and bitters.

Fill with club soda or cider. Stir.

sweet and sour bourbon

45 ml bourbon
120 ml orange juice
½ tsp sugar
Pinch of salt
Maraschino cherry

Mix all ingredients, except cherry, with ice in a shaker or blender.

Strain into a chilled cocktail glass.

Garnish with cherry.

thistle

60 ml Scotch whisky
30 ml sweet vermouth
Several dashes of Angostura bitters

Mix all ingredients with ice in a shaker or blender.

Strain into a chilled cocktail glass.

three-base hit

30 ml bourbon
30 ml light rum
30 ml brandy
2 tsp lemon juice
1 tsp sugar

Mix all ingredients with ice in a shaker or blender.

Strain into a chilled cocktail glass.

tommy latta

45 ml Scotch whisky
½ tsp dry vermouth
½ tsp lemon juice
½ tsp sugar

Mix all ingredients with ice in a shaker or blender.

Strain into a chilled cocktail glass.

twin hills

60 ml Scotch whisky
30 ml Bénédictine
1 tsp lemon juice
1 tsp sugar
Lemon slice

Shake all ingredients, except lemon slice, with ice cubes.

Strain into a chilled cocktail glass.

Garnish with lemon slice.

urquhart castle

45 ml Scotch whisky
Several dashes of dry vermouth
Several dashes of Cointreau or triple sec
Several dashes of Angostura bitters

Mix all ingredients with ice in a shaker or blender.

Pour into an old-fashioned glass.

walters

45 ml Scotch whisky
1 tsp orange juice
1 tsp lemon juice

Shake all ingredients with ice cubes.

Strain into a chilled cocktail glass.

The bartender at the Taj Mahal Hotel presented a customer with his bill and the man was outraged.

'Mumbai is the most expensive city in the country,' he complained. 'Back in Bangalore you can drink as much as you want in a bar without paying, sleep in a fancy hotel for free and wake up to find a thousand rupees on the bedside table.'

'That can't be true,' the bartender said, 'has it really happened to you?'

'No,' the man admitted, 'but my wife tells me it happens to her all the time.'

whisky cobbler

1 tsp sugar
Club soda
60 ml Scotch whisky
Maraschino cherry

Dissolve sugar in a little club soda in a wine glass.

Fill with ice cubes and add Scotch. Stir.

Garnish with cherry.

whisky daisy

60 ml Scotch whisky
Juice of ½ a lemon
½ tsp sugar
1 tsp grenadine
Maraschino cherry

Shake all ingredients, except cherry, with ice cubes.

Strain into a chilled cocktail glass.

Add cherry.

whisky fizz

45 ml Scotch whisky
Several dashes of Angostura bitters
½ tsp sugar
Club soda

Mix all ingredients, except club soda, with ice cubes in a highball glass.

Fill with club soda.

whisky rickey

45 ml Scotch whisky
Juice of ½ a lemon
1 tsp sugar
Club soda
Lemon peel

Mix whisky, lemon juice and sugar with ice cubes in a highball glass.

Fill with soda.

Twist lemon peel over the drink and drop into the glass.

whisky sour

45 ml Scotch whisky
Juice of ½ a lemon
½ tsp sugar
½ lemon slice
Maraschino cherry

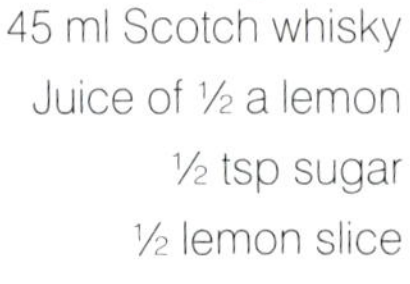

Shake Scotch, lemon juice and sugar with ice cubes.

Strain into a chilled cocktail glass.

Garnish with lemon slice and cherry.

THE GLENLIVET
12
SINGLE MALT SCOTCH WHISKY
THE GLENLIVET
15
SINGLE MALT SCOTCH WHISKY
FRENCH OAK RESERVE
THE GLENLIVET
18
SINGLE MALT SCOTCH WHISKY

BEEFEATER
LONDON

Seagram's
IMPERIAL BLUE
Superior Grain
WHISKY
Seagram Quality

Seagram's
ROYAL STAG
Seagram's
The King of the Forest
ROYAL
STAG
DELUXE
WHISKY
A Blend of Imported Scotch Malts and Select Indian Grain Spirits
Seagram Quality

GIN

Some people do not care for the taste of gin. In that case vodka can be substituted for gin in almost all the recipes given here. It is not the ideal solution because gin has its own special flavour and aroma for which there is no real substitute. For instance, there is no comparison between a gin Martini and a vodka Martini. But to each her own.

abbey cocktail

45 ml gin
Juice of ¼ orange
Dash of Angostura bitters
Maraschino cherry

Shake all ingredients, except cherry, with ice cubes.

Strain into a chilled cocktail glass.

Add cherry.

admiral benbow

60 ml gin
30 ml dry vermouth
2 tbsp lemon juice
Maraschino cherry

Pour all ingredients, except cherry, into a mixing glass with several ice cubes. Stir well.

Strain into a chilled cocktail glass.

Add cherry.

30 ml gin
30 ml Chartreuse (yellow)
Several dashes of Angostura bitters
Lemon peel

Mix all ingredients, except lemon peel, with ice in a shaker or blender.

Strain into a chilled cocktail glass.

Add lemon peel.

alfredo

45 ml gin 45 ml Campari Orange peel	*Mix all ingredients, except orange peel, with ice in a shaker or blender.* *Pour into an old-fashioned glass.* *Twist orange peel over drink and drop into the glass.*

anita's satisfaction

45 ml gin Several dashes of Angostura bitters 1 tsp grenadine	*Mix all ingredients with ice in a shaker or blender.* *Strain into a chilled cocktail glass.*

artillery

45 ml gin 2 tsp sweet vermouth Several dashes of Angostura bitters	*Stir all ingredients with ice cubes.* *Strain into a chilled cocktail glass.*

balmoral martini

60 ml gin Several dashes of dry vermouth 30 ml Scotch whisky Lemon peel	*Stir gin and vermouth with ice cubes in a mixing glass.* *Strain into a chilled cocktail glass.* *Float Scotch whisky on top.* *Garnish with lemon peel.*

barbary coast

15 ml gin 15 ml light rum 15 ml crème de cacao (white) 15 ml Scotch whisky 1 tbsp light cream	*Shake all ingredients with ice cubes.* *Strain into a cocktail glass.*

beaulieu buck

60 ml gin	*Mix all ingredients, except ginger ale and lemon wedge, with ice in a shaker or blender.*
15 ml Cointreau or triple sec	
Several dashes of dry vermouth	*Pour into a highball glass.*
Ginger ale	*Fill with ginger ale.*
Lemon wedge	*Squeeze lemon wedge over the drink and drop into the glass*

beauty spot

30 ml gin	*Shake all ingredients, except grenadine, with ice cubes.*
15 ml sweet vermouth	
15 ml dry vermouth	*Strain into a cocktail glass with a dash of grenadine at the bottom of the glass.*
1 tsp orange juice	
Dash of grenadine	*Do not stir.*

bermuda highball

30 ml gin	*Pour all ingredients, except club soda or ginger ale, into a highball glass with several ice cubes.*
30 ml brandy	
30 ml dry vermouth	*Fill with club soda or ginger ale.*
Club soda or ginger ale	*Stir gently.*

between the sheets

30 ml gin	*Mix all ingredients with ice in a shaker or blender.*
30 ml cognac	*Strain into a chilled cocktail glass.*
30 ml Cointreau or triple sec	

bijou

15 ml gin
15 ml Chartreuse (green)
10 ml sweet vermouth
Dash of Angostura bitters
Pineapple wedge

Stir all ingredients.

Strain into an old-fashioned glass filled with crushed ice.

Add pineapple wedge.

brave cow

45 ml gin
45 ml Tia Maria or Kahlúa
Lemon peel

Pour gin and the liqueur into an old-fashioned glass filled with ice cubes.

Twist lemon peel over the drink and drop into the glass. Stir.

bridesmaid

60 ml gin
1 tsp lemon juice
1 tsp sugar
Dash of Angostura bitters
Ginger ale
Lemon slice

Pour all ingredients, except ginger ale and lemon slice, into a highball glass filled with ice cubes and stir gently.

Add ginger ale.

Add lemon slice.

bronx

45 ml gin
15 ml dry vermouth
15 ml sweet vermouth
2 tbsp orange juice
Orange peel

Mix all ingredients, except orange peel, with ice in a shaker or blender.

Strain into a chilled cocktail glass.

Garnish with orange peel.

(For a dry Bronx cocktail do not add sweet vermouth.)

b.v.d.

25 ml gin
25 ml light rum
25 ml dry vermouth

Mix all ingredients with ice in a shaker or blender.

Strain into a chilled cocktail glass.

chelsea sidecar

30 ml gin
10 ml Cointreau or triple sec
1 tsp lemon juice

Shake all ingredients with ice cubes.

Strain into a chilled cocktail glass.

clover club

45 ml gin
1½ tbsp lemon juice
1 tsp grenadine

Shake all ingredients with ice cubes.

Strain into a chilled cocktail glass.

club cocktail

45 ml gin
25 ml sweet vermouth
Maraschino cherry

Stir gin and vermouth with ice cubes.

Strain into a cocktail glass.

Add cherry.

cooperstown

30 ml gin
15 ml dry vermouth
15 ml sweet vermouth
Sprig of mint leaves

Shake all ingredients, except mint leaves, with ice cubes.

Strain into a cocktail glass.

Add sprig of mint leaves.

copenhagen

30 ml gin
30 ml aquavit
10 ml dry vermouth
1 green olive

Stir all ingredients, except olive, with ice cubes.

Strain into a chilled cocktail glass.

Add olive.

damn-the-weather

30 ml gin
30 ml Cointreau or triple sec
15 ml sweet vermouth
1 tsp orange juice

Shake all ingredients with ice cubes.

Strain into a chilled cocktail glass.

delmonico

15 ml gin
15 ml dry vermouth
15 ml sweet vermouth
15 ml brandy
Lemon peel

Stir all ingredients, except lemon peel, with ice cubes.

Strain into a cocktail glass.

Add lemon peel.

dry martini

I don't think anyone will dispute that the Martini is the king of cocktails. There might be hundreds of cocktails involving all sorts of liqueurs, syrups, juices, spirits and paper umbrellas but there is only one cocktail with genuine mystique: the Martini. More Martinis are consumed every evening than all the other cocktails combined. It is immune to change in taste and fashion. It has not only endured over the years, it has prospered.

The drink first appeared in 1912 in the Knickerbocker Hotel in New York when the head bartender, Martini di Arma di Taggia, mixed equal parts of gin and vermouth with orange bitters and strained it into a chilled glass. It was an instant hit. Since then the Martini has gone from equal parts of gin and vermouth to something in the neighbourhood of a 20:1 gin:vermouth ratio.

Ian Fleming's creation James Bond initiated the myth that a Martini should be shaken, not stirred. He was, in fact, very precise on how he liked his Martini. In *Dr No* he ordered it medium dry with a slice of lemon peel. Later, in *Casino Royale* (the first version) he made his requirements more specific: three measures of gin, one measure of vodka and half a measure of vermouth, shaken until chilled. And always shaken, never stirred. Hardcore Martini aficionados like him can be a pain in the neck. Be careful not to 'bruise' the gin, some busybody will tell you. Another will want two, even three olives instead of one. You will be asked for the twist of lemon to be rubbed along the rim of the glass. Everyone has a view on the brand of gin and vermouth to be used, the garnish that is to be added and even the number of ice cubes that should be used to chill the concoction.

Making a Martini is simple. Making a great Martini, however, is an entirely different matter. It is about getting the gin–vermouth balance right. No matter how you make your Martini there is one strict rule that has to be followed. Use plenty of ice and mix the drink thoroughly and quickly so that the mixture is chilled without the ice melting too much. Chill the empty glass in the freezer before filling it. Always mix Martinis in small quantities, two or three glasses at a time, so that it doesn't lose its chill. If you are using a lemon twist (though I prefer the olive for the tiny amount of salt it adds to the drink from the brine it is preserved in) as garnish, it should, ideally, be squeezed delicately over the surface of the drink so that some of its oil floats on top.

Then there is the my-Martini-is-drier-than-yours business. How dry a Martini can get is again determined by the ratio of gin to vermouth. The larger the proportion of gin, the drier the drink. There was a film (I forget the name) in which Clark Gable swilled a drop of vermouth in a glass and tossed it out before filling the glass with gin. Winston Churchill, it is said, made his Martinis by pouring gin in a jug and then, to make it dry, glancing briefly at an unopened bottle of vermouth across the room.

60 ml gin
Dry vermouth to taste
Lemon peel or green olive

Pour gin and vermouth in an ice-filled shaker in the ratio of 5:1. (For an extra-dry Martini use as little as one or two drops of vermouth.)

Shake and strain into a chilled Martini glass.

Garnish with lemon peel or an olive.

derby

60 ml gin

Several dashes of Angostura bitters

Fresh mint leaves

Mix all ingredients, except mint leaves, with ice in a shaker or blender.

Pour into an old-fashioned glass.

Lightly tear several mint leaves to release their aroma. Add as garnish. Stir.

A man walked into a bar and slumped down on an empty bar stool. Looking up, he said to the bartender, 'I just lost my job, my wife, my car and my house. Give me a drink.'

The bartender replied, 'Listen buddy, if you're drinking to forget, could you pay first?'

dundee

30 ml gin

25 ml Scotch whisky

15 ml Drambuie

1 tsp lemon juice

Lemon peel

Mix all ingredients, except lemon peel, with ice in a shaker or blender.

Pour into an old-fashioned glass.

Twist lemon peel over the drink and drop into the glass.

emerald isle

60 ml gin

30 ml crème de menthe (green)

Several dashes of Angostura bitters

Stir all ingredients with ice cubes.

Strain into a chilled cocktail glass.

english highball

30 ml gin

10 ml brandy

10 ml sweet vermouth

Ginger ale or club soda

Maraschino cherry

Pour gin, brandy and vermouth into a highball glass over ice cubes.

Fill with ginger ale or club soda.

Add cherry and stir gently.

fifty-fifty cocktail

45 ml gin

45 ml dry vermouth

Stir all ingredients with ice cubes.

Strain into a chilled cocktail glass.

fine and dandy

45 ml gin
25 ml Cointreau or triple sec
1 tsp lemon juice
Dash of Angostura bitters

Mix all ingredients with ice in a shaker or blender.

Strain into a chilled cocktail glass.

flying dutchman

60 ml gin
30 ml Cointreau or triple sec

Shake gin and Cointreau or triple sec with ice cubes.

Strain into an old-fashioned glass over ice cubes.

gibson

60 ml gin
15 ml dry vermouth
2 cocktail onions

Pour gin and vermouth into a mixing glass with plenty of ice cubes.

Stir for at least 30 seconds to chill well.

Strain into a Martini glass.

Skewer the onions with the end of a cocktail stick or a toothpick. Add as garnish.

gilroy

30 ml gin
30 ml cherry brandy
15 ml dry vermouth
1 tbsp lemon juice
Several dashes of Angostura bitters

Mix all ingredients with ice in a shaker or blender.

Pour into an old-fashioned glass.

gimlet

60 ml gin
10 ml Rose's lime cordial
Lemon slice

Mix all ingredients, except lemon slice, with ice in a shaker or blender.

Pour into an old-fashioned glass.

Add lemon slice.

gin aloha

45 ml gin
45 ml Cointreau or triple sec
1 tsp unsweetened pineapple juice
Dash of Angostura bitters
Pineapple wedge

Shake all ingredients, except pineapple wedge, with ice cubes.

Strain into an old-fashioned glass.

Garnish with pineapple wedge.

gin-and-it

60 ml gin
30 ml sweet vermouth

Combine both ingredients in a chilled cocktail glass without ice.

gin-and-sin

30 ml gin
2 tbsp lemon juice
1 tsp orange juice
Dash of grenadine

Shake all ingredients with ice cubes.

Strain into a chilled cocktail glass.

gin-and-tonic

60 ml gin
Tonic water
Lemon wedge

Pour gin into a highball glass with ice cubes.

Fill with tonic water.

Add lemon wedge.

gin buck

45 ml gin
1 tsp lemon juice
Ginger ale

Pour gin and lemon juice into an old-fashioned glass over ice cubes.

Fill with ginger ale. Stir gently.

gin cobbler

1 tsp sugar
Club soda
60 ml gin
Lemon slice

Dissolve sugar in club soda in a goblet.

Fill with ice cubes. Add gin. Stir gently.

Add lemon slice.

gin cooler

½ tsp sugar
60 ml gin
Club soda or ginger ale
Lemon slice

Stir sugar with 60 ml club soda or ginger ale in a highball glass.

Fill with ice cubes. Add gin. Stir.

Fill with club soda or ginger ale. Stir gently.

Add lemon slice.

gin highball

60 ml gin
Ginger ale or club soda
Lemon peel

Pour gin into a highball glass over ice cubes.

Fill with ginger ale or club soda.

Add lemon peel.

gin old-fashioned

¼ tsp sugar
Several dashes of Angostura bitters
60 ml gin
Lemon peel

Pour sugar and bitters into an old-fashioned glass.

Stir till sugar dissolves, adding a tsp of water if necessary to complete the process.

Add gin and 2 or 3 ice cubes. Stir well.

Twist lemon peel over the drink and drop into the glass.

gin rickey

45 ml gin	*Pour gin into a highball glass with ice cubes.*
Club soda	*Fill with club soda.*
Juice of ½ a lemon	*Add lemon juice. Stir gently.*

gin side car

45 ml gin	*Mix all ingredients with ice in a shaker or blender.*
25 ml Cointreau or triple sec	*Pour into an old-fashioned glass.*
1 tsp lemon juice	

golf martini

45 ml gin	*Pour all ingredients, except olive, in a mixing glass.*
15 ml dry vermouth	*Stir with ice cubes.*
Several dashes of Angostura bitters	*Strain into a chilled cocktail glass.*
1 green olive	*Add olive.*

green devil

45 ml gin	*Shake all ingredients, except mint leaves, with ice cubes.*
45 ml crème de menthe (green)	*Strain into an old-fashioned glass over ice cubes.*
1 tsp lemon juice	*Lightly tear the mint leaves to release their aroma and drop into the glass.*
Fresh mint leaves	

gypsy

45 ml sweet vermouth	*Stir all ingredients, except cherry, with ice cubes.*
45 ml gin	*Strain into a chilled cocktail glass.*
Maraschino cherry	*Add cherry.*

honolulu

60 ml gin
1 tsp pineapple juice
1 tsp orange juice
½ tsp lemon juice
Dash of Angostura bitters

Shake all ingredients with ice cubes.

Strain into a chilled cocktail glass.

horse's neck with gin

Lemon peel
60 ml gin
1 tbsp lemon juice
Ginger ale

Place peel in a highball glass so that the top of the peel overlaps the rim of the glass, with the rest spiralling down into the glass.

Fill glass with ice cubes.

Pour gin and lemon juice into the glass.

Fill with ginger ale. Stir gently.

hudson bay

30 ml gin
15 ml light rum
15 ml cherry brandy
1 tbsp orange juice
2 tsp lemon juice
Lemon slice

Shake all ingredients, except lemon slice, with ice cubes.

Strain into an old-fashioned glass filled with ice cubes.

Add lemon slice.

jewel

30 ml gin
30 ml sweet vermouth
30 ml Chartreuse (green)
Several dashes of Angostura bitters
Lemon peel

Mix all ingredients, except lemon peel, with ice in a shaker or blender.

Strain into a chilled cocktail glass.

Twist lemon peel over the drink and drop into the glass.

kiss-in-the-dark

10 ml gin
10 ml cherry brandy
10 ml dry vermouth

Stir all ingredients with ice cubes.
Strain into a chilled cocktail glass.

knickerbocker

15 ml sweet vermouth
10 ml dry vermouth
45 ml gin
Lemon peel

Stir all ingredients, except lemon peel, with ice cubes.

Strain into a chilled cocktail glass.

Add a twist of lemon peel.

leap frog

45 ml gin
1 tbsp lemon juice
Ginger ale

Mix gin and lemon juice with ice cubes in a highball glass.

Fill with chilled ginger ale.

london cocktail

45 ml gin
25 ml Cointreau or triple sec
1 tbsp lemon juice

Mix all ingredients with ice in a shaker or blender.

Pour into a chilled cocktail glass.

maiden's blush

45 ml gin
30 ml Cointreau or triple sec
½ tsp lemon juice
½ tsp grenadine

Mix all ingredients with ice in a shaker or blender.

Strain into a chilled cocktail glass.

maiden's prayer

45 ml gin
25 ml Cointreau or triple sec
1 tsp orange juice
1 tsp lemon juice

Mix all ingredients with ice in a shaker or blender.

Strain into a chilled cocktail glass.

mint collins

60 ml gin	*Put gin, lemon juice, sugar and mint leaves with ice in a blender.*
1 tsp lemon juice	*Blend till the leaves are chopped.*
1 tsp sugar	*Pour into a highball glass half-filled with ice.*
4-5 fresh mint leaves	*Fill with soda. Stir gently.*
Club soda	*Add lemon slices.*
Lemon slices	

minted gin

45 ml gin	*Shake all ingredients, except mint leaves and lemon slice, with ice cubes.*
1 tbsp lemon juice	*Strain into a chilled cocktail glass.*
½ tsp sugar	*Add lemon slice.*
Fresh mint leaves	*Lightly tear the mint leaves to release their aroma and drop into the glass.*
Lemon slice	

mississippi mule

45 ml gin
10 ml crème de cassis
½ tsp lemon juice

Mix all ingredients with ice in a shaker or blender.

Pour into an old-fashioned glass with ice.

orange blossom

45 ml gin
2 tbsp orange juice
Orange slice

Mix all ingredients, except orange slice, with ice in a shaker or blender.

Strain into a chilled cocktail glass.

Add orange slice.

orange buck

45 ml gin
2 tbsp orange juice
1 tsp lemon juice
Ginger ale

Shake all ingredients, except ginger ale, with ice cubes.

Strain into a highball glass over ice cubes.

Fill with ginger ale. Stir gently.

orange fizz

60 ml gin
3 tbsp orange juice
1 tbsp lemon juice
30 ml Cointreau or triple sec
1 tsp sugar
Several dashes of Angostura bitters
Club soda
Orange slice

Shake all ingredients, except club soda and orange slice, with ice cubes.

Strain into a highball glass half-filled with ice.

Fill with soda. Stir gently.

Add orange slice.

palm beach

45 ml gin
30 ml sweet vermouth
1½ tsp grapefruit juice

Shake all ingredients with ice cubes.

Strain into a chilled cocktail glass.

pimm's

Pimm's is a very English drink. The very name, Pimm's, conjures up Oxford and Cambridge boat races, Wimbledon, picnic hampers and languid outdoor lunches. A bright sun in the sky would make a perfect Pimm's day, but that is always dicey in England. Pimm's is always drunk before sunset and never in winter. It is a deceptively potent drink; as the English say, it has the kick of a mule.

Pimm's was concocted in the 1840s by the owner of an oyster bar in the financial district of London, the area still known as 'the City'. James Pimm offered the gin-based drink containing quinine and a secret mix of herbs to his customers as an aid to digestion. Many drinking establishments of the day mixed house spirits and served and sold them in tankards which they called 'cups'. That is how this particular drink ended up being called the Pimm's No. 1 Cup.

By the 1920s Pimm's was sold all over England and quickly became fashionable among the upper classes. Somewhere along the way caramel colouring was added to the mixture, giving it its amber colour. After World War II the Pimm family extended their range using other spirits as the base for the drink. Pimm's No. 2 Cup was based on Scotch, No. 3 used brandy, No. 4 rum, No. 5 rye and No. 6 vodka. Other than the original, only Pimm's No. 6 survives today. It is produced in much smaller quantities and is difficult to find.

Be warned that while Pimm's has a pleasant syrupy smell, it tastes quite revolting on its own. It has to be mixed with carbonated lemonade. Some recipes suggest adding tonic water or ginger ale and lemon juice, or even Cointreau. I find that absurd. But on a hot day a jugful of Pimm's mix with sliced strawberries and oranges floating in it can be very enticing.

45 ml Pimm's No. 1
1 bottle Seven Up (or any carbonated lemonade that is clear)
1 sprig of fresh mint
1 lemon slice
Skin of 1 cucumber, cut lengthwise

Pour Pimm's No. 1 into a highball glass.

Add ice cubes and top up the glass with Seven Up.

Place the cucumber skin or wedge so that it stands upright in the glass and garnish with a sprig of mint leaves and a slice of lemon. A layer of pale froth will appear on top to make your drink all the more pleasurable.

FOR A PARTY: Make the drink in a large jug and substitute the lemon slice with orange slices and strawberry halves. Instead of the skin of cucumber, add cucumber slices cut in rounds.

pimlico cooler

45 ml gin
6 tbsp orange juice
Ginger ale

Pour gin and orange juice into a highball glass filled with ice cubes.

Add chilled ginger ale. Stir gently.

pink gin

60 ml gin
Several dashes of Angostura bitters

Mix gin and bitters with plenty of ice cubes in a mixing glass.

Strain into a chilled cocktail glass.

pink lady

45 ml gin
2 tsp lemon juice
1 tsp cream
1 tsp grenadine

Shake all ingredients with ice cubes.

Strain into a chilled cocktail glass.

(The glass may be sugar-frosted by moistening the rim with grenadine before dipping into sugar.)

pink pussycat

60 ml gin
6 tbsp pineapple juice
4 tbsp grapefruit juice
1 tsp grenadine

Shake all ingredients with ice cubes.

Strain into a chilled cocktail glass.

plaza cocktail

30 ml gin
10 ml sweet vermouth
10 ml dry vermouth
Maraschino cherry

Shake all ingredients, except cherry, with ice cubes.

Strain into a chilled cocktail glass.

Add cherry.

princeton

40 ml gin
25 ml dry vermouth
½ tsp lemon juice

Shake all ingredients with ice cubes.

Strain into a chilled cocktail glass.

racquet club

60 ml gin
15 ml dry vermouth
Several dashes of Angostura bitters

Shake all ingredients with ice cubes.

Strain into a chilled cocktail glass.

red lion

30 ml gin
30 ml Grand Marnier
1 tbsp orange juice
1 tbsp lemon juice

Mix all ingredients with ice in a shaker or blender.

Strain into a chilled cocktail glass.

renaissance

45 ml gin
15 ml dry sherry
1 tbsp cream
Powdered nutmeg

Shake all ingredients, except nutmeg, with ice.

Strain into a chilled cocktail glass.

Sprinkle lightly with nutmeg.

rolls royce royale

60 ml gin
15 ml dry vermouth
15 ml sweet vermouth
15 ml Bénédictine

Stir all ingredients with ice cubes.

Strain into a chilled cocktail glass.

roselyn

30 ml gin
10 ml dry vermouth
½ tsp grenadine
Lemon peel

Stir all ingredients, except lemon peel, with ice cubes.

Strain into a chilled cocktail glass.

Add lemon peel.

san francisco

30 ml gin
30 ml dry vermouth
30 ml sweet vermouth
Several dashes of Angostura bitters
Maraschino cherry

Mix all ingredients, except cherry, with ice in a shaker or blender.

Strain into a chilled cocktail glass.

Add cherry.

sensation cocktail

45 ml gin
Juice of ¼ lemon
Fresh mint leaves

Shake all ingredients, except mint leaves, with ice cubes.

Strain into a chilled cocktail glass.

Lightly tear the mint leaves to release their aroma and drop into the glass.

seventh heaven

60 ml gin
2 tsp grapefruit juice
Fresh mint leaves

Shake all ingredients, except mint leaves, with ice cubes.

Strain into a chilled cocktail glass.

Lightly tear the mint leaves to release their aroma and drop into the glass.

shady grove

45 ml gin
Juice of ½ a lemon
1 tsp sugar
Ginger ale

Shake all ingredients, except ginger ale, with ice.

Strain into a highball glass filled with ice cubes.

Fill with ginger ale. Stir gently.

singapore sling

Singapore Sling is one of the most exotic cocktails. The name itself evokes panama hats and cane furniture on some tropical veranda. When you sip your Singapore Sling you expect Somerset Maugham or Joseph Conrad to walk in through the door. I am, of course, thinking of the Long Bar at the Raffles Hotel in Singapore where the cocktail was invented almost a century ago and where I first drank it in the 1960s before they ruined the place by modernizing it. Singapore was then a laidback, sleepy town, quite unlike the bustling metropolis it is today.

Singapore Sling is a complicated cocktail to make and is best ordered from a good bartender. There are as many recipes for Singapore Sling as there are bartenders. All the recipes call for the use of cherry brandy and gin but some bartenders prefer to add Cointreau over Bénédictine. Sometimes soda water is omitted to make the drink stronger. Some bartenders go so far as to dump whatever fruit juice is handy into the shaker. They should resist the urge. Over the years I have discovered that only one juice works for this swinging cocktail: lemon juice. Trust me.

60 ml gin
30 ml Bénédictine
30 ml cherry-flavoured liqueur (preferably Cherry Heering)
Juice of 1 lemon
1 tsp sugar
Several dashes of Angostura bitters
Club soda
Slice of lemon

Mix gin, lemon juice, sugar and Angostura bitters in a highball glass.

Add crushed ice.

Add the two liqueurs, fill with soda and stir.

Garnish with a slice of lemon.

smile

45 ml gin
1 tsp grenadine
½ tsp lemon juice

Shake all ingredients with ice cubes.

Strain into a chilled cocktail glass.

southside

60 ml gin
½ tsp lemon juice
1 tsp sugar
Fresh mint leaves

Shake all ingredients, except mint leaves, with ice cubes.

Strain into a chilled cocktail glass.

Lightly tear the mint leaves to release their aroma and drop into the glass. Stir.

strawberry cream cooler

45 ml gin
½ cup fresh strawberries
2 tbsp lemon juice
2 tsp cream
1 tsp sugar
Club soda

Put all ingredients, except club soda, into a blender.

Blend for 10 to 15 seconds at high speed.

Pour into a highball glass.

Fill with ice cubes and a splash of club soda. Stir.

suffering bastard

Several dashes of Angostura bitters
45 ml gin
45 ml brandy
1 tsp Rose's lime cordial
Ginger ale
Fresh mint leaves
Cucumber slice
Lemon slice

Swirl bitters around a highball glass to coat it thoroughly. Discard excess bitters.

Add several ice cubes to glass along with gin, brandy, and lime cordial. Stir.

Fill with ginger ale. Stir gently.

Add mint leaves and cucumber and lemon slices.

sweet martini

60 ml gin
15 ml sweet vermouth
Dash of Angostura bitters
Orange peel

Mix all ingredients, except orange peel, with ice cubes in a mixing glass.

Strain into a chilled cocktail glass.

Twist orange peel over the drink and drop into the glass.

tango

45 ml gin
10 ml sweet vermouth
10 ml dry vermouth
2 tbsp orange juice
Several dashes of Cointreau or triple sec

Mix all ingredients with ice in a shaker or blender.

Pour into an old-fashioned glass.

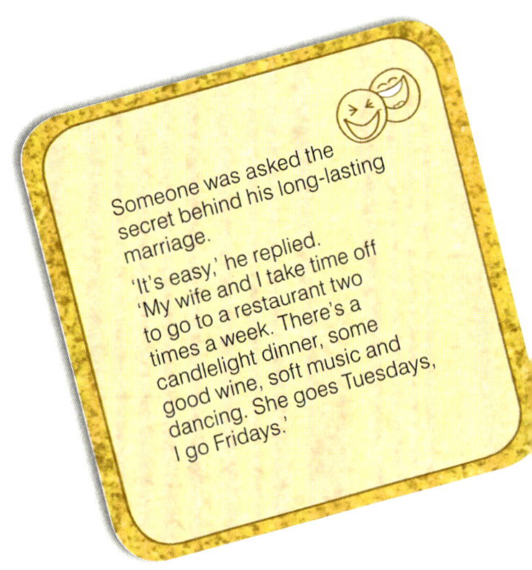

victory

45 ml gin	*Shake all ingredients with ice cubes.*
15 ml brandy	*Strain into a chilled cocktail glass.*
15 ml sweet vermouth	

xanthia

30 ml gin	*Shake all ingredients with ice cubes.*
30 ml cherry brandy	*Strain into a chilled cocktail glass.*
30 ml Chartreuse (yellow)	

tom collins

Tom Collins is another name for Gin Fizz. If you substitute gin with Scotch you have got yourself a John Collins. Use of Irish whiskey makes it Mike Collins and rum makes it Charlie Collins. For a good Charlie Collins, make sure you add a dash of Angostura bitters.

60 ml gin	*Shake all ingredients, except club soda and lemon peel, with ice cubes.*
Juice of ½ a lemon	*Strain into a highball glass.*
1 tsp sugar	*Add several ice cubes.*
Club soda	*Fill with club soda. Stir gently.*
Lemon peel or maraschino cherry	*Garnish with lemon peel or maraschino cherry.*

BEEFEATER
SEAGRAM'S
FUEL
VODKA
ABSOLUT 
Country of Sweden
PEPPAR
ABSOLUT
KURANT
ABSOLUT
Country of Sweden
VODKA
This superb vodka
was distilled from grain grown
in the rich fields of southern Sweden.
It has been produced at the famous
old distilleries near Åhus
in accordance with more than
400 years of Swedish tradition.
Vodka has been sold under the name
Absolut since 1879.
40% ALC./VOL. (80 PROOF) 1 LITER
IMPORTED
ABSOLUT
Country of Sweden
MANDRIN
ABSOLUT
Country of Sweden
CITRON

VODKA

Indians may have a soft corner for whisky but vodka is the world's most popular spirit. When it comes to cocktails you will find that vodka is more of an essential ingredient than any other spirit. Its enthusiasts like the fact that it is almost tasteless and very versatile when it comes to mixing drinks.

absolut a.m.

- 30 ml Absolut Mango
- 6 tbsp apple juice
- Mango slice or apple wedge
- Powdered cinnamon

Pour the vodka and apple juice over ice in a highball glass.

Garnish with mango slice or apple wedge.

Sprinkle powdered cinnamon on top.

bailey's comet

- 30 ml vodka
- 30 ml Bailey's Irish Cream

Combine the ingredients with ice cubes in an old-fashioned glass.

balalaika

- 45 ml vodka
- 30 ml Cointreau or triple sec
- 1 tsp lemon juice
- Maraschino cherry

Shake all ingredients, except cherry, with plenty of ice cubes.

Strain into a chilled cocktail glass.

Add cherry.

beer buster

- 60 ml vodka, ice cold
- Several dashes of Tabasco sauce
- Beer, ice cold

Pour all ingredients into a chilled beer glass. Stir gently.

bikini

60 ml vodka
30 ml light rum
1 tbsp cream
1 tsp sugar

Shake all ingredients with ice cubes.

Strain into a chilled cocktail glass.

black cossack

45 ml vodka, ice cold
1 small bottle or can Guinness stout beer, chilled
Lemon peel

Pour ice-cold vodka into a wine glass.

Follow with well-chilled Guinness.

Add lemon peel.

black russian

45 ml vodka
25 ml Tia Maria or Kahlúa
Coca-Cola

Mix vodka and liqueur with ice in a shaker or blender.

Pour into an old-fashioned glass filled with ice.

Add a dash of cola.

blue lagoon

60 ml vodka
30 ml blue curaçao
Seven Up
Maraschino cherry

Pour vodka and curaçao over ice into a highball glass.

Fill with Seven Up. Stir gently.

Garnish with cherry.

blue shark

30 ml vodka
30 ml tequila
15 ml blue curaçao

Mix all ingredients with ice in a shaker or blender. Strain into a chilled cocktail glass.

bolshoi

60 ml vodka
15 ml rum
15 ml crème de cassis
1 tsp lemon juice
1 tsp sugar

Shake all ingredients till sugar dissolves. Pour over ice cubes into an old-fashioned glass.

borodino

30 ml vodka
30 ml gin
15 ml Cointreau or triple sec
Orange peel

Shake all the ingredients, except orange peel, with ice cubes.

Strain into a chilled cocktail glass.

Add orange peel.

buckeye martini

70 ml vodka
10 ml dry vermouth
Black olive

Stir vodka and vermouth with ice cubes.

Strain into a chilled cocktail glass.

Add olive.

bull frog

45 ml vodka
120 ml Seven Up
30 ml Cointreau or triple sec
Lemon slice

Pour all ingredients, except lemon slice, into an old-fashioned glass half-filled with ice cubes. Stir.

Add lemon slice.

cape codder

45 ml vodka
½ tsp lemon juice
2 tsp cranberry juice
1 tsp sugar

Mix all ingredients with ice in a shaker or blender.

Strain into a chilled cocktail glass.

caribbean cruise

30 ml vodka
10 ml light rum
10 ml Malibu
120 ml pineapple juice
1 tsp grenadine
1 slice lemon or pineapple wedge or maraschino cherry

Shake vodka, rum and Malibu with ice.

Pour into a highball glass filled with ice.

Add pineapple juice and grenadine. Stir.

Garnish with lemon or pineapple wedge and cherry.

cayman cup

60 ml vodka
15 ml Cointreau or triple sec
4 tbsp mango juice
4 tbsp orange juice
½ tbsp lemon juice
Mango slice

Mix all ingredients, except mango slice, with ice in a shaker or blender.

Pour into a highball glass.

Garnish with mango slice, if in season.

cherry vodka

60 ml vodka
30 ml cherry brandy
1 tsp lemon juice

Shake all ingredients with ice cubes.

Strain into a chilled cocktail glass.

chi-chi

60 ml vodka
2 tbsp cream of coconut
1 cup pineapple juice
Pineapple wedge

Mix all ingredients, except pineapple wedge, with ice in a blender.

Pour into a highball glass.

Garnish with pineapple wedge.

chiquita

45 ml vodka
15 ml banana liqueur
1 ripe banana, sliced
2 tbsp lemon juice
1 tsp sugar

Put all ingredients into a blender with ice.

Blend at low speed for fifteen seconds.

Pour into a large wine glass.

cosmopolitan

60 ml vodka
15 ml Cointreau or triple sec
1 tsp lemon juice
1 tbsp cranberry juice

Mix all ingredients in a shaker with ice cubes.

Strain into a chilled cocktail glass.

curaçao cooler

30 ml blue curaçao
30 ml vodka
1 tsp lemon juice
2 tsp orange juice
Lemon peel
Orange peel

Shake curaçao, vodka and lemon juice with ice cubes.

Strain into a highball glass.

Add two large ice cubes.

Fill with orange juice. Stir.

Twist each of the peels over the drink and drop into glass.

desert sunrise

40 ml vodka
3 tbsp orange juice
3 tbsp pineapple juice
Dash of grenadine

Pour vodka and juices over ice cubes in a highball glass.

Top it slowly with grenadine so that it floats on top.

Do not stir.

dragon fire

30 ml Absolut Peppar
3 dashes crème de menthe (green)

Pour the ingredients over ice cubes in an old-fashioned glass.

Stir.

electric jam

40 ml vodka
15 ml blue curaçao
2 tsp lemon juice
Seven Up

Pour all ingredients over ice cubes into a highball glass.

Stir gently.

espresso kahlúa martini

60 ml Kahlúa
60 ml vodka
1 cup fresh-brewed espresso

Combine all ingredients in a cocktail shaker with ice cubes.

Strain into a chilled cocktail glass.

flying grasshopper

45 ml vodka
15 ml crème de menthe (green)
15 ml crème de menthe (white)

Mix all ingredients with ice in a shaker or blender.

Strain into a chilled cocktail glass.

genoa

45 ml vodka
30 ml Campari
3 tsp orange juice
Orange peel

Shake all the ingredients, except orange peel, with ice cubes.

Strain into an old-fashioned glass containing a couple of ice cubes.

Add orange peel.

godmother

45 ml vodka
25 ml amaretto

Pour into an old-fashioned glass over ice cubes.

green dragon

60 ml vodka
30 ml Chartreuse (green)

Shake the ingredients with ice.
Strain into a chilled cocktail glass.
(This cocktail is also known as Green Island.)

gypsy dram

60 ml vodka
15 ml Bénédictine
1 tsp lemon juice
1 tsp orange juice
Orange slice

Mix all ingredients, except orange slice, with ice in a shaker or blender.
Strain into a chilled cocktail glass.
Garnish with orange slice.

gypsy spell

45 ml vodka
15 ml Bénédictine
15 ml brandy
15 ml Cointreau or triple sec

Mix all ingredients with ice in a shaker or blender.
Strain into a chilled cocktail glass.

hammer horror

30 ml vodka
30 ml Tia Maria or Kahlúa
1 scoop vanilla ice cream
Chocolate flakes

Blend all ingredients, except chocolate flakes, with ice in a blender for a few seconds.
Strain into a chilled cocktail glass.
Sprinkle chocolate flakes.

handball cooler

60 ml vodka
Club soda
1 tsp orange juice

Pour vodka into a highball glass filled with ice cubes.
Fill almost to the top with club soda.
Top with orange juice. Stir gently.

harvey wallbanger

45 ml vodka 30 ml Galliano	*Pour vodka, Galliano and orange juice into a wine glass with several ice cubes. Stir well.*
120 ml orange juice	*Top with a little extra Galliano.*
Orange peel	*Garnish with orange peel.*

headless horseman

60 ml vodka	*Pour vodka into a highball glass and add ice cubes.*
Several dashes of Angostura bitters	*Add bitters.*
Ginger ale	*Fill with ginger ale. Stir gently.*
Orange slice	*Garnish with orange slice.*

ice pick

60 ml vodka
Iced tea (without milk)
Lemon wedge
Sugar (optional)

Fill a highball glass with some ice cubes.

Add vodka.

Fill with iced tea.

Squeeze lemon wedge into the glass and drop it in.

Add sugar if desired. Stir.

jericho's breeze

30 ml vodka
10 ml blue curaçao
1 tsp lemon juice
Seven Up
1 tsp orange juice
Maraschino cherry

Mix all ingredients, except Seven Up and cherry, with ice cubes in a shaker.

Strain into a large wine glass filled with ice cubes.

Add Seven Up and stir gently.

Garnish with cherry.

kangaroo cocktail

45 ml vodka
10 ml dry vermouth
Lemon wedge

Pour vodka and vermouth into a highball glass over ice cubes.

Garnish with lemon wedge.

kiss and tell

30 ml vodka
30 ml Galliano
15 ml dry vermouth
15 ml blue curaçao
4 tbsp orange juice
2 tbsp passion fruit juice
Maraschino cherry

Shake all the ingredients, except cherry, with ice cubes.

Pour into a highball glass.

Garnish with cherry.

kremlin colonel

60 ml vodka 1 tsp lemon juice 1 tsp sugar Fresh mint leaves	*Shake all ingredients, except mint leaves, with ice cubes.* *Strain into a chilled cocktail glass.* *Tear mint leaves in half to release their aroma and drop into the glass. Stir.*

kretchma

30 ml vodka 30 ml crème de cacao (white) 1 tsp lemon juice ½ tsp grenadine	*Shake all ingredients with ice cubes.* *Strain into a chilled cocktail glass.*

madras

45 ml vodka 120 ml cranberry juice 2 tbsp orange juice 1 tsp cream Maraschino cherries	*Shake all ingredients, except cherry, with ice cubes.* *Pour into a highball glass filled with ice cubes.* *Garnish with cherries held together by a toothpick.*

mandrico

30 ml Absolut Mandrin
Coca-Cola
Orange wedge

Pour the ingredients, except the wedge, over ice cubes in a highball glass.

Garnish with orange wedge.

mango cooler

60 ml vodka
30 ml Cointreau or triple sec
½ cup mango juice
1 tsp lemon juice
1½ tsp orange juice
Orange slice

Pour all ingredients, except orange slice, into a highball glass half-filled with ice cubes. Stir.

Garnish with orange slice.

mint vodka collins

60 ml vodka
30 ml crème de menthe (green)
1 tsp lemon juice
½ tsp sugar
Club soda
Fresh mint leaves

Pour all ingredients, except club soda and mint leaves, into a highball glass half-filled with ice cubes.

Add club soda. Stir.

Lightly tear mint leaves to release their aroma and drop into the glass.

moscow mule

60–90 ml vodka
1 tsp lemon juice
Ginger ale
Lemon slice

Shake vodka and lemon juice with ice cubes.

Pour into an old-fashioned glass. Stir.

Fill with ginger ale.

Garnish with lemon slice.

orange delight

30 ml vodka
30 ml Cointreau or triple sec
1 tsp lemon juice
2 tsp orange juice
Orange slice

Mix all ingredients, except orange slice, with ice in a shaker or blender.

Strain into a chilled cocktail glass.

Garnish with orange slice.

peter's cheer

30 ml vodka
30 ml cherry brandy
15 ml dry vermouth
3 tsp orange juice

Mix all ingredients with ice in a shaker or blender.

Strain into a chilled cocktail glass.

pink ink

45 ml vodka
Pineapple or grapefruit juice
1 tsp grenadine

Pour vodka into a highball glass filled with ice cubes.
Fill with juice.
Add grenadine for colour and stir.

polynesian cocktail

Lemon wedge
Powdered sugar
45 ml vodka
10 ml cherry brandy
Juice of 1 lemon

Rub rim of a cocktail glass with lemon wedge.
Roll it in powdered sugar till rim is evenly coated.
Shake all ingredients with ice cubes.
Strain into the glass.

red apple

60 ml vodka
4 tbsp apple juice
½ tsp lemon juice
½ tsp grenadine
Dash of Angostura bitters

Shake all ingredients with ice cubes.
Strain into a chilled cocktail glass.

russian bear

30 ml vodka
15 ml crème de cacao (white)
1 tsp cream

Stir all ingredients with ice cubes.
Strain into a chilled cocktail glass.

russian cocktail

15 ml crème de cacao (white)
15 ml gin
15 ml vodka

Shake all ingredients with ice cubes.
Strain into a chilled cocktail glass.

russian rob roy

45 ml vodka
15 ml dry vermouth
15 ml Scotch whisky
Lemon peel

Stir all ingredients, except lemon peel, in a mixing glass.

Pour into a chilled cocktail glass.

Garnish with lemon peel.

russian rose

60 ml vodka
2 tsp grenadine
Dash of Angostura bitters

Mix all ingredients with ice in a shaker.

Strain into a chilled cocktail glass.

salty dog

Pinch of salt
Pinch of powdered sugar
Lemon wedge
60 ml vodka
Grapefruit juice

Mix salt and sugar and spread out on a saucer or small plate.

Rub the rim of an old-fashioned glass with lemon wedge and roll it in a salt-and-sugar mix till rim is evenly coated.

Fill glass with several ice cubes, vodka and grapefruit juice. Stir.

screwdriver

60 ml vodka
Freshly squeezed juice of 1 large orange

Shake vodka and orange juice well with ice cubes. Or pour into a blender and blend with ice at high speed for five seconds.

Strain into an old-fashioned glass filled with ice.

sea breeze

60 ml vodka
4 tbsp grapefruit juice
6 tbsp cranberry juice
Lemon wedge

Shake all ingredients, except lemon wedge, with ice cubes.

Strain into an old-fashioned glass filled with ice.

Add lemon wedge.

sex on the beach

30 ml vodka
30 ml peach-flavoured brandy
6 tbsp cranberry juice
6 tbsp pineapple juice
Lemon or peach slice (optional)

Shake all ingredients, except lemon or peach slice, with ice cubes.

Pour into a chilled cocktail glass.

Garnish with lemon or peach slice.

sure rider

60 ml vodka
30 ml sweet vermouth
½ cup orange juice
Juice of ½ a lemon
½ tsp grenadine
Maraschino cherry

Shake all ingredients, except cherry, with ice cubes.

Strain into a chilled cocktail glass.

Garnish with cherry.

sweet marian

30 ml vodka
15 ml amaretto
1 tsp cream

Shake all ingredients with ice cubes.

Strain into a chilled cocktail glass.

twister

60 ml vodka
Juice of ½ a lemon
Lemon peel
Seven Up

Pour vodka and lemon juice into a highball glass filled with ice cubes.

Drop in lemon peel.

Fill with Seven Up. Stir gently.

velvet hammer

45 ml vodka
30 ml crème de cacao (white)
1 tsp cream

Shake all ingredients with ice cubes.

Strain into a cocktail glass.

vodka and apple juice

60 ml vodka
Apple juice

Pour vodka over ice cubes in a highball glass.

Fill with apple juice. Stir.

vodka-and-tonic

60 ml vodka
Tonic water
Lemon wedge

Pour vodka into a highball glass half-filled with ice cubes.

Add tonic. Stir gently.

Garnish with lemon wedge.

vodka collins

60 ml vodka
Juice of ½ a lemon
1 tsp sugar
Club soda
Maraschino cherry

Shake all ingredients, except club soda and cherry, with ice cubes.

Strain into a highball glass filled with ice cubes.

Fill with club soda. Stir gently.

Garnish with cherry.

vodka cooler

45 ml vodka
15 ml sweet vermouth
1 tbsp lemon juice
½ tsp sugar
Club soda

Mix all ingredients, except club soda, with ice in a shaker or blender.

Pour into a highball glass half-filled with ice.

Fill with club soda. Stir gently.

bloody mary

Bloody Mary is one of the most popular cocktails in the world. Its main ingredients are vodka and tomato juice. However, it is what you add to the combination that will differentiate a great Bloody Mary from a mediocre one.

The story goes that Bloody Mary was concocted in the Ritz Hotel in Paris for Ernest Hemingway. The doctors had forbidden the writer to drink, and his wife, Mary, had him under close watch. The barman at the Ritz devised an ingenious drink that packed in loads of alcohol but could not be detected on the writer's breath. Hemingway was so pleased that he had got the better of his 'bloody wife' that he named it after her. (Like all bar stories, this one too should be listened to with a grain of salt.)

I am willing to bet that you will not find a better recipe for Bloody Mary than the one here. It is a recipe I have perfected based on tips I got from Walter, the barman at the UN headquarters in New York in the 1970s.

60 ml vodka
180 ml tomato juice
Several dashes of Tabasco sauce
Several dashes of Worcestershire sauce
15 ml sherry
1 tsp horseradish sauce
Juice of 1 lemon
A pinch of coarsely ground black pepper
Salt to taste
A wedge of lemon
Celery stick

Rub the rim of a highball glass with a piece of cut lemon and dip the rim in a saucer of salt until it is evenly coated.

Mix all the ingredients well with ice cubes.

Pour the mixture into the glass.

Add a lemon wedge and the celery stick as garnish.

vodka daisy

60 ml vodka
Juice of ½ a lemon
½ tsp sugar
1 tsp grenadine
Maraschino cherry

Shake all ingredients, except cherry, with ice cubes.

Strain into an old-fashioned glass.

Add ice cubes and cherry.

vodka gimlet

60 ml vodka
15 ml Rose's lime cordial

Stir vodka and lime cordial with ice cubes.

Strain into a chilled cocktail glass.

vodka grand marnier

45 ml vodka
15 ml Grand Marnier
1 tsp lemon juice
Orange slice

Shake vodka, Grand Marnier and lemon juice with ice.

Strain over ice cubes in an old-fashioned glass.

Garnish with orange slice.

vodka grasshopper

30 ml vodka	*Shake all ingredients with ice cubes.*
10 ml crème de menthe (green)	*Strain into a cocktail glass.*
10 ml crème de cacao (white)	

vodka martini

75 ml vodka	*Stir vodka and vermouth well with ice cubes.*
Several drops of dry vermouth	*Strain into a chilled cocktail glass.*
Lemon peel or green olive	*Garnish with lemon peel or olive.*

vodka melon

Fresh mint leaves	*Lightly crush the mint leaves to release their aroma and drop into an old-fashioned glass.*
60 ml vodka	*Add ice cubes.*
1 cup watermelon juice	*Pour in vodka and the juices. Stir.*
1 tsp lemon juice	

vodka old-fashioned

½ tsp sugar	*Dissolve sugar with bitters and water in an old-fashioned glass.*
Several dashes of Angostura bitters	*Add vodka.*
1 tsp water	*Fill glass to the rim with ice cubes. Stir.*
60 ml vodka	*Twist lemon peel over the drink and drop into the glass.*
Lemon peel	

vodka sour

60 ml vodka
1 tsp lemon juice
1 tsp sugar
Lemon slice
Maraschino cherry

Shake all ingredients, except lemon slice and cherry, with ice cubes.

Strain into a chilled cocktail glass.

Garnish with lemon slice and cherry.

vodka stinger

45 ml vodka
15 ml crème de menthe (white)

Shake vodka and crème de menthe with ice cubes.

Strain into a chilled cocktail glass.

white carnation

45 ml vodka
1½ tbsp lemon juice
2 tbsp pineapple juice
Club soda

Mix all ingredients, except club soda, with ice in a shaker or blender.

Pour into a highball glass.

Fill with club soda. Stir gently.

white russian

60 ml vodka
30 ml crème de cacao (white)
2 tsp cream

Pour the vodka and the liqueur in an old-fashioned glass over ice cubes.

Add cream. Stir.

ABSOLUT
Country of Sweden
APEACH
Be seduced by the complex flavors of natural peach, blended with vodka distilled from grain grown in the rich fields of southern Sweden. The distilling and flavoring of vodka is an age-old Swedish tradition dating back more than 400 years. Vodka has been sold under the name Absolut since 1879.
40% ALC./VOL. (80 PROOF) 750 ML.
IMPORTED
PEACH FLAVORED VODKA
PRODUCED AND BOTTLED IN ÅHUS, SWEDEN
V&S VIN&SPRIT AB (PUBL)

RUM

Originating as it has from sugar cane, rum mixes well with other tropical fruit products like pineapple juice and coconut cream.

acapulco

45 ml light rum
15 ml Cointreau or triple sec
1 tbsp lemon juice
1 tsp sugar
Fresh mint leaves

Mix all ingredients, except mint leaves, with ice in a shaker or blender.

Strain into a chilled cocktail glass.

Lightly tear some mint leaves to release their aroma and drop into the glass.

admiral nelson

30 ml light rum
30 ml gin
1 tsp Cointreau or triple sec
1 tbsp lemon juice
Orange slice

Mix all ingredients, except orange slice, with ice in a shaker or blender.

Pour into an old-fashioned glass.

Add orange slice.

admiral vernon

45 ml light rum
15 ml Grand Marnier
1 tbsp lemon juice
1 tsp sugar

Mix all ingredients with ice in a shaker or blender.

Strain into a chilled cocktail glass.

banana mango

45 ml light rum
10 ml banana liqueur
1 tbsp mango juice
1 tbsp lemon juice
Fresh mango slice

Shake all ingredients, except mango slice, with ice cubes.

Pour into a highball glass half-filled with ice cubes.

Add mango slice.

beachcomber

45 ml light rum
15 ml Cointreau or triple sec
1 tbsp lemon juice

Mix all ingredients with ice in a shaker or blender.

Strain into a chilled cocktail glass.

bee's knees

45 ml light rum
1½ tbsp orange juice
1 tbsp lemon juice
1 tsp honey
Several dashes of Angostura bitters
Orange peel

Shake all ingredients, except orange peel, with ice cubes.

Strain into a chilled cocktail glass.

Twist orange peel over the drink and drop into the glass.

black devil

60 ml light rum
15 ml dry vermouth
Black olive

Stir rum and vermouth with ice cubes.

Strain into a chilled cocktail glass.

Add olive.

blue hawaiian

30 ml light rum
30 ml blue curaçao
4 tbsp pineapple juice
2 tbsp cream of coconut
Slice of fresh pineapple (optional)
Maraschino cherry

Combine all ingredients, except pineapple and cherry, with crushed ice in a blender at high speed.

Pour into a highball glass.

Garnish with pineapple slice, if desired, and cherry.

bolero

45 ml light rum
30 ml calvados
30 ml sweet vermouth
Lemon peel

Mix all ingredients, except lemon peel, with ice cubes.

Strain into a chilled cocktail glass.

Twist lemon peel over the drink and drop into the glass.

bolo

45 ml light rum
1 tbsp lemon juice
1 tbsp orange juice
½ tsp sugar
Lemon slice

Shake all ingredients, except lemon slice, with ice cubes.

Strain into a chilled cocktail glass.

Garnish with lemon slice.

boston cooler

Juice of ½ a lemon
1 tsp sugar
60 ml club soda
60 ml light rum
Club soda or ginger ale
Orange or lemon peel

Pour lemon juice, sugar and soda in a highball glass. Stir.

Fill glass with ice cubes. Add rum.

Fill with club soda or ginger ale. Stir again.

Add a spiral of orange or lemon peel and dangle it over the rim of the glass.

caipirinha

1 lemon
Fresh mint leaves
1 tsp sugar
60 ml cachaça

Cut lemon into eight equal pieces. Remove seeds.

Muddle lemon pieces together with mint leaves and sugar in an old-fashioned glass.

Fill glass with crushed ice.

Pour cachaça and stir.

calypso cooler

60 ml light rum
2 tbsp pineapple juice
1 tbsp lemon juice
1 tsp sugar
Dash of Angostura bitters
Powdered nutmeg

Mix all ingredients, except nutmeg, with ice in a shaker or blender.

Strain into a chilled cocktail glass.

Sprinkle lightly with nutmeg.

carib

30 ml light rum
30 ml gin
1 tbsp lemon juice
1 tsp sugar
Orange slice

Shake all ingredients, except orange slice, with ice cubes.

Strain over ice into an old-fashioned glass.

Garnish with orange slice.

corkscrew

45 ml light rum
15 ml dry vermouth
15 ml peach liqueur
Lemon slice

Shake all ingredients, except lemon slice, with ice cubes.

Strain into a chilled cocktail glass.

Add lemon slice.

costa del sol

60 ml light rum
45 ml sweet vermouth
1 tsp sugar
1 tsp lemon juice
Club soda
Maraschino cherry

Half-fill a highball glass with ice cubes.

Add rum, vermouth, sugar and lemon juice. Stir.

Add club soda.

Garnish with cherry.

cuba libre

60 ml light or dark rum (the best Cuba Libre is made with dark rum)
Coca-Cola
Lemon wedge

Half-fill a highball glass with ice cubes.

Add rum.

Fill with cola. Stir gently.

Squeeze lemon wedge over drink and drop into the glass.

cuban special

30 ml light rum
15 ml Cointreau or triple sec
1 tsp pineapple juice
Juice of ½ a lemon
Maraschino cherry

Shake all ingredients, except cherry, with ice cubes.

Strain into a chilled cocktail glass.

Garnish with cherry.

daiquiri

60 ml light rum
Juice of ½ a lemon
½ tsp sugar
Lemon slice

Mix all ingredients, except lemon slice, with ice in a shaker or blender.

Strain into a chilled cocktail glass.

Add lemon slice.

derby daiquiri

45 ml light rum
1 tbsp lemon juice
2 tbsp orange juice
½ tsp sugar

Put all ingredients into a blender along with ice.

Blend at low speed.

Pour into a chilled cocktail glass.

derby special

45 ml light rum
15 ml Cointreau or triple sec
2 tbsp orange juice
1 tbsp lemon juice

Mix all ingredients with ice in a blender.

Pour into a chilled cocktail glass.

el presidente

45 ml golden rum
15 ml dry vermouth
30 ml dark rum
30 ml Cointreau or triple sec
2 tsp lemon juice
¼ tsp grenadine

Shake all ingredients with ice cubes.

Strain into a chilled cocktail glass.

enhanced planter's punch

75 ml dark rum
30 ml Cointreau or triple sec
4 tbsp orange juice
2 tbsp pineapple juice
2 tbsp lemon juice
Sugar to taste
Dash of grenadine
Club soda, cold
Pineapple slice
Orange slice
Maraschino cherry

Mix all ingredients, except soda, pineapple and orange slices and cherry, with ice in a shaker or blender.

Pour into a large highball glass.

Fill with cold club soda. Stir gently.

Garnish with pineapple and orange slices and cherry.

fiji fizz

45 ml dark rum
15 ml bourbon or Scotch whisky
15 ml cherry brandy
Several dashes of Angostura bitters
Coca-Cola, cold
Lemon peel

Mix all ingredients, except cola and lemon peel, with ice in a shaker or blender.

Pour into a chilled highball glass.

Fill with cold cola.

Garnish with lemon peel.

fort de france

45 ml golden rum
15 ml brandy
15 ml Cointreau or triple sec
1 tbsp pineapple juice
2 tbsp lemon juice
Lemon slice

Mix all ingredients, except lemon slice, with ice in a shaker or blender.

Pour into a highball glass.

Garnish with lemon slice.

fort lauderdale

45 ml light rum
15 ml sweet vermouth
Juice of ¼ orange
Juice of ¼ lemon
Orange slice

Shake all ingredients, except orange slice, with ice cubes.

Strain into an old-fashioned glass over ice cubes.

Add orange slice.

golden friendship

30 ml amaretto
30 ml sweet vermouth
30 ml light rum
Ginger ale
Maraschino cherry

Mix amaretto, vermouth and rum in a highball glass with ice cubes.

Fill with ginger ale. Stir gently.

Garnish with cherry.

guava daiquiri

45 ml light rum
2 tbsp guava juice
1 tbsp lemon juice
1 tsp crème de banana (optional)

Mix all ingredients with plenty of ice in a blender, till the mixture becomes snowy.

Pour into a chilled cocktail glass.

happy apple

45 ml golden rum
6 tbsp apple juice
1 tbsp lemon juice
Lemon peel

Mix all ingredients, except lemon peel, with ice in a shaker or blender.

Pour over ice into an old-fashioned glass.

Twist lemon peel over the drink and drop into the glass.

havana club

60 ml light rum
15 ml dry vermouth

Mix both ingredients with ice in a shaker or blender.

Strain into a chilled cocktail glass.

havana cocktail

45 ml light rum
3 tbsp pineapple juice
½ tsp lemon juice

Shake all ingredients with ice cubes.

Strain into a chilled cocktail glass.

hustler

60 ml light rum
1½ tsp passion fruit juice
Juice of 1 lemon
1 tsp sugar

Shake all ingredients well with ice cubes, till sugar dissolves.

Strain into a chilled cocktail glass.

iced rum tea

60 ml light rum
1 cup black tea
1 tsp sugar
1 tsp lemon juice
Lemon slice
4 fresh mint leaves

Pour rum, tea, sugar and lemon juice into a highball glass filled with ice cubes. Stir.

Garnish with lemon slice and partially torn mint leaves.

(To prevent the tea from clouding, let it cool to room temperature before combining with ice.)

long island iced tea

Long Island Iced Tea contains no tea. Within its innocence it packs in quite a wallop. A superior Long Island Iced Tea contains equal parts of gin, vodka, rum, triple sec and tequila, all white drinks, and is topped with Pepsi or Coca-Cola. The combination of the five kinds of alcohol makes a heady cocktail.

A bartender by the name of Robert Butt has been credited with creating the cocktail in the 1970s at the Oak Beach Inn in Hampton Bays, Long Island. The other, more interesting story, is that the drink was invented by bored Long Island housewives who added a little of everything in their bar cabinet so their husbands would not find out they had been drinking.

15 ml light rum
15 ml vodka
15 ml gin
15 ml tequila
15 ml Cointreau or triple sec
Juice of 1 lemon
Coca-Cola
Lemon wedge

Fill a highball glass half with crushed ice.

Add rum, vodka, gin, tequila, Cointreau or triple sec and lemon juice.

Stir to mix the ingredients well and top the glass with cola.

Garnish with lemon wedge.

jade

45 ml light rum
15 ml crème de menthe (green)
15 ml Cointreau or triple sec
1 tsp lemon juice
1 tsp sugar
Lemon slice

Shake all ingredients, except lemon slice, with ice cubes.

Strain into a chilled cocktail glass.

Add lemon slice.

jamaica elegance

45 ml golden or dark rum
15 ml brandy
1 tbsp pineapple juice
2 tbsp lemon juice
1 tsp sugar
Lemon slice

Shake all ingredients, except lemon slice, with ice cubes.

Strain into a highball glass.

Add ice to fill glass.

Add lemon slice.

(Given the name of the cocktail, it should, ideally, be made with Jamaican rum.)

jamaica sunday

60 ml dark rum
1 tsp honey
2 tsp lemon juice
Seven Up
Lemon slice

Stir honey in a mixing glass with rum till it dissolves.

Half-fill an old-fashioned glass with ice cubes.

Add the honey–rum mix and lemon juice.

Add Seven Up. Stir gently.

Garnish with lemon slice.

(As the name suggests, this cocktail too is best made with Jamaican rum.)

jolly roger

30 ml light rum
30 ml Drambuie
½ tsp lemon juice
Several dashes of Scotch whisky
Club soda

Mix all ingredients, except club soda, with ice in a shaker or blender.

Pour into a highball glass.

Fill with club soda. Stir.

kill devil

60 ml light or golden rum
30 ml brandy
1 tbsp honey
Several pinches of freshly grated ginger

Stir all ingredients with a little water till honey dissolves.

Add ice cubes. Stir till cold.

Pour into an old-fashioned glass, adding additional ice if necessary.

kingston

45 ml dark rum
25 ml gin
Juice of ½ a lemon
1 tsp grenadine

Mix all ingredients with ice in a shaker or blender.

Strain into a chilled cocktail glass.

kingston cocktail

45 ml dark rum
30 ml Tia Maria or Kahlúa
1 tsp lemon juice

Mix all ingredients with ice in a shaker or blender.

Strain into a chilled cocktail glass.

little devil

30 ml light rum
45 ml Cointreau or triple sec
15 ml gin
Juice of ½ a lemon

Shake all ingredients with ice cubes.

Strain into a chilled cocktail glass.

little princess

45 ml light rum
45 ml sweet vermouth

Shake both ingredients with ice cubes.

Strain into a chilled cocktail glass.

lounge lizard

30 ml dark rum
15 ml amaretto
Coca-Cola
Lemon slice

Pour rum and amaretto into an ice-filled highball glass.

Fill with cola.

Garnish with lemon slice.

mango daiquiri

60 ml light rum
1 tbsp lemon juice
1 tsp sugar (optional)
Diced, half-ripe Alfonso mango

Mix all ingredients with ice in a blender till smooth.

Pour into a chilled cocktail glass.

mariposa

30 ml light rum
15 ml brandy
1 tsp lemon juice
1 tsp orange juice
Dash of grenadine

Shake all ingredients with ice cubes.

Strain into a chilled cocktail glass.

mai tai

Most cocktails have one or two types of alcohol in them, but three-ingredient cocktails are not uncommon. These are usually a mix of a spirit with two different liqueurs to give it extra sweetness. The Mai Tai is one of them. The name, in Tahitian, means 'out of this world', and this one does not disappoint.

Mai Tai was invented by Victor Bergon, better known as Trader Vic, in his bar in Oakland, California, in 1944. The original recipe calls for dark Jamaican rum but any dark rum will be a good substitute. If you cannot find amaretto you can use a non-alcoholic almond syrup and add a little extra rum.

60 ml rum
30 ml Cointreau or triple sec
30 ml amaretto
2 tsp lemon juice
1 tsp sugar
Several dashes of Angostura bitters
Maraschino cherry

Shake the ingredients (except cherry) with ice until the sugar dissolves.

Strain into an old-fashioned glass about one-third full with crushed ice.

Garnish with the cherry.

(Instead of the cherry, you can tear a few mint leaves to release their flavour and add as garnish.)

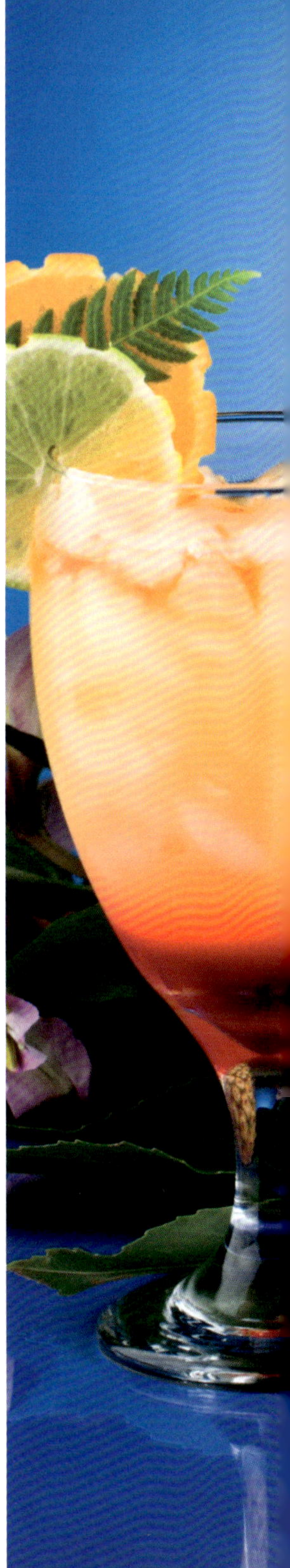

miami

45 ml light rum
15 ml crème de menthe (white)
½ tsp lemon juice

Shake all ingredients with ice cubes.

Strain into a chilled cocktail glass.

midnight express

45 ml dark rum
15 ml Cointreau or triple sec
¼ tsp lemon juice

Shake all ingredients with ice cubes.

Pour over ice into an old-fashioned glass.

mojito

Juice of 1 lemon
1 tsp sugar
Fresh mint leaves
60 ml light rum
Sprig of fresh mint leaves
Club soda, cold (optional)

Squeeze lemon juice into an old-fashioned glass.

Add sugar and mint leaves. Muddle till sugar dissolves.

Fill glass with ice cubes and pour in rum.

Swizzle till glass frosts, adding additional ice and rum as needed.

Garnish with sprig of fresh mint leaves.

You may top off the drink with cold club soda if you wish.

monkey wrench

60 ml light rum
4 tsp grapefruit juice
Seven Up
Maraschino cherry

Half-fill a highball glass with ice cubes.

Add rum and grapefruit juice and stir.

Top with Seven Up. Stir gently.

Add cherry.

navy grog

30 ml dark rum
15 ml light rum
1 tbsp lemon juice
1 tbsp orange juice
1 tbsp pineapple juice
1 tbsp guava juice
¼ tsp sugar
Fresh mint leaves

Put all ingredients, except mint leaves, with ice into a blender.

Blend at low speed.

Pour into an old-fashioned glass.

Add ice to fill glass to the rim.

Partially tear some mint leaves and float on drink.

ocho ríos

45 ml dark rum
2 tbsp guava juice
1 tbsp cream
1 tbsp lemon juice
½ tsp sugar

Put all ingredients with ice into a blender.

Blend at low speed.

Strain into a chilled cocktail glass.

outrigger

30 ml golden rum
30 ml brandy
30 ml Cointreau or triple sec
½ tsp lemon juice

Mix all ingredients with ice in a shaker or blender.

Strain into a chilled cocktail glass.

pago pago

45 ml golden rum
1 tsp lemon juice
15 ml Chartreuse (green)
10 ml crème de cacao (white)
Several dashes of pineapple juice

Shake all ingredients well with ice cubes.

Strain into a chilled cocktail glass.

palm island

45 ml golden rum
45 ml Grand Marnier

Pour both into an old-fashioned glass with several ice cubes. Stir.

piña colada

60 ml light rum
3 tsp coconut milk
3 tsp crushed pineapple
Maraschino cherry

Place all ingredients, except cherry, with ice in a blender.

Blend at high speed.

Pour into a highball glass.

Add cherry.

pineapple daiquiri

60 ml light rum
15 ml Cointreau or triple sec
6 tbsp pineapple juice
1½ tsp lemon juice

Mix all ingredients with ice in a shaker or blender.

Strain into a chilled cocktail glass.

pink creole

45 ml golden rum
1 tbsp lemon juice
1 tsp cream
1 tsp grenadine
Maraschino cherry

Shake all ingredients, except cherry, with ice cubes.

Strain into a chilled cocktail glass.

Add cherry.

pink veranda

30 ml golden rum
30 ml dark rum
1 tbsp cranberry juice
1 tsp sugar

Shake all ingredients well with ice cubes.

Pour into an old-fashioned glass.

Add more ice if desired.

planter's punch

60 ml dark rum
6 tbsp orange juice
30 ml Cointreau or triple sec
1 tsp pineapple juice
Juice of ½ a lemon
1 tsp sugar
Dash of Angostura bitters
Orange or lemon slice

Mix all ingredients, except fruit slice, with ice in a shaker or blender.

Pour into a highball glass.

Garnish with orange or lemon slice.

polynesian paradise

45 ml golden rum
1 tsp sugar
1½ tbsp lemon juice
15 ml sweet vermouth
10 ml Cointreau or triple sec

Put all ingredients with ice into a blender.

Blend at low speed for 10 to 15 seconds.

Strain into a chilled deep-saucer cocktail glass.

port antonio

30 ml golden rum
15 ml dark rum
15 ml Tia Maria or Kahlúa
1 tsp lemon juice
1 tsp sugar
Lemon slice

Shake all ingredients, except lemon slice, with ice cubes.

Pour over ice into an old-fashioned glass.

Add lemon slice.

presidente cocktail

45 ml light rum
15 ml dry vermouth
15 ml white curaçao
Dash of grenadine
Lemon peel

Mix all ingredients, except lemon peel, with ice in a shaker or blender.

Strain into a chilled cocktail glass.

Twist lemon peel over the drink and drop into the glass.

puerto rican pink lady

50 ml golden rum
1½ tbsp lemon juice
1 tsp grenadine

Put all ingredients with ice into a blender.

Blend at low speed.

Strain into a chilled cocktail glass.

rum and coconut cooler

75 ml light rum
1 tbsp cream of coconut
1 tbsp lemon juice
Club soda
Lemon slice
Maraschino cherry

Shake rum, cream of coconut and lemon juice with ice cubes.

Strain into a highball glass half-filled with ice.

Add a splash of club soda.

Garnish with lemon slice and cherry.

rum and pineapple cooler

75 ml light rum
4 tbsp pineapple juice
½ tsp lemon juice
1 tsp sugar
Dash of Angostura bitters
Club soda
Pineapple wedge

Shake rum, pineapple juice, lemon juice, sugar and bitters with ice cubes.

Strain into a highball glass.

Add a splash of club soda and ice to fill glass.

Garnish with pineapple wedge.

rum bloody mary

1 tsp lemon juice
30 ml light rum
120 ml tomato juice
Several dashes of Worcestershire Sauce
Several dashes of Tabasco Sauce
Pinch of freshly ground black pepper
Pinch of salt

Rub lemon juice on the rim of a highball glass and dip into a saucer of salt till the rim is coated with salt.

Stir all ingredients well with ice cubes in a mixing glass.

Pour into the highball glass.

rum citrus cooler

60 ml light rum
2 tbsp orange juice
½ tsp lemon juice
15 ml Cointreau or triple sec
1 tsp sugar
Seven Up
Lemon slice

Shake all ingredients, except Seven Up and lemon slice, with ice cubes.

Strain into a highball glass half-filled with ice.

Add Seven Up. Stir.

Garnish with lemon slice.

rum cobbler

60 ml light rum
1 tsp sugar
60 ml club soda
Maraschino cherry

Dissolve sugar in club soda in an old-fashioned glass.

Fill with ice cubes.

Add rum. Stir.

Garnish with cherry.

rum coconut fizz

65 ml light rum
½ tsp lemon juice
1 tsp cream of coconut
Club soda
Lemon slice

Shake all ingredients, except club soda and lemon slice, with ice cubes.

Strain into a highball glass half-filled with ice.

Fill with club soda. Stir.

Add lemon slice.

rum cooler

½ tsp sugar 60 ml club soda 60 ml light rum Extra club soda or ginger ale Lemon or orange peel	*Stir sugar in 60 ml club soda in a highball glass till it dissolves.* *Fill glass with ice. Add rum.* *Fill with club soda or ginger ale. Stir again.* *Insert a spiral of orange or lemon peel (or both) and dangle over rim of glass.*

rum fix

Juice of ½ a lemon 1 tsp sugar 1 tsp water 60 ml light rum Lemon slice	*Stir lemon juice, sugar and water in a highball glass.* *Fill glass with ice. Add rum. Stir again.* *Add lemon slice.*

rum highball

60 ml light or dark rum	*Pour rum over ice cubes into a highball glass.*
Ginger ale or club soda	*Fill with ginger ale or club soda.*
Lemon peel	*Add lemon peel. Stir.*

rum martini

60 ml light rum	*Shake rum and vermouth with ice cubes.*
1 tsp dry vermouth	*Strain into a chilled cocktail glass.*
Several dashes of Angostura bitters	*Add Angostura bitters. Stir.*
Lemon slice	*Garnish with lemon slice.*

rum pineapple fizz

60 ml golden rum	*Put all ingredients, except club soda and lemon slice, with ice into a blender.*
1/3 cup diced fresh pineapple	*Blend at low speed.*
1 tsp sugar	*Pour into a highball glass.*
1 tsp lemon juice	*Add ice cubes to almost fill the glass.*
Club soda	*Top with soda.*
Lemon slice	*Drop in lemon slice.*

saint augustine

45 ml light rum	*Shake all ingredients, except lemon peel, with ice cubes.*
2 tbsp grapefruit juice	*Strain into a chilled sugar-rimmed cocktail glass.*
1 tsp Cointreau or triple sec	*Twist lemon peel over the drink and drop into the glass.*
Lemon peel	

san juan

45 ml light rum
25 ml brandy
1 tsp grenadine
1 tbsp lemon juice

Mix all ingredients with ice in a shaker or blender.

Strain into a chilled cocktail glass.

scorpion

60 ml light rum
30 ml brandy
4 tbsp orange juice
3 tbsp lemon juice
½ tsp sugar

Mix all ingredients with ice in a blender.

Pour into a chilled wine goblet.

september morn

45 ml light rum
½ tsp lemon juice
1 tsp grenadine

Shake all ingredients with ice cubes.

Strain into a chilled cocktail glass.

(The glass rim may be moistened with grenadine before dipping into sugar.)

sevilla

30 ml dark rum
30 ml sweet vermouth
Orange peel

Mix rum and vermouth with ice in a shaker or blender.

Strain into a chilled cocktail glass.

Twist orange peel over the drink and drop into the glass.

shark's tooth

45 ml golden rum
30 ml sweet vermouth
15 ml gin
½ tsp lemon juice
2 tsp passion fruit juice
Dash of Angostura bitters
Orange peel
Maraschino cherry

Shake all ingredients, except orange peel and cherry, with ice cubes.

Strain into a chilled cocktail glass.

Twist orange peel over the drink and drop into the glass.

Add cherry.

sloppy joe's

30 ml light rum
30 ml dry vermouth
15 ml Cointreau or triple sec
½ tsp grenadine
Juice of 1 lemon

Mix all ingredients with ice in a shaker or blender.

Strain into a chilled cocktail glass.

A man walks into a bar in a fancy restaurant and asks for whisky.
The barman pours out a double. 'That will be five rupees.'
'Only five rupees?' the man asks puzzled.
'That's right,' the barman replies.
'If that's the price, I will have another double,' says the delighted customer.
Everyone in the bar is also enjoying drinks at such prices.
'Look, I would like to thank the owner,' the man says after an hour of drinking.
'He is upstairs with my wife,' the barman says.
'What's he doing with your wife?'
'What I am doing to his business.'

strawberry daiquiri

45 ml light rum
Juice of ½ a lemon
1 tsp sugar
8 fresh strawberries

Mix all ingredients with ice in a blender till smooth.

Pour into a chilled cocktail glass.

sweet 'n' silky

30 ml light rum
30 ml Cointreau or triple sec
1 tbsp cream

Mix all ingredients with ice in a shaker or blender.

Strain into a chilled cocktail glass.

tahiti club

60 ml golden rum 1 tbsp pineapple juice 1 tsp lemon juice Orange slice Maraschino cherry	*Shake all ingredients, except orange slice and cherry, with ice cubes.* *Pour into an old-fashioned glass.* *Add ice cubes to fill glass.* *Add orange slice and cherry.*

ti punch

1 lemon 60 ml light rum 1 tsp sugar	*Cut the lemon in four pieces and squeeze juice into an old-fashioned glass. Remove any seeds and drop in the lemon pieces.* *Add rum and sugar. Stir till sugar dissolves.* *Fill the glass with crushed ice.*

tobago

30 ml golden rum 30 ml gin 2 tsp lemon juice 1 tsp guava juice Lemon peel	*Put all ingredients, except lemon peel, with ice into a blender.* *Blend at low speed.* *Pour over ice cubes in an old-fashioned glass.* *Twist lemon peel over the drink and drop into the glass.*

villa hermosa

30 ml dark rum
30 ml Tia Maria or Kahlúa
1 tbsp cream

Mix all ingredients with ice in a shaker or blender.

Strain into a chilled cocktail glass.

white witch

30 ml light rum
15 ml crème de cacao (white)
15 ml Cointreau or triple sec
Juice of ½ a lemon
Club soda, cold
Fresh mint leaves

Mix all ingredients, except lemon, club soda and mint leaves, with ice in a shaker or blender.

Pour into a highball glass.

Add lemon juice.

Fill with cold club soda. Stir gently.

Garnish with mint leaves, lightly torn to release the aroma.

x.y.z

60 ml dark rum
30 ml Cointreau or triple sec
1 tsp lemon juice
Maraschino cherry

Shake all ingredients, except cherry, with ice cubes.

Strain into a chilled cocktail glass.

Add cherry.

yaka-hula-hicky-dula

45 ml light rum
45 ml dry vermouth
3 tbsp pineapple juice

Mix all ingredients with ice in a shaker or blender.

Strain into a chilled cocktail glass.

MARTELL
XO
COGNAC
J Martell
1715
MARTELL
XO
40%vol
70cle
J Martell

TEQUILA

Unless otherwise stated, white (colourless) tequila is preferred for making these cocktails.

acapulco orange blossom

45 ml tequila
25 ml Bénédictine
4 tbsp orange juice
Orange slice

Mix all ingredients, except orange slice, with ice in a shaker or blender.

Strain over ice cubes into an old-fashioned glass.

Garnish with orange slice.

big blue shark

30 ml tequila
30 ml vodka
25 ml blue curaçao

Mix all ingredients with ice in a shaker or blender.

Strain into a chilled cocktail glass.

bloody maria

30 ml tequila
2 tsp tomato juice
1 tsp lemon juice
Dash of Tabasco sauce
Salt to taste
Lemon slice

Shake all ingredients, except lemon slice, with ice cubes.

Strain over ice cubes into an old-fashioned glass.

Add lemon slice.

blue margarita

2 tbsp lemon juice
Salt
60 ml tequila
30 ml blue curaçao
Lemon slice

Rub rim of cocktail glass with lemon juice. Dip rim in salt.

Shake lemon juice, tequila and curaçao with ice.

Strain into a chilled cocktail glass.

Garnish with lemon slice.

margarita

Had it not been for the Margarita the popularity of tequila might have been confined to Mexico. The Margarita is a relative newcomer on the cocktail scene. The recipe first turned up in written form in London, of all places, in 1937, in the *Café Royale Cocktail Book* but the drink really took off in the 1970s. Most bar books before that period don't even mention Margaritas.

Margaritas are made in 2:1:1 proportions: that is two of tequila, one of triple sec and one of freshly squeezed lemon juice. Don't add sugar to the mix the way some Indian bartenders tend to do. That's gross. If you prefer your drink on the sweeter side, add more of triple sec or Cointreau and less lemon juice.

If you have a blender at home try making frozen Margaritas. It is tricky but after several unsuccessful attempts you just might master the art. You can also mix peach, strawberry or melon Margaritas in the blender. A Margarita made with alphonso mangoes is a delicious drink for a lazy summer afternoon. The one that has impressed me the most so far was made with the sweet-and-sour prickly pear in Dos Caminos, a Mexican restaurant in downtown Manhattan. The restaurant also makes great guacamole which goes very well with this cocktail.

60 ml tequila
30 ml triple sec or Cointreau
2 tbsp lemon juice
Salt
Lemon slice

Mix tequila, triple sec or Cointreau and lemon juice with ice cubes in a shaker or blender.

Rub the rim of a chilled cocktail glass with a piece of lemon and dip the rim of the glass in a saucer of salt until it is evenly coated.

Strain and pour the mixture into the glass.

Garnish with lemon slice.

brave bull

45 ml tequila
25 ml Tia Maria or Kahlúa
Lemon peel

Mix all ingredients, except lemon peel, with ice in a shaker or blender.

Pour into an old-fashioned glass.

Twist lemon peel over the drink and drop into the glass.

caramba

45 ml tequila
6 tbsp grapefruit juice
1 tsp sugar
Club soda

Mix all ingredients, except club soda, with ice in a shaker or blender.

Pour into a highball glass filled with ice.

Top with club soda. Stir gently.

changuirongo

45 ml tequila
Ginger ale
Lemon wedge

Pour tequila and ginger ale over ice cubes in a highball glass. Stir gently.

Garnish with lemon wedge.

chapala

45 ml tequila
15 ml Cointreau or triple sec
1 tsp orange juice
1 tsp lemon juice
½ tsp grenadine
Orange slice

Mix all ingredients, except orange slice, with ice in a shaker or blender.

Pour into an old-fashioned glass.

Garnish with orange slice.

esmeralda

45 ml tequila
Juice of 1 lemon
1 tsp honey
Dash of Angostura bitters
Lemon slice

Mix all ingredients, except lemon slice, with ice in a shaker or blender.

Strain into a chilled cocktail glass.

Add lemon slice.

gentle ben

30 ml tequila
30 ml vodka
6 tbsp orange juice
30 ml gin
Orange slice

Mix all ingredients, except gin and orange slice, in a shaker or blender with ice cubes.

Pour into an old-fashioned glass.

Float gin on top.

Garnish with orange slice.

mango margarita

1 fresh mango peeled and sliced
60 ml tequila
30 ml Cointreau or triple sec
30 ml lemon juice

Mash the mango slices into a smooth paste in a blender.

Add tequila, triple sec or Cointreau and lemon juice.

Blend for a few seconds more, then add ice.

Blend again until the drink becomes the consistency of a milkshake.

Pour into a chilled cocktail glass with a salted rim.

matador

45 ml tequila
6 tbsp pineapple juice
1 tsp lemon juice
½ tsp sugar

Mix all ingredients with ice in a shaker or blender.

Strain into a chilled cocktail glass.

(You can use honey or grenadine in place of sugar if you wish.)

mexicana

45 ml tequila
2 tbsp lemon juice
1 tsp pineapple juice
1 tsp grenadine

Shake all ingredients with ice cubes.

Strain into a chilled cocktail glass.

mexicola

45 ml tequila
Coca-Cola
Lemon slice

Pour tequila over ice cubes in a highball glass.

Follow with cola.

Squeeze in a few drops of lemon juice. Stir.

Drop in the lemon slice.

pacific sunshine

45 ml tequila
45 ml blue curaçao
1 tsp lemon juice
Dash of Angostura bitters
Lemon slice

Mix all ingredients, except lemon slice, with ice cubes.

Pour into a chilled cocktail glass with a salted rim.

Garnish with lemon slice.

piña

45 ml tequila
6 tbsp fresh pineapple juice
1 tsp lemon juice
1 tsp honey or sugar
Lemon slice

Mix all ingredients, except lemon slice, with ice in a shaker or blender.

Pour into an old-fashioned glass.

Garnish with lemon slice.

rosita

30 ml tequila
15 ml dry vermouth
15 ml sweet vermouth
30 ml Campari
Lemon slice

Stir all ingredients, except lemon slice, in a highball glass with ice cubes.

Add lemon slice.

sangrita

2 cups tomato juice
1 cup orange juice
2 tsp lemon juice
1 tsp Tabasco sauce
2 tsp minced onion
1-2 tsp Worcestershire sauce
Several pinches freshly ground white or black pepper
Salt to taste

Shake all ingredients with ice cubes.

Strain into an old-fashioned glass.

(Sangrita is traditionally a Mexican peppery mixture of tart oranges, tomato juice, onions, hot chillies and other seasonings. It is usually drunk with neat tequila as a chaser.)

silk stockings

45 ml tequila
30 ml crème de cacao (white)
3 tbsp cream
Dash of grenadine
Powdered cinnamon

Shake all ingredients, except cinnamon, with ice cubes.

Strain into a chilled cocktail glass.

Sprinkle lightly with cinnamon.

strawberry margarita

1 tsp lemon juice Salt	*If desired, rub rim of cocktail glass with lemon juice, dip rim in salt.*
30 ml tequila	*Put all ingredients in a blender with ice.*
15 ml Cointreau or triple sec	*Blend for twenty seconds.*
Fresh strawberries	*Strain into a chilled glass.*

sunset

45 ml tequila 1 tsp lemon juice	*Put tequila, lemon juice, grenadine and ice in a blender.*
1 tsp grenadine	*Blend at low speed.*
Lemon slice	*Pour into an old-fashioned glass.*
	Add ice cubes to fill glass.
	Garnish with lemon slice.

tequila collins

45 ml tequila 1 tsp lemon juice	*Pour tequila, lemon juice and sugar over ice cubes in a highball glass. Stir.*
Sugar to taste	*Fill with club soda. Stir gently.*
Club soda	*Add cherry.*
Maraschino cherry	

tequila daiquiri

45 ml tequila
1 tsp lemon juice
1 tsp sugar

Mix all ingredients with ice in a shaker or blender.

Strain into a chilled cocktail glass.

tequila fizz

60 ml tequila
1 tsp lemon juice
1 tsp sugar
Several dashes of Angostura bitters
Club soda

Shake all ingredients, except club soda, with ice cubes.

Strain into a highball glass half-filled with ice.

Fill with soda. Stir.

tequila gimlet

45 ml tequila
30 ml Rose's lime cordial
Lemon wedge

Pour tequila and lime cordial over ice cubes into an old-fashioned glass. Stir.

Garnish with lemon wedge.

tequila guayaba

45 ml tequila
2 tsp guava juice
1 tsp orange juice
1 tsp lemon juice
Orange peel

Shake all ingredients, except orange peel, with ice cubes.

Pour into an old-fashioned glass.

Add ice cubes to fill glass.

Twist orange peel over the drink and drop into the glass.

tequila old-fashioned

1 sugar cube	*Place sugar cube in an old-fashioned glass and saturate with bitters.*
Several dashes of Angostura bitters	*Muddle till sugar dissolves.*
45 ml golden tequila	*Add ice, tequila and a little water. Stir.*
Lemon peel	*Garnish with lemon peel.*

tequila pink

45 ml tequila	*Shake all ingredients with ice cubes.*
30 ml dry vermouth	*Strain into a chilled cocktail glass.*
Dash of grenadine	

tequila sour

60 ml tequila	*Shake tequila, lemon juice and sugar with ice cubes.*
1 tbsp lemon juice	*Strain into a chilled cocktail glass.*
1 tsp sugar	*Add lemon slice and cherry.*
Lemon slice	
Maraschino cherry	

tequila straight

Pinch of salt	*Take a pinch of salt between the thumb and index finger of your right hand. Put it on the back of your left hand.*
45 ml tequila	*Hold the jigger of tequila in the same hand and the lemon wedge in the right hand.*
¼ lemon	*Taste salt, drink the tequila, and then suck the lemon.*

tequila sunrise

45 ml tequila
Juice of ½ a lemon
4 tsp orange juice
2 tsp grenadine

Mix all ingredients, except grenadine, with ice in a shaker or blender.

Pour into a highball glass.

Carefully pòur the grenadine over the back of a spoon so that it floats. Do not stir.

BRANDY

Cognac is the best known of the large variety of brandies and most people like to drink it neat, without any mixers and mostly even without ice. But brandy is also the main ingredient of some famous cocktails, Brandy Alexander and Stinger among them. Bénédictine & Brandy, aka B&B, is so popular that now you can buy it bottled. In the recipes that follow, 'brandy' refers only to grape brandies. Wherever a recipe calls for cognac, any other good grape brandy can be used as substitute.

30 ml brandy
30 ml curaçao (white)
1 tbsp lemon juice
½ tsp sugar
Orange peel

Mix all ingredients, except orange peel, with ice in a shaker or blender.

Strain into a chilled cocktail glass.

Twist orange peel over the drink and drop into the glass.

alhambra

45 ml brandy
15 ml sherry
15 ml Drambuie
Orange slice
Lemon peel

Mix all ingredients, except orange slice and lemon peel, with ice in a shaker or blender.

Pour into an old-fashioned glass.

Garnish with orange slice. Twist lemon peel over the drink and drop into the glass.

apple blossom

45 ml brandy
2 tbsp apple juice
1 tsp lemon juice
Lemon slice

Mix all ingredients, except lemon slice, with ice in a shaker or blender.

Strain into a chilled cocktail glass.

Garnish with lemon slice.

apple brandy cooler

60 ml brandy
30 ml light rum
120 ml apple juice
1 tbsp lemon juice
1 tsp sugar or to taste
1 tsp dark rum
Lemon slice

Mix all ingredients, except dark rum and lemon slice, with ice in a shaker or blender.

Pour into a highball glass.

Top with a float of dark rum and garnish with lemon slice.

b & b

30 ml cognac
30 ml Bénédictine

Pour both ingredients into a brandy snifter.

Swirl till blended.

beach street cooler

45 ml brandy
15 ml Cointreau or triple sec
1 tbsp lemon juice
Coca-Cola, chilled

Mix all ingredients, except cola, with ice in a shaker or blender.

Pour into a chilled highball glass.

Fill with cola. Stir gently.

behind the sheet

45 ml cognac
30 ml light rum
25 ml Cointreau or triple sec
1 tbsp lemon juice

Mix all ingredients with ice in a shaker or blender.

Strain into a chilled cocktail glass.

bombay

30 ml brandy
30 ml dry vermouth
15 ml sweet vermouth
15 ml Cointreau or triple sec
Orange slice

Mix all ingredients, except orange slice, with ice in a shaker or blender.

Pour into an old-fashioned glass.

Garnish with orange slice.

brandy alexander

30 ml brandy
25 ml crème de cacao
1½ tbsp cream
Powdered nutmeg (optional)

Shake all ingredients, except nutmeg, with ice cubes.

Strain into a chilled cocktail glass.

Sprinkle lightly with nutmeg.

brandy cobbler

1 tsp sugar
60 ml club soda
60 ml brandy

Dissolve sugar in club soda in an old-fashioned glass.

Fill with ice cubes.

Add brandy. Stir.

brandy deluxe

45 ml brandy
15 ml sherry
15 ml Drambuie
½ lemon slice
Lemon peel

Shake all ingredients, except lemon slice and peel, with ice cubes.

Pour over ice into an old-fashioned glass.

Add lemon slice. Twist lemon peel over the drink and drop into the glass.

brandy fix

90 ml brandy
1 tsp sugar
1 tsp water
Juice of ½ a lemon

Add all ingredients to an old-fashioned glass.

Fill with ice cubes. Stir.

brandy gump

45 ml brandy
Juice of ½ a lemon
½ tsp grenadine
Lemon slice

Shake all ingredients, except lemon slice, with ice cubes.

Strain into an old-fashioned glass filled with ice cubes.

Garnish with lemon slice.

brandy highball

60 ml brandy
Ginger ale or club soda
Lemon peel

Pour brandy over ice cubes into a highball glass.

Fill with ginger ale or club soda. Stir gently.

Garnish with a long strip of lemon peel.

brandy manhattan

60 ml brandy
15 ml sweet vermouth
Dash of Angostura bitters
Maraschino cherry

Stir brandy, vermouth and bitters with ice cubes.

Strain into a chilled cocktail glass.

Add cherry.

brandy old-fashioned

1 sugar cube	*Place sugar cube in an old-fashioned glass.*
Several dashes of Angostura bitters	*Sprinkle with bitters and a dash of cold water.*
90 ml brandy	*Add ice cubes and brandy. Stir.*
Lemon peel	*Twist lemon peel over the drink and drop into the glass.*

brandy sangaree

½ tsp sugar	*Dissolve sugar in water. Add brandy.*
1 tsp water	
60 ml brandy	*Pour over ice cubes into a highball glass.*
Club soda	*Fill with club soda. Stir.*
30 ml port	*Float port on top.*
Powdered nutmeg	*Sprinkle lightly with nutmeg.*

brandy smash

1 sugar cube	*Muddle sugar cube with club soda and some mint leaves in an old-fashioned glass.*
30 ml club soda	
Fresh mint leaves	
60 ml brandy	*Add brandy and ice cubes.*
Lemon peel	*Add lemon peel.*

brandy sour

60 ml brandy 2 tbsp lemon juice 1 tsp sugar Maraschino cherry	*Shake brandy, lemon juice and sugar with ice cubes.* *Strain into a chilled wine or cocktail glass.* *Add cherry.*

brandy swizzle

60 ml brandy Juice of 1 lemon 1 tsp sugar Several dashes of Angostura bitters Club soda	*Put brandy, lemon juice and sugar in a highball glass.* *Add bitters.* *Fill with ice cubes and soda. Stir.*

brandy toddy

½ tsp sugar 1 tsp water 60 ml brandy Lemon peel	*Dissolve sugar in water in an old-fashioned glass.* *Add brandy and ice cubes. Stir.* *Twist lemon peel over the drink and drop into the glass.*

brandy vermouth cocktail

15 ml sweet vermouth 60 ml brandy Dash of Angostura bitters	*Stir all ingredients with ice cubes.* *Strain into a chilled cocktail glass.*

brantini

45 ml brandy 30 ml gin Dash of dry vermouth Lemon peel	*Stir liquors with ice cubes and strain into a chilled cocktail glass.* *Add lemon peel.*

carrol

45 ml brandy
15 ml sweet vermouth
Maraschino cherry

Stir brandy and vermouth with ice cubes.

Strain into a chilled cocktail glass.

Add cherry.

champs-élysées

30 ml brandy
15 ml Chartreuse (yellow)
Juice of ¼ of a lemon
½ tsp sugar
Dash of Angostura bitters
Maraschino cherry

Shake all ingredients, except cherry, with ice cubes.

Strain into a chilled cocktail glass.

charles cocktail

45 ml sweet vermouth
45 ml brandy
Dash of Angostura bitters

Stir all ingredients with ice cubes.

Strain into a chilled cocktail glass.

cherry blossom

45 ml brandy
15 ml cherry brandy
30 ml Cointreau or triple sec
1½ tsp grenadine
2 tsp lemon juice
Maraschino cherry

Shake all ingredients, except cherry, with ice cubes.

Strain into a chilled cocktail glass.

Add cherry.

cherry hill

30 ml brandy
30 ml cherry brandy
15 ml dry vermouth
Orange peel

Mix all ingredients, except orange peel, with ice in a shaker or blender.

Strain into a chilled cocktail glass.

Twist orange peel over the drink and drop into the glass.

chicago cocktail

60 ml brandy
30 ml Cointreau or triple sec
Dash of Angostura bitters

Stir all ingredients with ice.

Strain into a chilled cocktail glass.

clabama

60 ml brandy
1 tbsp lemon juice
30 ml Cointreau or triple sec
½ tsp sugar
Lemon peel

Shake all ingredients, except lemon peel, with ice cubes.

Strain into a chilled cocktail glass.

Twist lemon peel over the drink and drop into the glass.

cognac highball

60 ml cognac
Ginger ale or club soda
Lemon peel

Pour cognac over ice cubes into a highball glass.

Fill with ginger ale or club soda.

Add lemon peel. Stir.

coterie

30 ml cognac
30 ml Chartreuse (yellow)
30 ml gin
1 tsp lemon juice
1 tsp sugar
Lemon slice

Mix all ingredients, except lemon slice, with ice cubes in a shaker or blender.

Strain into a chilled cocktail glass.

Add lemon slice.

depth charge

30 ml calvados
30 ml cognac
2 tsp lemon juice
1 tsp grenadine
Lemon peel

Shake all ingredients, except lemon peel, with ice cubes.

Strain into a chilled cocktail glass.

Add lemon peel.

devil's smile

30 ml brandy
30 ml Cointreau or triple sec
2 tbsp lemon juice
15 ml amaretto

Mix all ingredients with ice in a shaker or blender.

Strain into a chilled cocktail glass.

dry cold deck

60 ml brandy
15 ml dry vermouth
10 ml crème de menthe (white)

Shake all ingredients with ice cubes.

Strain into a chilled cocktail glass.

east india

45 ml brandy
30 ml Cointreau or triple sec
30 ml dark rum
½ tsp pineapple juice
Dash of Angostura bitters
Lemon peel

Shake all ingredients, except lemon peel, with ice cubes.

Strain into a chilled cocktail glass.

Add lemon peel.

femina

45 ml brandy
15 ml Bénédictine
1 tbsp orange juice
Orange slice

Shake all ingredients, except orange slice, with ice cubes.

Strain over ice cubes into an old-fashioned glass.

Add orange slice.

french connection

45 ml cognac
25 ml amaretto

Mix cognac and amaretto with ice cubes in an old-fashioned glass.

froupe

40 ml brandy
40 ml sweet vermouth
30 ml Bénédictine

Stir all ingredients well with ice cubes.

Strain into a chilled cocktail glass.

gazette

45 ml brandy
30 ml sweet vermouth
1 tsp lemon juice
1 tsp sugar

Mix all ingredients with ice in a shaker or blender.

Strain into a chilled cocktail glass.

golden chain

30 ml cognac
30 ml Galliano
1 tbsp lemon juice
15 ml Chartreuse (yellow)
Lemon slice

Mix all ingredients, except lemon slice, with ice in a shaker or blender.

Strain into a chilled cocktail glass.

Garnish with lemon slice.

harvard

45 ml brandy
10 ml sweet vermouth
Dash of Angostura bitters
1 tsp grenadine
2 tsp lemon juice

Shake all ingredients with ice cubes.

Strain into a chilled cocktail glass.

lady be good

45 ml brandy
15 ml crème de menthe (white)
15 ml sweet vermouth

Shake all ingredients with ice cubes.

Strain into a chilled cocktail glass.

loudspeaker

30 ml brandy
30 ml gin
10 ml Cointreau or triple sec
1 tbsp lemon juice

Shake all ingredients with ice cubes.

Strain into a chilled cocktail glass.

mcbrandy

60 ml brandy
2 tbsp apple juice
1 tsp lemon juice
Lemon slice

Shake all ingredients, except lemon slice, with ice cubes.

Strain into a chilled cocktail glass.

Add lemon slice.

metropolitan

40 ml brandy
40 ml sweet vermouth
½ tsp sugar
Dash of Angostura bitters

Shake all ingredients with ice cubes.

Strain into a chilled cocktail glass.

netherland

30 ml brandy
30 ml Cointreau or triple sec
Dash of Angostura bitters

Put all ingredients into an old-fashioned glass with ice cubes. Stir.

€ 400

THE WORLD'S MOST EXPENSIVE COCKTAIL

You can try the Side Car for € 400 (Rs 22,000) in the Hemingway Bar of the Ritz Hotel in Paris. This elixir is a mixture of lemon juice, Cointreau and a cognac more than a century old that was nearly seized from the hotel by the Nazis during the German occupation.

olympic

30 ml brandy 30 ml Cointreau or triple sec 2 tbsp orange juice	*Mix all ingredients with ice in a shaker or blender.* *Strain into a chilled cocktail glass.*

picasso

45 ml cognac 15 ml Dubonnet (red) 1 tbsp lemon juice 1 tsp sugar Orange peel	*Shake all ingredients, except orange peel, with ice cubes.* *Strain into a chilled cocktail glass.* *Twist orange peel over the drink and drop into the glass.*

quaker

45 ml brandy 15 ml rum 1 tbsp lemon juice 1 tsp grenadine Lemon peel	*Shake all ingredients, except lemon peel, with ice cubes.* *Strain into a chilled cocktail glass.* *Twist lemon peel over the drink and drop into the glass.*

santa fe

45 ml brandy 1 tbsp grapefruit juice ½ tbsp dry vermouth 1 tsp lemon juice	*Shake all ingredients with ice cubes.* *Strain into a chilled cocktail glass.*

side car

30 ml Cointreau or triple sec 60 ml cognac Juice of ½ a lemon	*Shake all ingredients with ice cubes.* *Strain into a chilled cocktail glass.*

sink or swim

45 ml brandy
15 ml sweet vermouth
Several dashes of Angostura bitters

Mix all ingredients with ice in a shaker or blender.

Strain into a chilled cocktail glass.

sir walter raleigh

45 ml brandy
25 ml light rum
15 ml Cointreau or triple sec
1 tsp lemon juice
1 tsp grenadine

Mix all ingredients with ice in a shaker or blender.

Strain into a chilled cocktail glass.

south pacific

45 ml brandy
1 tbsp lemon juice
10 ml crème d'ananas
10 ml crème de menthe (white)
Pineapple wedge

Shake all ingredients, except pineapple wedge, with ice cubes.

Strain over ice cubes into an old-fashioned glass.

Add pineapple wedge.

southern cross

45 ml brandy
15 ml Cointreau or triple sec
Tonic water
Lemon wedge

Pour brandy and Cointreau over ice cubes in a highball glass.

Fill with tonic water.

Garnish with lemon wedge.

stinger

30 ml crème de menthe (white)
45 ml cognac

Shake crème de menthe and cognac with ice cubes,

Strain into a chilled cocktail glass.

vanderbilt special

60 ml cognac
30 ml cherry brandy
Dash of Angostura bitters
1 tsp sugar
Lemon peel

Shake all the ingredients, except lemon peel, with ice cubes.

Strain into a chilled cocktail glass.

Garnish with lemon peel.

washington

45 ml brandy
30 ml dry vermouth
½ tsp sugar
Several dashes of Angostura bitters

Mix all ingredients with ice in a shaker or blender.

Strain into a chilled cocktail glass.

whitehall club

30 ml brandy
15 ml gin
15 ml Grand Marnier
4 tbsp orange juice
2 tbsp lemon juice
½ tsp sugar

Mix all ingredients in a shaker or blender.

Strain into an old-fashioned glass filled with crushed ice.

APERITIFS AND BITTERS

Aperitifs are usually drunk neat, without added liquor or mixers, since they are meant to whet the appetite before food is laid on the table. But aperitifs, vermouth in particular, also go into making some good cocktails.

achampanado

90 ml dry vermouth
½ tsp sugar
Juice of ¼ of a lemon
Club soda

Pour vermouth over ice cubes into a highball glass.

Add sugar and lemon juice. Stir till sugar dissolves.

Fill glass with club soda. Stir gently.

addington

60 ml dry vermouth
60 ml sweet vermouth
Club soda
Orange peel

Pour vermouths over several ice cubes into a highball glass. Stir.

Fill with club soda.

Twist orange peel over the drink and drop into the glass.

adonis

90 ml sherry
30 ml sweet vermouth
Dash of Angostura bitters
Orange peel

Mix sherry, vermouth and bitters with ice cubes in a mixing glass.

Strain into a chilled cocktail glass.

Twist orange peel over the drink and drop into the glass.

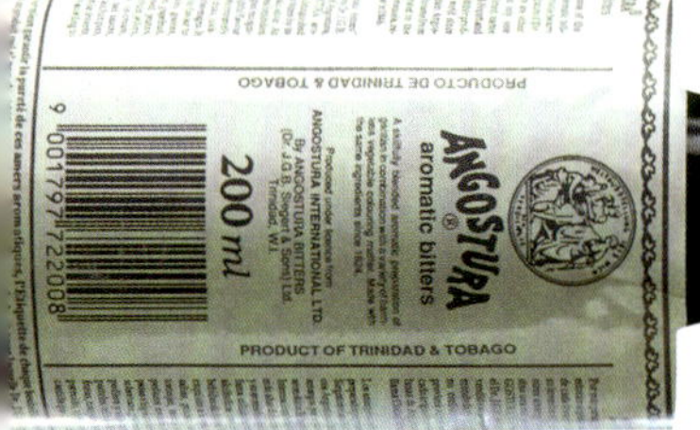

affinity

30 ml sweet vermouth
30 ml dry vermouth
30 ml Scotch whisky
Several dashes of Angostura bitters
Maraschino cherry

Stir vermouths, Scotch and bitters with ice cubes in a mixing glass.

Strain into a chilled cocktail glass.

Garnish with cherry.

americano

60 ml sweet vermouth
60 ml Campari
Club soda
Orange peel

Mix vermouth and Campari with ice cubes in a mixing glass.

Strain into an old-fashioned glass.

Add several ice cubes and club soda. Stir gently.

Twist orange peel over the drink and drop into the glass.

aquatini

60 ml aquavit
Dash of dry vermouth
Lemon peel

Mix aquavit and vermouth with ice cubes in a mixing glass.

Strain into a chilled cocktail glass.

Garnish with lemon peel.

aquavit fizz

75 ml aquavit
30 ml cherry brandy
½ tsp lemon juice
1 tsp sugar
Club soda
Maraschino cherry

Shake aquavit, cherry brandy, lemon juice and sugar with ice cubes.

Strain over ice into a highball glass.

Add club soda. Stir.

Add cherry.

aruba cooler

90 ml dry vermouth
45 ml Cointreau or triple sec
Club soda

Pour dry vermouth and Cointreau or triple sec over ice cubes into a highball glass.

Fill with club soda. Stir gently.

californian

4 tbsp orange juice
1 tsp sugar
60 ml sweet vermouth
30 ml Scotch whisky
Orange peel

Dip the rim of a chilled cocktail glass into orange juice.

Coat the rim with sugar placed on a board or plate.

Shake all ingredients, except orange peel, with ice cubes.

Strain into the cocktail glass.

Garnish with orange peel.

cardinal

30 ml gin
30 ml Campari
15 ml dry vermouth
Lemon peel

Stir gin, Campari and vermouth with ice cubes.

Strain into a chilled cocktail glass.

Twist lemon peel over the drink and drop into the glass.

combo

60 ml dry vermouth
30 ml Cointreau or triple sec
30 ml cognac
Several dashes of Angostura bitters
½ tsp sugar

Shake all ingredients with ice cubes.

Strain over ice cubes into an old-fashioned glass.

duplex

60 ml dry vermouth
60 ml sweet vermouth
Several dashes of Angostura bitters

Stir all ingredients with ice cubes in a mixing glass.

Strain into a chilled cocktail glass.

gin and campari

45 ml gin
45 ml Campari
Lemon or orange peel

Stir gin and Campari with ice cubes in a mixing glass.

Strain over ice cubes into an old-fashioned glass.

Twist lemon or orange peel over the drink and drop into the glass.

green room

60 ml dry vermouth
30 ml brandy
15 ml Cointreau or triple sec
Orange peel

Stir vermouth, brandy and Cointreau or triple sec with ice cubes in a mixing glass.

Strain into a chilled cocktail glass.

Twist orange peel over the drink and drop into the glass.

midnight sun

45 ml aquavit
1 tsp grapefruit juice
½ tsp lemon juice
1 tsp sugar
Dash of grenadine
Lemon slice

Shake all ingredients, except lemon slice, with ice cubes.

Strain into a chilled cocktail glass.

Add lemon slice.

negroni

25 ml Campari 25 ml gin 25 ml sweet vermouth	*Stir all ingredients with ice cubes in a mixing glass.* *Strain into a chilled cocktail glass.* *(It may also be served with ice cubes in an old-fashioned glass with a splash of club soda and a lemon slice.)*

punt e mes negroni

25 ml Punt e Mes 25 ml gin 25 ml sweet vermouth	*Stir all ingredients with ice cubes in a mixing glass.* *Strain into a chilled cocktail glass.* *(It may also be served with ice cubes in an old-fashioned glass with a splash of club soda and a lemon slice.)*

roman cooler

30 ml Punt e Mes 30 ml gin ½ tsp lemon juice 1 tsp sugar Club soda Lemon peel	*Shake all ingredients, except club soda and lemon peel, with ice cubes.* *Pour into a highball glass.* *Fill with soda.* *Twist lemon peel over the drink and drop into the glass.*

A man walks into a bar and orders a beer. He sips it and sets it down. A monkey swings across the bar and pisses in his glass.

The man asks the barman who owns the monkey.

The barman replies, 'The piano player.'

The man walks over to the piano player and says, 'Do you know your monkey pissed in my beer?'

The pianist relies, 'No, but if you hum it I can play it.'

southwest one

25 ml Campari
25 ml vodka
1½ tbsp lime juice
7 ml sugar syrup
7 ml grenadine

Shake all ingredients except grenadine with ice.

Strain into a chilled old-fashioned glass and top with grenadine.

trio

25 ml dry vermouth
25 ml sweet vermouth
25 ml gin

Stir all ingredients with ice cubes in a mixing glass.

Strain into a chilled cocktail glass.

vermouth cassis

90 ml dry vermouth
30 ml crème de cassis
Club soda

Mix vermouth and cassis with ice cubes in a highball glass.

Fill with club soda.

Stir gently.

vermouth cooler

60 ml sweet vermouth 30 ml vodka 1 tbsp lemon juice 1 tsp sugar Club soda Lemon slice	*Shake all ingredients, except club soda and lemon slice, with ice cubes.* *Strain over ice cubes into a highball glass.* *Fill with club soda. Stir gently.* *Add lemon slice.*

vermouth triple sec

30 ml dry vermouth 15 ml triple sec 30 ml gin Several dashes of Angostura bitters Lemon peel	*Shake all ingredients, except lemon peel, with ice cubes.* *Strain into a chilled cocktail glass.* *Twist lemon peel over the drink and drop into the glass.*

victor

45 ml sweet vermouth 30 ml brandy 30 ml gin Orange peel	*Mix all ingredients, except orange peel, with ice in a shaker or blender.* *Strain into a chilled cocktail glass.* *Twist orange peel over the drink and drop into the glass.*

wyoming swing

60 ml sweet vermouth 60 ml dry vermouth 4 tsp orange juice 1 tsp sugar Orange slice	*Mix all ingredients, except orange slice, with ice in a shaker or blender.* *Pour over ice cubes into a highball glass.* *Garnish with orange slice.*

yellow rattler

30 ml dry vermouth
30 ml sweet vermouth
30 ml gin
4–6 tbsp orange juice

Mix all ingredients with ice in a shaker or blender.

Strain into a chilled wine glass.

zanzibar

60 ml dry vermouth
30 ml gin
1 tsp lemon juice
1 tsp sugar
Several dashes of Angostura bitters
Lemon peel

Mix all ingredients, except lemon peel, with ice in a shaker or blender.

Strain into a chilled cocktail glass.

Twist lemon peel over the drink and drop into the glass.

zaza

60 ml Dubonnet (red)
30 ml gin
Orange slice

Stir Dubonnet and gin with ice cubes.

Strain over ice cubes into an old-fashioned glass.

Add orange slice.

FENI

Both coconut and cashew feni are quite versatile. They can be substituted for gin, vodka and white rum in just about any cocktail recipe. You can make a Cuba Libre by adding feni instead of rum (and call it Goa Libre for all I care!). Or perhaps a feni-and-tonic instead of the gin staple?

blue lagoon feni

60 ml cashew feni 30 ml blue curaçao Juice of 1 lemon Club soda Maraschino cherry	*Pour all ingredients, except club soda and cherry, into a highball glass.* *Add ice cubes and club soda to taste. Stir gently.* *Garnish with cherry.*

feni caipirinha

1 lemon Fresh mint leaves 1 tsp sugar 60 ml feni	*Cut lemon into eight equal pieces. Remove seeds.* *Muddle lemon pieces together with mint leaves and sugar in an old-fashioned glass.* *Fill glass with crushed ice.* *Pour feni and stir.*

feni cosmopolitan

60 ml cashew feni
30 ml Cointreau or triple sec
4 tbsp cranberry juice
Juice of 1 lemon
Lemon slice

Mix all ingredients, except lemon slice, with ice cubes in a shaker.

Strain into a chilled cocktail glass.

Add lemon slice.

feni mojito

Juice of 1 lemon
1 tsp sugar
Several fresh mint leaves
60 ml cashew feni
Club soda (optional)

Squeeze lemon juice into a chilled old-fashioned glass.

Add sugar and some mint leaves, and muddle till sugar is dissolved.

Fill glass with ice cubes and pour in the feni.

You may top off with club soda if you wish.

goa libre

60 ml coconut feni
Coca-Cola
Lemon wedge

Half-fill a chilled highball glass with ice cubes.

Add feni and fill with cola. Stir gently.

Squeeze lemon wedge over drink and drop into glass.

maheshwar margarita

This is the best feni cocktail I have come across, courtesy my friend Raja Richard Holkar. It is a variation of the Margarita in which you use feni instead of tequila. Everything else remains the same. I have named the cocktail after the Holkar fort on the banks of the Narmada, where I first tasted it.

60 ml cashew feni
30 ml Cointreau or triple sec
Juice of 1 lemon

Shake all ingredients with plenty of ice cubes.

Strain into a chilled cocktail glass rimmed with salt.

LIQUEURS

Liqueur cocktails tend to be on the sweeter side because the base ingredient, the liqueur, is sweet. You will find that many recipes call for the addition of a citrus juice. This gives the mixture a balanced, invigorating taste.

alfonso special

45 ml Grand Marnier
30 ml gin
1 tsp dry vermouth
1 tsp sweet vermouth
Several dashes of Angostura bitters

Mix all ingredients with ice in a shaker or blender.

Strain into a chilled cocktail glass.

amaretto and cream

45 ml amaretto
1 tsp cream

Shake amaretto and cream with ice cubes.

Strain into a chilled cocktail glass.

amaretto sour

45 ml amaretto
2 tsp lemon juice
Orange slice

Shake amaretto and lemon juice with ice cubes.

Strain into a chilled cocktail glass.

Add orange slice.

b-52

30 ml Grand Marnier
25 ml Tia Maria or Kahlúa
1 tbsp lemon juice
4 tbsp orange juice

Mix all ingredients with ice in a shaker or blender.

Strain into a chilled cocktail glass.

b & b collins

60 ml cognac
30 ml Bénédictine
1 tbsp lemon juice
1 tsp sugar
Club soda
Lemon slice

Shake cognac, lemon juice and sugar with ice cubes.

Strain into a highball glass half-filled with ice.

Add soda. Stir.

Float Bénédictine on drink.

Add lemon slice.

barracuda

30 ml Bénédictine
30 ml gin
4 tbsp grapefruit juice

Mix all ingredients with ice in a shaker or blender.

Strain into a chilled cocktail glass.

bee sting

30 ml Bénédictine
30 ml bourbon
1 tbsp lemon juice
4 tbsp orange juice

Mix all ingredients with ice in a shaker or blender.

Strain into a chilled cocktail glass.

beverly's hills

45 ml Cointreau or triple sec
15 ml cognac
15 ml Tia Maria or Kahlúa

Mix all ingredients with ice in a shaker or blender.

Strain into a chilled cocktail glass.

boccie ball

45 ml amaretto
3 tbsp orange juice
Club soda

Pour all ingredients into a highball glass over ice cubes.

Stir gently.

bulldog

45 ml cherry brandy
15 ml gin
Juice of ½ a lemon

Shake all ingredients with ice cubes.

Strain into a chilled cocktail glass.

café romano

30 ml Sambuca
30 ml Tia Maria or Kahlúa
1 tbsp cream

Mix all ingredients with ice in a shaker or blender.

Strain into a chilled cocktail glass.

canyon quake

25 ml Baileys Irish Cream 25 ml brandy 30 ml amaretto 4 tbsp light cream	*Combine all ingredients with ice in a blender.* *Blend till smooth.* *Pour into a chilled cocktail glass.*

caribbean jewel

60 ml Malibu 30 ml strawberry liqueur 90 ml pineapple juice 60 ml lychee juice Strawberry slice	*Fill a shaker with ice cubes. Add all ingredients, except strawberry slice, and shake hard.* *Strain into a highball glass over ice cubes.* *Garnish with strawberry slice.*

carthusian cooler

30 ml Chartreuse (yellow) 30 ml bourbon Club soda	*Put ice cubes in a highball glass.* *Add Chartreuse and bourbon.* *Fill with soda. Stir gently.*

chartreuse cognac frappé

25 ml Chartreuse (yellow) 25 ml cognac	*Stir Chartreuse and cognac in a mixing glass.* *Pour over ice cubes into a wine glass.*

chartreuse cooler

45 ml Chartreuse (yellow) 120 ml orange juice 1 tbsp lemon juice Seven Up Orange slice	*Mix all ingredients, except Seven Up and orange slice, with ice in a shaker or blender.* *Pour into a highball glass.* *Fill with Seven Up. Stir gently.* *Add orange slice.*

cherry daiquiri

30 ml cherry brandy
30 ml light rum
Juice of ½ a lemon

Mix all ingredients with ice in a shaker or blender.

Strain into a chilled cocktail glass.

cherry fizz

60 ml cherry brandy
Juice of ½ a lemon
Club soda
Maraschino cherry

Shake cherry brandy and lemon juice with ice cubes.

Strain into a highball glass with two ice cubes.

Fill with club soda.

Add cherry.

cherry gilroy

15 ml cherry brandy
10 ml gin
Juice of ½ a lemon
15 ml dry vermouth
Dash of Angostura bitters

Shake all ingredients with ice cubes.

Strain into a chilled cocktail glass.

cherry sour

45 ml cherry brandy
25 ml gin
Juice of ½ a lemon

Mix all ingredients with ice in a shaker or blender.

Strain into a chilled cocktail glass.

chinchilla

30 ml Bénédictine
30 ml Cointreau or triple sec
1 tbsp light cream
Orange slice

Mix all ingredients, except orange slice, with ice in a shaker or blender.

Strain into a chilled cocktail glass.

Garnish with orange slice.

cholula

30 ml Bénédictine
15 ml Tia Maria or Kahlúa
1½ tbsp cream

Mix all ingredients with ice in a shaker or blender.

Strain into a chilled cocktail glass.

coffee grand marnier

15 ml Tia Maria or Kahlúa
15 ml Grand Marnier
1 tbsp orange juice
Orange slice

Stir all ingredients, except orange slice, without ice.

Pour over ice cubes into a large wine glass.

Add orange slice.

connoisseur's treat

60 ml cognac
30 ml Grand Marnier
30 ml Galliano

Stir all ingredients in a mixing glass with ice cubes.

Strain into a chilled cocktail glass.

cranberry delight

30 ml Malibu
6 tbsp cranberry juice
Lemon slice

Pour Malibu and cranberry juice into an old-fashioned glass filled with ice cubes.

Garnish with lemon slice.

curaçao cool

45 ml blue curaçao
30 ml light rum
150 ml orange juice
2 tbsp lemon juice
Orange peel

Mix all ingredients, except orange peel, with ice in a shaker or blender.

Pour into a highball glass filled with ice.

Twist orange peel over the drink and drop into the glass.

dorchester night cap

30 ml Galliano
30 ml cognac
15 ml crème de menthe (white)

Stir all ingredients in a mixing glass with ice cubes.

Strain into a chilled brandy snifter filled with several ice cubes.

espress yourself

30 ml Tia Maria or Kahlúa
30 ml Baileys Irish Cream
10 ml hazelnut liqueur
10 ml light rum
30 ml espresso coffee

Shake all ingredients with ice cubes.

Strain into a cocktail glass.

ferrari

60 ml sweet vermouth
30 ml amaretto
Lemon peel

Pour vermouth and amaretto over ice cubes into an old-fashioned glass. Stir.

Add lemon peel.

foreign affair

30 ml Sambuca
30 ml cognac
Lemon peel

Mix all ingredients, except lemon peel, with ice in a shaker or blender.

Strain into a chilled cocktail glass.

Twist lemon peel over the drink and drop into the glass.

frisco

45 ml Bénédictine
45 ml bourbon
Lemon peel

Stir Bénédictine and bourbon with ice cubes.

Strain into a chilled cocktail glass.

Twist lemon peel over the drink and drop into the glass.

golden dragon

45 ml Chartreuse (yellow)
45 ml cognac
Lemon peel

Stir Chartreuse and cognac with ice cubes in a mixing glass.

Strain into a chilled cocktail glass.

Twist lemon peel over the drink and drop into the glass.

grand hotel

45 ml Grand Marnier
45 ml gin
15 ml dry vermouth
Dash of lemon juice
Lemon peel

Mix all ingredients, except lemon peel, with ice in a shaker or blender.

Strain into a chilled cocktail glass.

Twist lemon peel over the drink and drop into the glass.

grasshopper

25 ml crème de menthe (green)
25 ml crème de cacao (white)
1½ tbsp light cream

Shake all ingredients with ice cubes.

Strain into a chilled cocktail glass.

hand glider

45 ml gin
25 ml cherry brandy
Coca-Cola
Lemon slice

Pour gin and cherry brandy into a highball glass filled with several ice cubes.

Fill with cola. Stir gently.

Add lemon slice.

ixtapa

45 ml Tia Maria or Kahlúa
15 ml tequila

Stir both ingredients in a mixing glass with ice cubes

Strain into a chilled cocktail glass.

jezebel

25 ml Tia Maria
Club soda
10 ml grenadine
Lemon slice

Fill a highball glass with ice cubes.

Pour Tia Maria and club soda over the cubes.

Add grenadine.

Gently squeeze lemon slice over the drink and drop it in.

kamikaze

30 ml Cointreau or triple sec
30 ml vodka
2 tbsp lemon juice

Mix all ingredients with ice cubes.

Strain into a chilled cocktail glass.

kowloon

30 ml Grand Marnier
30 ml Tia Maria or Kahlúa
4–6 tbsp orange juice
Orange slice

Combine all ingredients, except orange slice, in a mixing glass. Stir well.

Pour into a chilled wine glass with plenty of ice cubes.

Garnish with orange slice.

kremlin

30 ml Tia Maria or Kahlúa
30 ml vodka
2 tbsp cream

Mix all ingredients with ice in a blender for a few seconds till smooth.

Pour into a chilled cocktail glass.

las hadas

30 ml Sambuca
30 ml Tia Maria or Kahlúa
Several freshly roasted coffee beans

Stir both liqueurs in a mixing glass with ice cubes.

Pour into a chilled wine goblet. Add additional ice if necessary.

Float coffee beans on top of drink.

(If the coffee beans are freshly roasted they will give a wonderful aroma.)

malibu and pineapple

30 ml Malibu
6 tbsp pineapple juice
Lemon slice

Pour Malibu and pineapple juice into an old-fashioned glass filled with ice cubes.

Garnish with lemon slice.

mandarin

30 ml Grand Marnier
15 ml cherry brandy
4 tbsp orange juice
2 tbsp lemon juice

Mix all ingredients with ice in a shaker or blender.

Strain into a chilled cocktail glass.

martinique

30 ml Bénédictine
30 ml light rum
120 ml pineapple juice

Mix all ingredients with ice in a shaker or blender.

Pour over ice cubes into a chilled highball glass.

mcclelland

60 ml gin
30 ml Cointreau or triple sec
Several dashes of Angostura bitters

Mix all ingredients with ice in a shaker or blender.

Strain into a chilled cocktail glass.

milano

30 ml gin
30 ml Galliano
Juice of ½ a lemon
Maraschino cherry

Shake all the ingredients, except cherry, with ice cubes.
Strain into a chilled cocktail glass.
Add cherry.

mint highball

60 ml crème de menthe (green)
Ginger ale or club soda
Lemon peel

Pour crème de menthe over ice cubes into a highball glass.
Fill with ginger ale or club soda.
Add lemon peel. Stir.

mixed mocha frappé

25 ml Tia Maria or Kahlúa
10 ml crème de menthe (white)
10 ml crème de cacao (white)
10 ml Cointreau or triple sec

Stir all ingredients without ice.
Pour over ice cubes into a large wine goblet.

montego mocha

30 ml Tia Maria or Kahlúa
10 ml Malibu
Black coffee
Whipped, thick cream

Pour Tia Maria or Kahlúa and rum in a glass with ice cubes.
Fill with coffee.
Top with cream.

peugeot

45 ml Cointreau or triple sec
25 ml calvados
4 tbsp orange juice

Mix all ingredients with ice in a shaker or blender.

Strain into a chilled cocktail glass.

pick-me-up

30 ml dry vermouth
30 ml cherry brandy
30 ml gin

Pour all ingredients into a highball glass filled with crushed ice. Stir.

pimlico

45 ml brandy
15 ml amaretto
15 ml crème de cacao (white)

Mix all ingredients with ice in a shaker or blender.

Strain into a chilled cocktail glass.

queen elizabeth

45 ml Bénédictine
25 ml dry vermouth
1½ tbsp lemon juice

Mix all ingredients with ice in a shaker or blender.

Strain into a chilled cocktail glass.

road runner

30 ml vodka
15 ml amaretto
1 tbsp coconut cream
Orange slice
Powdered sugar
Powdered nutmeg

Combine vodka, amaretto and coconut cream with ice in a shaker or blender.

Rub edge of a chilled cocktail glass with orange slice.

Dip edge in a sugar and nutmeg mixture.

Pour cocktail into the glass.

Sprinkle lightly with nutmeg.

rolls royce

30 ml Cointreau or triple sec
30 ml cognac
2 tbsp orange juice

Mix all ingredients with ice in a shaker or blender.

Strain into a chilled cocktail glass.

sambuca coffee frappé

30 ml Sambuca
15 ml Tia Maria or Kahlúa
Freshly roasted coffee beans

Stir liqueurs without ice.

Pour over crushed ice into a large wine glass.

Place the glass on a saucer along with six coffee beans to munch while sipping.

smitten

30 ml Tia Maria or Kahlúa
30 ml light rum
6 tbsp pineapple juice
1 tbsp coconut cream
5 fresh strawberries
Freshly squeezed juice of ½ a lemon
Strawberry slice
Lemon slice

Mix all ingredients, except strawberry and lemon slices, in a blender with ice.

Pour into a tall glass.

Garnish with strawberry and lime slices.

sombrero

45 ml Tia Maria or Kahlúa
2 tbsp cream

Pour liqueur over several ice cubes into an old-fashioned glass.

Carefully pour cream over the back of a spoon so that it floats.

30 ml Bénédictine
30 ml gin
120 ml orange juice

Mix all ingredients with ice in a shaker or blender.

Pour over ice cubes into an old-fashioned glass.

sunburn

30 ml cognac
30 ml Tia Maria or Kahlúa
2 tsp orange juice
2 tsp lemon juice
Orange slice

Shake all the ingredients, except orange slice, with ice cubes.

Strain into a chilled cocktail glass.

Add orange slice.

sundowner

30 ml Bénédictine
30 ml light or golden rum
120 ml orange juice

Mix all ingredients with ice in a shaker or blender.

Pour over ice cubes into a highball glass.

vanderbilt

10 ml cherry brandy
45 ml brandy
1 tsp sugar
Several dashes of Angostura bitters

Stir all ingredients with ice cubes.

Strain into a chilled cocktail glass.

via veneto

50 ml brandy
15 ml Sambuca
2 tsp lemon juice
1 tsp sugar

Shake all ingredients with ice cubes.

Pour over crushed ice into an old-fashioned glass.

widow's kiss

30 ml brandy
15 ml Chartreuse (yellow)
15 ml Bénédictine
Dash of Angostura bitters

Stir all ingredients with ice cubes.

Strain into a chilled cocktail glass.

JACOB'S CREEK
RESERVE
Shiraz
SEAGRAM'S
nine hills
shiraz
nashik valley vintage 2007
red wine
JACOB'S CREEK
RESERVE
Chardonnay
CHAMPAGNE
G.H. MUMM
MAISON FONDÉE EN 1827
A REIMS-FRANCE
Brut
MUMM
JACOB'S CREEK
SHIRAZ CABERNET
Named after Jacob's Creek, site of Johann Gramp's first vineyard in the Barossa Valley
JACOB'S CREEK
CHARDONNAY

WINE, CHAMPAGNE, PORT AND SHERRY

wine

Wine cocktails are recommended for those who like their cocktails on the lighter side.

american dream

1 glass red wine
15 ml bourbon
10 ml sweet vermouth
Club soda
Maraschino cherry

Half-fill a highball glass with ice cubes.

Pour in wine, bourbon and vermouth.

Top with club soda. Stir.

Add cherry.

bishop

1 tsp lemon juice
1 tsp orange juice
1 tsp sugar
1 glass red wine
Maraschino cherry

Shake lemon juice, orange juice and sugar with ice cubes.

Strain into a highball glass.

Add two ice cubes.

Fill with wine. Stir.

Add cherry.

cocomacoque

45 ml light rum	*Shake all ingredients, except wine.*
Juice of ½ a lemon	*Pour into a large wine glass over ice cubes.*
4 tbsp pineapple juice	*Top with wine.*
4 tbsp orange juice	
60 ml red wine	

crimean cocktail

1 glass dry white wine	*Stir wine, Cointreau or triple sec and lemon rind with ice cubes.*
1 tsp Cointreau or triple sec	*Pour into an old-fashioned glass.*
Grated rind of 1 lemon	*Fill with cold club soda. Stir.*
Club soda, cold	*Add lemon slice.*
Lemon slice	

hillary wallbanger

1 glass dry white wine	*Half-fill a highball glass with ice cubes.*
15 ml Galliano	*Pour in wine, Galliano and orange juice. Stir.*
4 tbsp orange juice	

little bishop

4 tbsp orange juice	*Mix orange juice, lemon juice and sugar with ice in a shaker or blender.*
2 tbsp lemon juice	*Pour into a highball glass.*
1 tsp sugar	*Add ice cubes.*
1 glass dry red wine	*Fill with wine.*
15 ml dark rum	*Top with a float of rum.*
Orange slice	*Add orange slice.*

sangria

Fruity and fizzy, and perfect for cooling off on a particularly sweltering summer day, Sangria is what the Americans call a pitcher drink. You cannot make just a glass of it; it has to be made in jugfuls.

From its humble roots in Spain the Sangria has travelled the world. It takes its name from the Spanish word *sangre*, meaning blood, which here refers to the colour since the drink is made with red wine. You can also use white wine if that is what you prefer. The drink will then be known as Sangria Blanco, and of course there is a sparkling wine or champagne version.

There is no hard and fast rule for making a Sangria; one of its attractions is its flexibility. It works well as a light thirst quencher, but some people like it as a potent cocktail that can set heads spinning. In southern Spain the drink is known as Zurra and is made with local peaches. The Spanish usually serve it without ice and prefer to make it with a very dry red wine. Adding ice is an American habit and I am all for it. You can use any seasonal fruit that tempts you. Let your imagination be your guide. But ensure that the fruits are firm. Use vodka or white rum if you don't have brandy in the house.

Just a few pointers: Don't use any wine you wouldn't normally drink. Never buy a pre-mixed bottle of Sangria. You will certainly regret it. And don't order it in a restaurant if all the bartender does is add some fruit and liquor to wine. Sangria turns out best when the mixture is left overnight in the refrigerator to marinate.

1 bottle red wine

Sugar to taste

1 whole orange, peeled and sliced into thin rounds

1 fresh peach, peeled, pitted and sliced thin

2 lemons with the peel, thinly sliced

4 tbsp brandy

4 tbsp Cointreau or triple sec

1 quarter of a 750 ml bottle of club soda

Pour wine into a large jug.

Add sugar and stir till it dissolves.

Add the fruit slices and liquor.

Let the mixture marinate in the refrigerator, preferably overnight or for at least four hours.

Pour club soda in large wine glasses half-filled with ice.

Add the Sangria together with the slices of fruit. Stir gently.

kir

1 glass dry white wine	*Chill cassis and wine.*
15 ml crème de cassis	*Mix together in a chilled wine glass.*

operator

1 glass dry white wine	*Half-fill an old-fashioned glass with ice cubes.*
3 tsp sparkling ginger ale	*Add all ingredients, except lemon slice. Stir.*
1 tsp lemon juice	*Garnish with lemon slice.*
Lemon slice	

quick thrill

90 ml red wine	*Put some ice cubes in a large wine glass.*
15 ml dark rum	*Pour in wine and rum. Stir.*
90 ml Coca-Cola or Pepsi	*Top with cola.*

sonoma cup

1 glass dry white wine	*Mix all ingredients, except club soda with ice in a shaker or blender.*
15 ml Cointreau	*Pour into a highball glass.*
6 tbsp orange juice	*Fill with cold club soda. Stir gently.*
Club soda, cold	*Add more ice if required.*

wine spritzer

1 glass dry white wine	*Pour wine into a wine goblet or highball glass with several ice cubes.*
Club soda, cold	*Fill with cold club soda.*
Lemon peel	*Twist lemon peel over the drink and drop into the glass.*

champagne

Diehard champagne enthusiasts consider it sacrilegious to add anything to it. They do have a point. I would use any good sparkling wine instead of champagne for cocktails. On the other hand, a dash of crème de cassis in a glass of champagne is a delightful and very popular French cocktail.

american flyer

45 ml light rum
2 tsp lemon juice
½ tsp sugar
1 glass champagne, cold

Mix all ingredients, except champagne, with ice in a shaker or blender.

Strain into a chilled wine goblet.

Fill with cold champagne.

americana

30 ml bourbon
½ tsp sugar
Dash of Angostura bitters
1 glass champagne, cold
Peach slice, fresh or canned

Stir bourbon, sugar and bitters in a chilled champagne glass.

Add cold champagne and peach slice.

black velvet

½ pint Guinness beer
½ pint champagne

Chill beer and champagne.

Pour carefully into a chilled highball glass.

Stir very gently without losing the fizz.

caribbean champagne

30 ml light rum 15 ml banana liqueur	*Pour rum, banana liqueur and bitters into a chilled champagne flute.*
Dash of Angostura bitters 1 glass champagne, cold	*Add cold champagne. Stir very gently without losing the fizz.*
Half a banana slice	*Add banana slice.*

champagne blues

1 glass champagne	*Chill champagne and curaçao.*
30 ml blue curaçao	*Pour champagne into a chilled champagne flute.*
Lemon peel	*Add curaçao. Stir gently without losing the fizz.*
	Twist lemon peel over the drink and drop into the glass.

bellini

The Bellini was created in Harry's Bar in Venice in 1948. The drink is named after the Venetian Renaissance painter Giovanni Bellini.

The Bellini at Harry's Bar is a mixture of prosecco, a sparkling wine from around Venice, and the juice of fresh white peaches which grow in abundance throughout Italy from June till September. Outside Italy most bartenders use champagne for their Bellinis and are not fussy about the colour of the peaches. But there is nothing as divine as the Mango Bellini, made from alphonso mangoes. It has become popular in upscale Indian restaurants in London.

classic bellini

1 fresh peach	*Peel the peach and purée it in a blender or food processor.*
1 tsp sugar	*Strain peach juice into a chilled champagne flute.*
1 glass champagne, cold	*Add sugar and mix till it dissolves.*
	Pour in cold champagne. Stir gently without losing the fizz.

mango bellini

1 alphonso mango, sliced	*Purée the mango in a blender until it is a smooth paste.*
1 glass champagne or any good sparkling wine, chilled	*Strain into a chilled champagne flute or a wine glass. The straining should separate the pulp from the juice.*
	Slowly add cold champagne. The glass should be one-third filled with mango juice and two-third with champagne. Stir gently.

champagne cocktail

1 sugar cube
Several dashes of Angostura bitters
1 glass champagne, cold
1 strawberry (optional)

Put sugar cube in a chilled champagne flute. Saturate it with bitters.

Fill with cold champagne. Stir gently without losing the fizz.

Add a strawberry as garnish.

champagne cup

15 ml cognac
15 ml Cointreau or triple sec
1 glass champagne, cold
Orange slice
Fresh mint leaves

Pour cognac and Cointreau or triple sec into a chilled large wine goblet.

Add a cube of ice.

Fill with cold champagne. Stir gently without losing the fizz.

Add orange slice and some mint leaves.

champagne manhattan

30 ml Scotch whisky or bourbon
10 ml sweet vermouth
Dash of Angostura bitters
1 glass champagne, cold
Maraschino cherry

Stir whisky, vermouth and bitters with ice in a mixing glass.

Strain into a chilled champagne glass.

Add cold champagne and cherry. Stir very gently without losing the fizz.

champagne normande

1 glass champagne, cold
30 ml calvados
½ tsp sugar
Dash of Angostura bitters

Pour calvados, sugar and bitters into a glass of cold champagne. Stir very gently without losing the fizz.

chapultepec

30 ml light rum
25 ml apricot liqueur
4 tbsp orange juice
1 tbsp lemon juice
Dash of grenadine
1 glass champagne, cold
Orange slice

Mix all ingredients, except champagne and orange slice, with ice in a shaker or blender.

Pour into a chilled champagne glass.

Pour cold champagne. Stir gently without losing the fizz.

Add orange slice.

chartreuse champagne

1 glass champagne, cold
15 ml Chartreuse (green)
15 ml cognac
Lemon peel

Pour Chartreuse, cognac and cold champagne into a champagne glass. Stir very gently without losing the fizz.

Twist lemon peel over the drink and drop into the glass.

cherry champagne

15 ml cherry brandy
1 glass champagne, cold
Maraschino cherry

Pour chilled cherry brandy into a chilled champagne glass.

Add cold champagne and cherry. Stir very gently without losing the fizz.

french 75

45 ml cognac
2 tbsp lemon juice
1 tsp sugar
1 glass champagne, cold

Shake cognac, lemon juice and sugar with ice cubes.

Strain into a highball glass with two large ice cubes.

Fill to the rim with cold champagne. Stir very gently without losing the fizz.

kir royale

1 glass champagne
15 ml crème de cassis

Mix cassis and cold champagne gently in a chilled champagne tulip glass.

This one is for you if you are put off by champagne's acidity and prefer something sweeter.

maharajah's burra-peg

1 sugar cube
Several dashes of Angostura bitters
30 ml cognac, chilled
1 glass champagne, cold

Saturate sugar cube with bitters.

Put into a chilled brandy snifter.

Add chilled cognac.

Fill with cold champagne. Stir gently without losing the fizz.

mimosa

1 glass champagne, cold
6 tbsp orange juice, cold
Several dashes of Grand Marnier or Cointreau (optional)
Orange slice

Pour cold champagne and cold orange juice into a champagne flute.

Add Grand Marnier or Cointreau.

Garnish with orange slice.

night and day

1 sugar cube
10 ml cognac
15 ml Cointreau or triple sec
10 ml Campari
1 glass champagne, cold

Place the sugar cube in a chilled champagne flute.

Pour in splashes of cognac, Cointreau and Campari.

Add cold champagne.

orange champagne

Peel of ½ an orange, in one spiral

1 tsp Cointreau or triple sec

1 glass champagne, cold

Place orange peel in chilled champagne glass.

Add Cointreau and cold champagne. Stir very gently without losing the fizz.

pushkin's punch

30 ml vodka

30 ml Grand Marnier

Dash of lemon juice

Dash of Angostura bitters

1 glass champagne, cold

Mix all ingredients, except champagne, with ice in a shaker or blender.

Strain into a large chilled wine goblet.

Fill with cold champagne. Stir gently without losing the fizz.

sparkling galliano

15 ml Galliano

½ tsp lemon juice

1 glass champagne, cold

2" long cucumber peel

Pour Galliano and lemon juice into a chilled champagne glass. Stir.

Add cold champagne and cucumber peel.

Stir again very gently without losing the fizz.

port

More often than not, cognac or some other brandy is added to port to make a cocktail that gives the famous Portuguese export an extra kick.

any port in a storm

90 ml port
30 ml cognac
2 tbsp lemon juice
Club soda

Mix port, cognac and lemon juice with ice in a shaker or blender.

Pour into a highball glass.

Add additional ice if necessary.

Fill with club soda. Stir gently.

60 ml port
30 ml sweet vermouth
1 tbsp lemon juice

Shake port, vermouth and lemon juice with ice.

Strain into a chilled cocktail glass.

montana

45 ml port
45 ml brandy
15 ml dry vermouth

Stir all ingredients in an old-fashioned glass filled with ice cubes.

port cobbler

120 ml port
25 ml cognac
½ tsp sugar
Lemon peel
Orange peel
Fresh mint leaves

Fill a highball glass with finely cracked ice.

Add port, brandy and sugar. Stir well.

Add more ice to fill glass to rim. Stir.

Twist lemon peel and orange peel over the drink and drop into the glass.

Tear some mint leaves partially and drop into the glass.

sherry

Sherry cocktails are a little stronger than wine cocktails and yet lighter than the cocktails made with spirits.

adonis

60 ml dry sherry

30 ml sweet vermouth

Several dashes of Angostura bitters

Stir sherry, vermouth and bitters with ice in a mixing glass.

Strain into a chilled cocktail glass.

andalusia

60 ml dry sherry

15 ml cognac or Spanish brandy

75 ml light rum

Stir all ingredients with ice cubes.

Strain into a chilled cocktail glass.

bamboo

60 ml sherry

30 ml dry vermouth

Dash of Angostura bitters

Lemon peel

Add ice cubes to a mixing glass.

Pour in sherry and vermouth.

Add bitters. Stir.

Strain into a chilled cocktail glass.

Add lemon peel.

creamy orange

60 ml cream sherry

2 tbsp orange juice

1 tbsp cream

2 tsp cognac or Spanish brandy

Shake all ingredients well with ice cubes.

Strain into a chilled cocktail glass.

granada

30 ml dry sherry
30 ml brandy
15 ml Cointreau or triple sec
Tonic water
Orange slice

Shake sherry, brandy and Cointreau or triple sec with ice cubes.

Pour into a highball glass.

Add ice cubes and tonic water. Stir.

Add orange slice.

mai maison

30 ml cream sherry
Juice of ½ a lemon
30 ml light rum

Shake all ingredients with ice cubes.

Strain into a chilled cocktail glass.

ozone

75 ml dry sherry
10 ml Scotch whisky
30 ml Campari
2 tbsp pineapple juice
1 tsp lemon juice
1 tsp grenadine

Mix all ingredients with ice in a shaker or blender.

Strain into a chilled cocktail glass.

screwdriver with sherry

60 ml sherry ½ cup orange juice 30 ml vodka	*Shake all ingredients with ½ cup crushed ice.* *Pour into an old-fashioned glass.* *Add more ice cubes if required.*

sherry and rum

30 ml cream sherry 45 ml light rum Maraschino cherry	*Stir sherry and rum with ice cubes.* *Strain into a chilled cocktail glass.* *Add cherry.*

sherry cobbler

75 ml sherry 30 ml cognac or Spanish brandy 1 tbsp orange juice ½ tsp sugar Orange slice	*Fill a highball glass with finely cracked ice.* *Add sherry, cognac, orange juice and sugar.* *Stir till sugar dissolves.* *Add more ice to fill glass to the rim. Stir.* *Add orange slice.*

sherry martini

60 ml gin 15 ml dry sherry Olive or lemon peel	*Stir gin and sherry with ice cubes.* *Strain into a chilled cocktail glass.* *Add olive or lemon peel.*

OTHER MIXED DRINKS

frozen cocktails

Serious drinkers have a problem with frozen cocktails. They consider them to be more desserts than booze. But I can assure you that you will find these summertime quaffs refreshingly frosty. In old times bartenders hated making frozen drinks because preparing and serving them was time consuming. Now technology has made the job easier. All a bartender has to do is to pull a handle on a fancy machine and out come frozen Margaritas, Daiquiris or Piña Coladas. Frozen cocktails should always be served in a deep-saucer champagne glass, if you have one, or in a wine glass, and they are best sipped slowly. Making frozen drinks at home can be tricky. Unless you have a very sturdy blender, I suggest you use crushed ice instead of ice cubes. Sometimes you may need a little more ice than a recipe specifies and it may take you a few tries before you get it right.

blizzard

30 ml brandy
30 ml Baileys Irish Cream
30 ml Tia Maria or Kahlúa
30 ml light rum
2 scoops vanilla ice cream
A splash of light cream
Powdered nutmeg

Combine all ingredients, except nutmeg, in a blender with a cup of crushed ice.

Blend till smooth.

Pour into a wine glass.

Sprinkle lightly with nutmeg.

frozen banana daiquiri

1 ripe banana
60 ml light rum
Juice of 1 lemon

Slice the banana into 1" pieces.

Combine all ingredients in a blender with a cup of crushed ice.

Blend till smooth and slushy.

Pour into a wine glass.

frozen daiquiri

60 ml light rum	*Combine all ingredients, except lemon wedge, with a cup of crushed ice in a blender.*
30 ml Cointreau or triple sec	*Blend till smooth and firm.*
3 tbsp lemon juice	*Pour into a chilled wine glass.*
1 tsp sugar	*Garnish with lemon wedge.*
Lemon wedge	

frozen guava daiquiri

60 ml light rum	*Put all ingredients into a blender.*
4 tbsp guava juice	*Blend for 10 to 15 seconds at low speed along with a cup of crushed ice.*
2 tbsp lemon juice	*Pour into a chilled wine glass.*

frozen margarita

½ lemon	*Rub lemon on the rim of a wine glass.*
Salt	*Dip the rim in a saucer of salt till it is well covered.*
45 ml tequila	*Combine ingredients with a cup of crushed ice in blender. Blend at low speed for 5 seconds. Then blend at high speed till firm.*
15 ml Cointreau or triple sec	*Pour into a wine glass.*
2 tbsp lemon juice	

frozen matador

45 ml tequila	*Combine all ingredients with a cup of crushed ice in a blender.*
4 tbsp pineapple juice	*Blend at low speed.*
1 tsp lemon juice	*Pour into a wine glass.*

frozen mint daiquiri

60 ml light rum
1 tsp lemon juice
Fresh mint leaves
1 tsp sugar

Combine all ingredients with a cup of crushed ice in a blender.

Blend at low speed.

Pour into a wine glass.

frozen peach daiquiri

60 ml light rum
1 tbsp lemon juice
¼ cup canned, sliced peaches

Put all ingredients into blender along with a cup of crushed ice.

Blend at low speed for 10 to 15 seconds.

Pour into a chilled wine glass.

frozen piña colada

60 ml light rum
4 tbsp cream of coconut
4 tbsp pineapple juice
Maraschino cherry

Put all ingredients, except cherry, in a blender with a cup of crushed ice.

Blend till smooth.

Pour into a wine glass.

Garnish with cherry.

frozen pineapple daiquiri

60 ml light rum
1 tbsp lemon juice
½ tsp sugar
4 canned pineapple chunks, drained

Put all ingredients into blender along with a cup of crushed ice.

Blend at low speed for 10 to 15 seconds.

Pour into a wine glass.

hot cocktails

While making hot cocktails take care not to boil the alcohol, otherwise it will evaporate. Hot drinks must always be served in sturdy glasses which have been freshly rinsed in hot water. When pouring into a glass it is advisable to put a spoon in it first to prevent the glass from cracking. Some people prefer to use mugs instead of glasses because they retain the heat better.

aberdeen angus

1 tsp lemon juice
1 tsp honey
Boiling water
60 ml Scotch whisky
30 ml Drambuie

Put lemon juice and honey into a heatproof mug.

Add a little boiling water. Stir till honey dissolves.

Add whisky.

Warm Drambuie in a small ladle.

Ignite. Pour into the mug while it's blazing.

Fill the mug with boiling water. Stir.

black striple

2 tsp honey
Boiling water
Lemon peel
Cinnamon stick
90 ml dark rum
Powdered nutmeg

Dissolve honey in a heatproof mug with a little boiling water.

Add lemon peel and cinnamon stick and more boiling water.

Float rum on top and blaze for a few seconds, if you wish.

Stir to extinguish flames.

Top with a sprinkling of nutmeg.

blue blazer

2 tsp honey
¼ cup boiling water
180 ml Scotch whisky
Lemon peel

Rinse 2 large mugs with boiling water.

Pour honey and ¼ cup boiling water into a mug. Stir till honey dissolves.

Heat whisky in a pan, till hot but not boiling.

Pour into second mug. Ignite it. (The flowing blue-flaming stream will be best appreciated in a dimly lit room.)

Pour the whisky, carefully, back and forth between the mugs.

When flames subside, pour the blazer into two thick glass goblets.

Twist lemon peel over the blazer and drop it into the drink.

(Only professionals should try this. Some bartenders wear fire-proof gloves when making a blue blazer.)

brandy blazer

½ orange
1 lemon
60 ml cognac
1 sugar cube
30 ml Tia Maria or Kahlúa
Maraschino cherry

Cut out the peel from the orange and lemon, removing and discarding the white bits as much as possible.

Put the cognac, sugar cube, orange and lemon peel in a small pan.

Heat gently without boiling.

Remove from heat, light a match and pass the flame close to the surface of the liquid. The alcohol will burn with a low, blue flame for about a minute.

Blow out the flame.

Add Tia Maria or Kahlúa.

Strain into a heat-resistant glass.

Add cherry.

café diable

2 cups black coffee
2 cinnamon sticks
8 whole cloves
Seeds of 4 green cardamoms
Grated rind of ½ an orange or lemon
90 ml Grand Marnier
60 ml Sambuca
150 ml cognac
2 tsp sugar

Simmer ½ cup of coffee, cinnamon, cloves, cardamom and orange or lemon rind for 2 to 3 minutes to release flavours, stirring constantly.

Add cognac, Grand Marnier and Sambuca.

When hot, ignite. Stir with a long-handled spoon till flames subside.

Add the remaining coffee and sugar.

Ladle into small coffee cups.

café di amaretto

30 ml amaretto
1 cup black coffee
Heavy cream

Add amaretto to a mug of hot black coffee. Stir.

Top with cream. Do not stir.

Sip through the cream.

english christmas hot punch

2 bottles red wine
Juice of 1 orange
Juice of 1 lemon
½ cup sugar
½ bottle dark rum
Orange and lemon slices

Heat wine and fruit juices in a pan, without allowing them to boil. Simmer for about 5 minutes.

Add sugar. Stir till it dissolves.

Transfer to a punch bowl.

Using the same pot, heat about a quarter of the rum till it starts seething. Do not boil. Ignite.

Pour the flaming rum into the punch bowl.

Add the rest of the rum. Stir.

Throw in some orange and lemon slices.

hot brandy toddy

1 tsp sugar or honey
Boiling water
60 ml brandy
Lemon slice
Powdered nutmeg

Put sugar or honey in a coffee mug.

Fill two-third of the mug with boiling water.

Add brandy. Stir.

Garnish with lemon slice and a light sprinkle of nutmeg.

hot drambuie toddy

60 ml Drambuie
½ tsp lemon juice
Lemon slice
120 ml boiling water
Cinnamon stick

Pour Drambuie and lemon juice into a preheated mug or cup. (Fill with boiling water; discard water after about a minute.)

Add lemon slice and boiling water.

Stir with cinnamon stick and leave it in the mug.

hot eggnog

1 egg
Salt
1 tsp sugar
¾ cup hot milk
60 ml cognac
30 ml dark rum
Powdered nutmeg

Put egg and a dash of salt into a mixing bowl.

Beat till very thick and lemon yellow in colour.

Add sugar and beat till sugar is blended in.

Add hot milk, cognac and rum. Stir well.

Pour into a mug that has been rinsed in hot water to make it warm.

Sprinkle lightly with nutmeg.

hot milk punch

60–90 ml whisky, rum, brandy or vodka
1 cup milk
1 tsp sugar
Pinch of powdered nutmeg

Heat all ingredients, except nutmeg, in a pan over low heat. Stir regularly to ensure the milk does not burn.

When piping hot, pour into a heatproof mug that has been rinsed in boiling water.

Sprinkle lightly with nutmeg.

(If glasses are used, warm them in advance and keep a spoon in the glass when pouring in hot liquid to prevent cracking.)

hot nail

60 ml Scotch whisky
30 ml Drambuie
Dash of lemon juice
Lemon slice
Boiling water
Cinnamon stick

Pour whisky, Drambuie and lemon juice into a warmed heatproof mug.

Add lemon slice and boiling water.

Add cinnamon stick as garnish.

hot tea toddy

60 ml light rum
½ tsp honey
Pinch of powdered cinnamon
Lemon slice
1 tea cup of hot black tea
½ tsp ginger juice

Add all ingredients, except ginger juice, to a pan.

Warm gently till it is just about to boil.

Add ginger juice.

Pour into a mug or goblet. Stir lightly.

hot toddy

1 tsp sugar or honey
3 cloves
Cinnamon stick
A thin lemon slice
Boiling water
60 ml bourbon
Powdered nutmeg

Put sugar, cloves, cinnamon and lemon slice in a heavy mug or heat-resistant goblet.

Add 30 ml boiling water. Stir till sugar dissolves.

Let the mixture stand for about 5 minutes.

Heat the bourbon and 60 ml water separately without boiling.

Add to the goblet. Stir.

Sprinkle lightly with nutmeg.

hot whisky toddy

1 sugar cube
Boiling water
60 ml Scotch whisky
Lemon slice
Powdered nutmeg

Put sugar cube in a mug and fill two-third of the mug with boiling water.

Add whisky. Stir.

Add lemon slice and sprinkle lightly with nutmeg.

irish coffee

Black coffee

1 tsp sugar or honey

45 ml Irish whiskey
or Scotch whisky

1 tsp cream

Rinse a wine glass or goblet with hot water.

Add a little hot coffee and sugar. Stir till sugar dissolves.

Add whisky.

Fill with hot coffee, allowing room for topping.

Take a spoon and place it over the glass. Slowly pour the cream over the back of the spoon so that it spreads and floats over the drink. Do not stir.

Sip coffee through the cream.

mulled cider

60 ml dark rum
Dash of Angostura bitters
4 cloves
Cinnamon stick
Pinch of powdered nutmeg
1 tsp honey or sugar
1 cup apple cider or apple juice
Lemon peel

Heat all ingredients, except lemon peel, in a pan. (Be careful not to boil.)

Strain into a warmed heatproof mug.

Add lemon peel.

mulled scotch

60 ml Scotch whisky
30 ml Drambuie
Several dashes of Angostura bitters
60 ml boiling water
Maraschino cherry

Pour Scotch and Drambuie into an old-fashioned glass.

Add bitters.

Add boiling water. Stir.

Add cherry.

swedish glogg

1 bottle dry red wine
½ cup sugar
16 cloves
8 cinnamon sticks
1 cup brandy
Raisins
Peeled, unsalted almonds

Combine wine, sugar, cloves and cinnamon in a large pan.

Bring to almost boiling point.

Reduce flame and simmer for 5 to 8 minutes.

Stir in brandy.

Put a few raisins and almonds into each heatproof mug or glass.

Add the hot mixture into the mugs or glasses.

Makes 6 servings

tom and jerry

Ingredients	Method
2 eggs	*Beat eggs to a fine foamy mixture, slowly adding sugar.*
¼ cup sugar	*Continue beating till very stiff and light lemon yellow in colour.*
60 ml dark rum	*Add rum, cinnamon and cloves.*
½ tsp powdered cinnamon	*Beat a little more to blend spices.*
4 powdered cloves	*Spoon into mugs or glasses.*
½ bottle whisky	*Add 60 ml whisky to each mug or glass.*
1 litre hot milk	*Fill with hot milk. Stir.*

Makes 6 servings

punch

The word 'punch' comes from the Hindi word 'paanch', because it is usually a mix of five ingredients. In summer, our markets are awash with plums, apples, peaches and juicy melons. All of these are potential ingredients for a deliciously cool punch. With a bottle of white or red wine as the base and a little help from sugar, it is possible to produce a variety of fruity mixtures. Besides wine, vodka and rum are popular for making punch. Gin-based punches have their passionate partisans. Personally, I find gin too assertive.

barbados bowl

8 ripe bananas
1 cup lemon juice
1 cup sugar
1 750 ml bottle of light rum
1 litre pineapple juice
½ litre mango juice
2 lemons, sliced

Chill all ingredients except bananas.

Cut 6 bananas into thin slices.

Blend in an electric blender with lemon juice and sugar till smooth.

Pour over a block of ice into a punch bowl. Remove block of ice.

Add rum, pineapple juice and mango juice. Stir well.

Let mixture ripen in refrigerator for 1 hour before serving.

Cut remaining 2 bananas into thin slices.

Float banana and lemon slices on punch.

Makes about 24 servings

A FEW HANDY TIPS ON PACKING A PUNCH:

- Buy the wine or liquor that suits your taste, not necessarily the most expensive one.
- Some varieties of punch do not take ice; a champagne punch, for example. In that case keep the mixture surrounded with crushed ice. That will keep it properly chilled. One way of doing this is by placing the punch bowl in a larger vessel filled to the brim with crushed ice.
- Some recipes require the fruit to be marinated in liquor or wine for a couple of days. These are exceptions. Generally an hour or so is all you need for priming the old and the weak, the tart and the sweet, for a delicious drink.
- Making a punch is an art, not a science. Trust your own sense of taste and improvise as much as you want. Just make sure you are generous with your portions of liquor or wine.

bengal lancer's punch

1 bottle dry red wine
90 ml dark rum
90 ml Cointreau or triple sec
1 cup lemon juice
1 cup pineapple juice
1 cup orange juice
2 tsp sugar
1 750 ml bottle of champagne
½ litre club soda
Lemon and orange slices, halved

Chill all ingredients.

Put all ingredients, except champagne, soda and lemon and orange slices, in a chilled punch bowl with a large slab of ice. Stir well.

Just before serving, add champagne and soda. Stir gently.

Add lemon and orange slices.

Makes about 24 servings

bombay punch

12 lemons
Sugar to taste
1 750 ml bottle of brandy
1 750 ml bottle of medium-dry sherry
1 cup Cointreau or triple sec
4 750 ml bottles of cold brut champagne
2 cups cold club soda

Squeeze juice from lemons and sweeten taste with sugar in a chilled punch bowl with a large slab of ice.

Add brandy, sherry and Cointreau or triple sec. Stir well.

Just before serving, add cold champagne and club soda. Stir gently to preserve carbonation.

Makes about 50 servings

brandy punch

12 lemons
4 oranges
Sugar to taste
½ cup grenadine
1 cup Cointreau or triple sec
2 750 ml bottles of brandy
1 750 ml bottle of cold champagne or club soda

Squeeze juice from fruit and pour into a chilled punch bowl with large slab of ice.

Add sugar and stir till it dissolves.

Add grenadine, Cointreau and brandy. Stir well.

Just before serving, add cold champagne or club soda. Stir gently.

(Spiral peels from the oranges will make a good garnish.)

Makes about 30 servings

cardinal punch

1 750 ml bottle of dry red wine
½ litre cognac
½ litre dark rum
90 ml sweet vermouth
½ cup sugar, or sugar to taste
1 750 ml bottle of brut champagne
½ litre club soda
Sliced oranges

Chill all ingredients.

Put red wine, cognac, rum, vermouth and sugar in a chilled punch bowl with a large slab of ice. Stir well.

Check for sweetness.

Pour in cold champagne and club soda. Stir gently.

Garnish with a few thinly sliced orange rings.

(Some people prefer more champagne than club soda, so feel free to adjust quantities to suit your taste.)

Makes about 46 servings

celebrity punch

1 750 ml bottle of dark rum
1 750 ml bottle of gin
1 litre grape juice
½ litre orange juice
½ litre ginger ale
Small jar of maraschino cherries
6 orange slices

Pour chilled spirits and fruit juices into a punch bowl with a large slab of ice. Stir well.

Gently stir in ginger ale and cherries with their juices.

Float orange slices as garnish.

Makes about 40 servings

champagne bleu

Peel of 2 oranges

½ a 750 ml bottle of blue curaçao

1 cup lemon juice

1 750 ml bottle of brut champagne

Chill all ingredients except orange peel.

Cut orange peel into strips 1½" to 2" long and ¼" wide.

Pour curaçao and lemon juice into a glass punch bowl. Stir.

Add champagne. Stir lightly.

Float orange peel in bowl.

Do not put ice in the bowl. It may be chilled further, if desired, by placing the glass bowl in a larger vessel filled with ice cubes.

Makes about 15 servings

devil's cup

1 cup brandy

½ cup lemon juice

60 ml Chartreuse (green)

60 ml Chartreuse (yellow)

60 ml Bénédictine

60 ml sugar

2 750 ml bottles of champagne

1 litre club soda

Chill all ingredients.

Pour brandy, lemon juice, liqueurs and sugar into a chilled punch bowl with a large slab of ice. Mix well.

Check sweetness.

Immediately before serving add cold champagne and club soda. Stir gently.

Makes about 25 servings

english christmas punch

2 750 ml bottles of dry red wine

3 cups black tea

Juice of 1 orange

Juice of 1 lemon

½ kg sugar

1 750 ml bottle of dark rum

Heat wine, tea and fruit juices in a large pan but do not boil.

This punch may be served from the pan or transferred to a heatproof punch bowl.

Put sugar into a large ladle and saturate with rum.

If ladle is not large enough for all the sugar, put the remainder in the punch bowl.

Ignite rum in ladle.

Pour blazing into punch. Stir well.

Extinguish flames.

Pour remaining rum into punch. Stir again.

Makes about 25 servings

fish house punch

1 litre cold water
1½ cups sugar
1 750 ml bottle of brandy
1 750 ml bottle of light rum
1 750 ml bottle of dark rum
23 cups lemon juice
180 ml Cointreau or triple sec

Put sugar into punch bowl.

Add about 1 cup of the measured water. Stir till sugar dissolves.

Add remaining ingredients, including water.

Let mixture ripen in refrigerator for about 1 hour.

Place a block of ice in the bowl.

Ladle punch over ice.

Add more cold water if a weaker mixture is desired.

Makes about 30 servings

fish house punch II

10 fresh ripe peaches
1 750 ml bottle of light rum
1 750 ml bottle of brandy
½ litre lemon juice
1 cup sugar
1 litre water

Skin peaches, take out the pits.

Blend peach flesh for 1 minute at high speed.

Pour over a large block of ice in a punch bowl.

Add remaining ingredients. Stir well to dissolve sugar.

Let punch ripen in refrigerator for about one hour before serving.

Makes about 15 servings

harvard punch

A 750 ml bottle of Scotch whisky
½ a 750 ml bottle of brandy
1 cup Grand Marnier or triple sec
1 cup orange juice
½ cup lemon juice
½ cup sugar or to taste
2 750 ml bottles of champagne or 2 litre club soda or ginger ale
Orange and lemon slices

Mix all ingredients, except champagne, soda or ginger ale and fruit slices, in a large, chilled container or punch bowl.

Cover and chill in refrigerator for 1 hour.

When ready to serve, add a large slab of ice to bowl.

Pour in champagne, club soda or ginger ale. Stir gently

Garnish with orange and lemon slices.

Makes about 30 servings

peach punch

1 750 ml bottle of dry white wine

¾ cup vodka

6 tbsp lemon juice

¼ cup sugar

½ kg fresh peaches, pitted and sliced

¾ cup seedless red grapes, halved

¾ cup seedless green grapes, halved

Combine dry white wine, vodka, lemon juice and sugar in a glass bowl. Stir till sugar dissolves.

Add peaches and grapes.

Refrigerate for at least 2 hours, or overnight, to blend flavours.

Serve with ice cubes.

Use a slotted spoon to include peaches and grapes with each serving.

Makes about 6 servings

whisky punch

3 cups orange juice

1 cup lemon juice

1 cup sugar

2 lemons, thinly sliced

1 750 ml bottle of Scotch whisky

1 litre club soda

Put fruit juices and sugar into a punch bowl. Stir till sugar dissolves.

Add lemon slices.

Place a large chunk of ice in the bowl.

Add whisky.

Refrigerate for 1 hour.

Add club soda before serving. Stir.

(Additional club soda may be added if desired.)

Makes about 15 servings

christmas cheer

eggnog

Eggnogs and hot mulled wine are to Christmas what bhang is to Holi. Eggnogs have descended from an English hot drink that used to be known as posset. The name itself comes from the word *noggin*, which, in an old dialect from East Anglia, means a small drinking cup. There are innumerable versions of eggnog that replace rum with whisky or vodka. Just don't try making it with something like tequila or feni which can be pungent and overpowering. Eggnogs can be made hot or cold. The recipe below is for the cold version. (For Hot Eggnog see p. 272.)

12 eggs
2 cups powdered sugar
½ litre cognac or good brandy
½ litre dark rum
1½ litre milk
½ litre cream
Grated nutmeg

Separate the yolks from the whites of the eggs.

Beat the yolks slowly while adding sugar till the mixture is even and golden.

Stir in cognac or brandy, rum, milk and cream.

Chill in the refrigerator till needed.

Just before serving, transfer mixture into a large glass bowl.

Beat the egg whites till even and mix in with a gentle stir.

Sprinkle lightly with nutmeg.

Do not add any ice to the bowl.

Makes about 25 servings

hot buttered rum

Hot buttered rum is a devilishly simple drink to mix. All you need is rum. All the other ingredients can be found in any self-respecting Indian kitchen: dalchini, laung and honey. And the purpose of the butter? According to the 1939 *Gun Club Drink Book*, its only purpose is to lubricate your moustache. Good enough.

4 cloves
2" thick cinnamon sticks
1 tsp butter
1 tsp honey or sugar
60 ml dark rum
60 ml light rum
1 tsp lemon juice
Lemon slices

Bring a large cup of water, cloves and cinnamon sticks to a boil.

Add butter and honey or sugar. Turn off the heat.

Let it stand for 1 to 2 minutes.

Pour in both rum and lemon juice. Stir gently.

Serve in heat-resistant glasses or mugs with a slice of lemon.

Add some cloves and cinnamon sticks in the glass.

(Just use double the amount of dark rum if you don't have light rum handy.)

hot mulled wine

Mulling is the technique of gently heating wine, beer or cider with spices, sometimes even with fruits like peaches and strawberries. A shot of spirit, like brandy, can also be added to give the mix more kick. The word 'mulled' comes from an old English word, no longer in use, meaning mixed or muddled, which is how you will feel if you have too many glasses of it.

There are many ways of preparing a hot mulled wine. Some people add boiling water to the wine but that's for wimps. There is no need to dilute the wine. If you prefer your drink on the robust side, go ahead and add a dash of brandy. Hot drinks should be warm enough but not so hot as to burn your lips. You should heat the wine and the ingredients just short of boiling point and let it cool a bit before serving

One can make a non-alcoholic variation of this concoction by using red grape juice. Pour a carton of it into a handi, add honey to taste, some cinnamon sticks and cloves. Heat all of these together gently without bringing to a boil.

1 750 ml bottle of red wine
20 cloves
4 large cinnamon sticks
8 tsp sugar or to taste
Peel of 2 lemons

Add all ingredients to a large pan.

Heat gently till hot. Do not boil.

Serve in glasses that are not likely to break.

Remove lemon peel before serving to prevent the drink from becoming bitter.

Makes 6 to 8 servings

AND WHEN YOU'VE HAD TOO MANY . . .

hangover cures

An old folk medicine for dog bites, probably of Scottish origin, recommends applying a few hairs of the dog that bit you to the wound in order to heal it. The 'hair of the dog' theory is also prevalent among drinkers who believe that driznking more alcohol will get rid of a hangover. Ernest Hemingway favoured a concoction of beer and tomato juice the next morning. I say, Yuck! This remedy, though, is supported by scientific evidence. So, apart from a Bloody Mary, which sometimes works as a highly improbable but effective hangover cure, I have listed below a few more recipes you could try, to begin your morning afresh after a night of indulgence. At the end of the day, however, time is the only true healer. Good luck!

gin bracer

60 ml gin
1 tsp tomato ketchup
2 tbsp lemon juice
Several dashes of Tabasco sauce
Pinch of salt
½ tsp Worcestershire sauce

Put all the ingredients into a blender.

Blend at low speed for 15 to 20 seconds.

Pour into a highball glass and add ice cubes to fill glass.

morning fizz

60 ml Scotch whisky
Half the white of an egg
½ tsp lemon juice
1 tsp sugar
Club soda

Shake whisky, egg white, lemon juice and sugar with ice cubes.

Strain into a highball glass.

Add club soda and ice to fill glass. Stir.

polynesian pick-me-up

½ cup pineapple juice
45 ml vodka
½ tsp curry powder
½ tsp lemon juice
1 tsp cream
Several dashes of Tabasco sauce
Chilli powder

Put all ingredients, except chilli powder, with crushed ice into a blender.

Blend for 10 seconds at high speed.

Pour into a chilled old-fashioned glass.

Sprinkle very lightly with chilli powder.

prairie oyster

45 ml cognac
2 tsp vinegar
15 ml Worcestershire sauce
1 tsp tomato ketchup
Several dashes of Angostura bitters
1 egg yolk
Chilli powder

Shake all ingredients, except egg yolk and chilli powder, with ice cubes.

Strain into a chilled old-fashioned glass.

Add 1 or 2 ice cubes to fill glass almost to the rim.

Place egg yolk on top of drink without breaking it.

Sprinkle yolk with chilli powder.

The oldest and most stunning of all morning-after drinks, this one should be swallowed in one long, determined gulp. Grit your teeth, then open your eyes very slowly. Hopefully your head will have cleared and you will be ready for another fun evening.

MOCKTAILS

I have always felt that those of us who drink alcohol are the lucky ones. We can get pickled. It is not so easy for teetotallers. Some years ago, at lunch at an Egyptian diplomat's home, I was served, to my horror, what was proudly presented as non-alcoholic 'beer'. I will not begin to describe what it tasted like, though many may venture to guess. The bottom line remains, if you take out the little alcohol beer has in it, it becomes undrinkable. It is the same with wine; you cannot substitute wine with grape juice.

Instead of imitations of wine, beer or any other spirit, those who do not drink alcohol should opt for mocktails. Mocktails are smooth blends of various beverages and ingredients. They can be made from anything—fresh fruit juices, syrups, cream, mint leaves, ground pepper, nutmeg, and so forth. A good mixture, with zany colours and perhaps fruit floating in the glass can be enjoyed by people of all ages who prefer not to touch alcohol for whatever reason—religious, personal, pregnancy or the fact that they have not reached drinking age. It is criminal to limit these fine folks to Coca-Cola at your parties.

Some mocktails are variations of well-known alcoholic drinks. You can make yourself a non-alcoholic Piña Colada, for instance, by taking rum out of a mix of pineapple juice and coconut cream. A Virgin Mary is simply Bloody Mary without the vodka and tastes just as delicious because vodka is tasteless.

You will find all sorts of bottled fruit concentrates and syrups from abroad in our upscale grocery shops. You name it and the guy behind the counter will probably have it: pineapple, banana, strawberry and raspberry extracts as well as more exotic stuff like grenadine and the non-alcoholic version of curaçao. With a little bit of imagination you can put together all kinds of drinks for your guests who are teetotallers.

banana milk shake

1 cup regular milk
1 ripe banana
2 scoops vanilla ice cream
Powdered cinnamon or nutmeg

Mix all ingredients, except cinnamon or nutmeg, in a blender with ice cubes.

Pour into a highball glass.

Sprinkle cinnamon or nutmeg.

blushing piña colada

1 ripe banana, peeled and sliced
1 thick slice pineapple, peeled
6 tbsp pineapple juice
1 scoop strawberry ice cream
2 tsp cream of coconut
2 tsp grenadine
Maraschino cherry

Chop the banana and the pineapple and put in a blender.

Add the pineapple juice and blend till smooth.

Add the ice cream with the cream of coconut and a little finely crushed ice.

Blend till smooth.

Pour into 2 cocktail glasses.

Pour the grenadine syrup slowly on top for effect.

Garnish with cherry.

bora bora

6 tbsp pineapple juice
½ tsp grenadine
1 tsp lemon juice
90 ml ginger ale
Maraschino cherry
Lemon slice

Half-fill a shaker with ice cubes.

Pour in pineapple juice, grenadine and lemon juice. Shake well.

Strain into an ice-filled highball glass.

Top with ginger ale. Stir gently.

Garnish with cherry and lemon slice.

brontosaurus

- 6 tbsp grapefruit juice
- ½ tsp grenadine
- ½ tsp lemon juice
- Seven Up

Half-fill a shaker with ice cubes and pour in grapefruit juice, grenadine and lemon juice. Shake well.

Strain into a highball glass filled with ice cubes.

Top it with Seven Up. Stir.

cinderella

- 4 tbsp orange juice
- 4 tbsp pineapple juice
- 1 tsp lemon juice
- ½ tsp sugar
- Club soda
- Lemon slice

Half-fill a shaker with ice cubes.

Add orange juice, pineapple juice, lemon juice and sugar. Shake well.

Strain into an ice-filled highball glass.

Top with club soda. Stir.

Garnish with lemon slice.

creamy creamsicle

- 1 cup fresh orange juice
- 2 scoops vanilla ice cream
- Orange slice

Combine both ingredients, except orange slice, in a blender.

Pour into highball glass.

Add orange slice.

flamingo

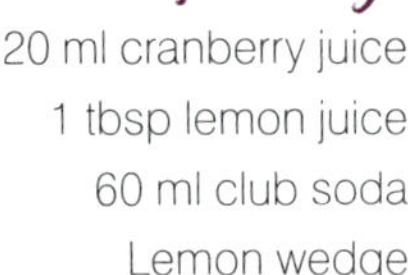

- 120 ml cranberry juice
- 1 tbsp lemon juice
- 60 ml club soda
- Lemon wedge

Shake juices with ice.

Pour into a highball glass.

Top with club soda. Stir.

Garnish with lemon wedge.

florida punch

2 litres orange juice
1 litre grapefruit juice
1 litre ginger ale
1 cup lemon juice
1 cup sugar
½ cup grenadine
1 tsp fresh ginger paste

Chill all ingredients.

Mix in a chilled punch bowl with a large cake of ice.

Makes about 30 servings

fruit smoothie

1 cup chilled orange juice
1 banana, chilled and sliced
½ cup chilled strawberries, sliced

Combine all ingredients in a blender.

Blend at low speed.

Pour into a highball glass over ice.

Garnish with slices of strawberries.

fuzzy lemon fizz

¾ cup peach juice
120 ml Seven Up
Lemon slice

Pour peach juice and Seven Up over ice cubes into a highball glass.

Garnish with lemon slice

grapeberry

60 ml cranberry juice
60 ml grapefruit juice
Lemon slice

Combine juices in large wine glass filled with ice cubes.

Add lemon slice.

innocent passion

120 ml passion fruit juice
2 tbsp cranberry juice
2 tbsp lemon juice
Club soda
Maraschino cherry

Combine juices in a highball glass filled with ice cubes.

Top with club soda. Stir.

kidsicle

250 ml regular milk
1 scoop vanilla ice cream
4 tbsp orange juice
Dash of grenadine
Seven Up
Maraschino cherry

Combine milk, ice cream and orange juice in a blender.

Blend till smooth.

Pour into a highball glass.

Add grenadine.

Fill with Seven Up. Stir.

Add cherry.

little engineer

120 ml pineapple juice
120 ml orange juice
15 ml grenadine

Pour all ingredients over ice cubes in a highball glass.

mocha float

2 cups club soda
½ cup chocolate syrup
1 tsp instant coffee
4 small scoops coffee ice cream
Chocolate shavings

Combine club soda, chocolate syrup and coffee. Mix well.

Pour into highball glasses filled with crushed ice.

Top with ice cream and chocolate shavings.

Makes 2 servings

orange-and-tonic

¾ cup orange juice
120 ml tonic water
Lemon wedge

Pour orange juice and tonic water over ice cubes into a highball glass. Stir gently.

Add lemon wedge.

pac man

2 tsp lemon juice
1 tsp grenadine
Dash of Angostura bitters
Ginger ale
Orange slice

Pour grenadine, lemon juice and bitters into a highball glass filled with ice cubes.

Top with ginger ale. Stir.

Slide the orange slice down the side of the glass.

peach melba

250 ml peach nectar
2 scoops vanilla ice cream
½ ripe peach peeled, pitted and sliced
½ cup strawberries, sliced

Mix all ingredients, except strawberries, in a blender.

Pour into highball glass.

Garnish with sliced strawberries.

pineapple and lemon agua fresca

2 pineapples
Juice of 3 lemons
½ litre water
2 tsp sugar

Peel the pineapples and chop the flesh, removing the core and 'eyes'.

Put pineapple flesh into a blender.

Add lemon juice and half the water.

Purée to a smooth pulp.

Stop the machine and scrape the mixture from the side of the blender once or twice during processing.

Place a strainer over a large bowl.

Tip the pineapple pulp into the strainer and press it through with a spoon.

Pour the strained mixture into a large pitcher.

Cover and chill in the refrigerator for about 1 hour.

Stir in the remaining water and sugar to taste.

Serve with ice.

Makes about 6 servings

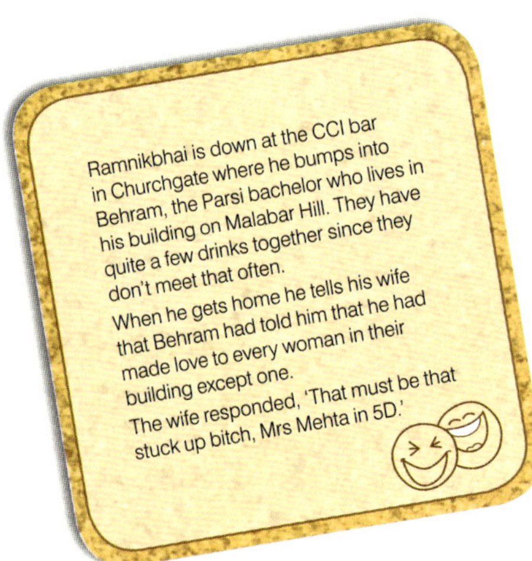
Ramnikbhai is down at the CCI bar in Churchgate where he bumps into Behram, the Parsi bachelor who lives in his building on Malabar Hill. They have quite a few drinks together since they don't meet that often.

When he gets home he tells his wife that Behram had told him that he had made love to every woman in their building except one.

The wife responded, 'That must be that stuck up bitch, Mrs Mehta in 5D.'

pomola

Coca-Cola
2 tbsp lemon juice
15 ml grenadine
Lemon slice
Maraschino cherry

Pour cola, lemon juice and grenadine over ice in a highball glass. Stir gently.

Garnish with lemon slice and cherry.

prohibition punch

6 tbsp lemon juice
1 tsp sugar
¼ litre apple juice
½ litre ginger ale
Orange slices

Put ice cubes in a jug.

Add lemon juice, apple juice and sugar. Stir till sugar dissolves.

Pour in ginger ale. Stir.

Serve in ice-filled highball glasses, garnished with orange slices.

Makes 4 to 6 servings

punchless piña colada

2 tbsp cream of coconut
2 tbsp pineapple juice
1 tsp lemon juice
Maraschino cherry

Combine all ingredients in blender with 1 cup of crushed ice.

Pour into a highball glass.

Add cherry.

(Add sugar to taste if the juices are unsweetened.)

rumless rickey

2 tbsp lemon juice
15 ml grenadine
Dash of Angostura bitters
Club soda
Lemon peel

Pour lemon juice, grenadine and bitters into an old-fashioned glass with 3–4 large ice cubes.

Top with club soda. Stir.

Add lemon peel.

shirley temple

Several dashes of grenadine
Ginger ale
Orange or pineapple slice
Maraschino cherry

Add grenadine to a highball glass filled with ice.

Top with ginger ale. Stir.

Garnish with orange or pineapple slice and cherry.

strawberry and orange smoothie

250 gm strawberries, chilled
½ cup plain yogurt, chilled
½ litre orange juice, chilled
Sugar to taste (optional)

Place strawberries and yogurt in a food processor or blender.

Process for about a minute till smooth and creamy.

Add orange juice. Process for about another 30 seconds, or till thoroughly combined.

Pour into highball glasses.

Sugar can be added while processing if desired.

Makes 4 to 6 servings

summertime barbarian

½ cup fresh strawberries
½ cup fresh pineapple
½ cup grapefruit juice
½ tsp sugar

Combine all ingredients with ice in a blender.

Blend till smooth.

Pour into highball glasses.

Makes 2 servings

sunburst

1 green apple, cored and chopped
3 carrots, peeled and chopped
1 mango, peeled and pitted
1 cup orange juice, chilled
½ cup strawberries
Orange wedge

Place apple, carrots and mango in a blender or food processor.

Process to a pulp.

Add orange juice and strawberries. Process again.

Pass through a strainer, pressing out all the juice with the back of a large spoon. Discard pulp.

Pour into an old-fashioned glass filled with ice cubes.

Slide orange wedge down the side of the glass.

virgin mary

120 ml tomato juice
½ tsp lemon juice
½ tsp Worcestershire sauce
Dash of Tabasco sauce
Salt, pepper to taste
Lemon slice

Rub the rim of a wine glass with lemon juice.

Dip in a saucer of salt to cover the rim.

Fill the glass with ice.

Add tomato juice.

Add the remaining ingredients, except lemon slice. Stir.

Add lemon slice.

volunteer

60 ml Rose's lime cordial
Several dashes of Angostura bitters
Tonic water

Fill a highball glass with ice cubes.

Add all ingredients. Stir gently.

yellow jacket

4 tbsp pineapple juice
4 tbsp orange juice
1 tbsp lemon juice
Lemon slice

Shake all ingredients with ice cubes.

Strain into an old-fashioned glass filled with ice cubes.

Garnish with lemon slice.

GLOSSARY

Here are some of the names and terms that frequently crop up in the world of alcoholic drinks.

ABV: Alcohol by Volume, or the alcoholic strength of a spirit. If a spirit is said to be 40 per cent ABV, it contains 40 per cent alcohol and 60 per cent water. By law, this information has to be provided on the packaging of all alcoholic products.

Ageing: Wood ageing is the process of maturing wines and spirits in wooden barrels before bottling them. The flavours that result depend on the kind of barrels used. While wines can be improved by ageing in bottles, spirits do not improve when preserved in bottles.

Angel's Share: The spirit that evaporates through the wood of barrels containing aging spirit.

Aperitif: Usually a wine that has been fortified by the addition of herbs and spices, it is traditionally drunk before a meal to stimulate the appetite. Dubonnet and Campari are two well-known brands.

Aqua vitae: The original Latin term for spirits meaning 'water of life'.

Bitters: Aromatic mixtures made from seeds, roots and leaves with an alcohol base. The most famous of these is the Angostura brand from Trinidad.

Botanicals: Vegetable products, such as herbs, peels and flowers, that give flavour to spirits and liqueurs.

Breathing: Breathing is the process of allowing wine to come in contact with air after a bottle is uncorked. This enhances the wine's aroma and improves the overall flavour of most red wines and some whites.

Chaser: A long drink drunk immediately after a shorter one, for example, a glass of beer after a shot of neat whisky.

Cobbler: A drink served in a tall glass filled with crushed ice and decorated with fresh fruit and mint sprigs. The base could be any spirit or wine.

Cocktail: A combination of spirits or liqueurs or wine and flavourings that is shaken or stirred with ice; a mixed drink intended to be drunk before dinner.

Collins: Any lemon drink in a tall glass, mixed with club soda and a spirit.

Daisy: A spirit that has lemon or lime juice but also another fruit syrup, such as grenadine, and is topped with soda.

Decanting: The process of pouring wine from a bottle into another vessel. This lets the wine breathe (see 'Breathing' above) and also removes any sediment at the bottom of the bottle.

Digestif: A beverage, usually alcoholic, that is taken after a meal to stimulate digestion.

Dram: Scottish and Irish word for a glass of spirit.

Fix: Same as a Daisy (above) except that the squeezed lemon is dropped into the cocktail.

Fizz: Another term for a Collins.

Frappé: Any drink that is served with crushed ice.

Garnish: A decoration or embellishment for a drink, such as a lemon slice, cherry, olive, pineapple wedge and mint leaves.

Highball: Any drink containing a spirit and club soda or any other fizzy mixer, served in a tall glass.

Maraschino cherry: Marinated cherries that come in jars with syrup and are bright red in colour.

Muddling: Pressing or crushing of various ingredients, such as sugar or fruit garnishes, in a serving glass before adding alcohol. A good Mojito, for instance, requires mint leaves to be muddled.

Mulling: Lightly heating wine, beer or cider with spices or fruit or even a little spirit. It is a popular Christmas party drink.

Neat: Alcohol served straight, with no ice.

Nightcap: Any drink taken immediately before retiring at night.

On the rocks: Any drink poured over ice only, usually in a short glass.

Peel: The skin of a fruit, most times that of a citrus fruit like lemon or orange. It is often twisted over a cocktail to release its oil before being dropped in the drink.

Pick-me-up: Any drink that is taken to cure a hangover the morning after a bit of indulgence.

Proof: The alcoholic strength of a beverage, calculated at twice the percentage of alcohol in it. Simply put, 80 proof means the liquor is 40 per cent alcohol.

Punch: A combination of spirits or wine with sweeteners and flavouring served at parties in large bowls, sometimes with fruits like strawberries and grapes floating in them.

Shooter: Also known as a 'shot'. A small portion of alcohol served straight from the bottle, with no ice, and drunk in a single gulp.

Sling: A tall drink made with lemon juice, sugar and spirits. The most famous is the Singapore Sling which contains gin and cherry brandy as its base.

Sour: A short drink made with lemon juice, sugar, spirits and perhaps a little soda.

Terroir: A French term for a group of vineyards in the same region sharing the same type of soil, weather conditions, grapes and farming techniques.

Toddy: A hot drink made with spirits, sugar and spices (such as cinnamon sticks, cloves and nutmeg) and mixed with hot water. In India, neera sapped from palm trees is also sometimes referred to as toddy.

Vintage: The year the grapes of a given wine were harvested. It has nothing to do with the year the wine was bottled. If a vintage date appears on a wine label, at least 95 per cent of the bottle's contents must be from that vintage.

Zest: Oils from the outer skin of citrus fruits that are twisted over certain cocktails.

INDEX